CARRY
THE
CODE

CARRY
THE
CODE
LIVING THE ETHOS

WARRIOR   GUARDIAN   SHEPHERD   PROTECTOR

MICHAEL DAVENPORT

RESOLUTE
GUARDIAN
— PRESS —

Carry the Code: Warrior • Guardian • Shepherd • Protector
Published by Resolute Guardian Press
Oklahoma City, Oklahoma

Library of Congress Control Number: 2025948451
ISBN (hardcover): 9798993096315
ISBN (paperback): 9798993096308
eISBN: 9798993096322

CONTENTS

Dedication

For Maria—my bride, my partner, and my greatest encourager. You have walked beside me in every season, steady and unshaken, reminding me who I am and why this mission matters. Your presence is the anchor that holds me fast.

For my Mom—whose faith, sacrifice, and quiet strength built the foundation beneath my feet. Your example taught me to work, to endure, and to believe when the odds were long.

This book is as much yours as mine. Every page carries your fingerprints. Without your love and example, there would be no *Carry the Code.*

Preface

This book was not written in an ivory tower or a quiet study. It was forged in the crucible of crisis—in the silence of squad cars after hard calls, in briefing rooms where decisions carried lives, and in the quiet of empty classrooms after another day of preparing others for the unthinkable.

I have worn many uniforms in my life—as a law enforcement officer, a negotiator, a martial artist, a credit union executive, a husband, and a son. In each role, I discovered the same truth: Leadership is not about position or rank. It is about presence. It is about showing up when others falter. It is about carrying the code.

The pages that follow are not theory. They are lessons lived, tested, and sometimes paid for in sweat, tears, and sacrifice. The Warrior, Guardian, Shepherd, and Protector are not archetypes on paper—they are living ethos. They are anchors that keep us steady when the storm is at full force, a guiding code of values and behavior.

I wrote this book now because I believe the need is urgent. Our culture is hungry for leaders of courage and conviction— not just in law enforcement or the military, but in boardrooms, classrooms, locker rooms, and homes. The next generation of leaders is watching us, measuring us, and deciding if the code is worth carrying forward. That decision will be shaped by what we model today.

This book is not mine alone. It belongs to the men and women who stood shoulder to shoulder with me. It belongs to the families who sacrificed so we could serve. It belongs to the parents, leaders, coaches, and spouses who never carried a badge but who carried weight just the same.

If there is one thing I ask as you turn these pages, it is this: Do not read *Carry the Code* as a collection of stories. Read it as a challenge. A mirror. A compass. Take from it what you can use, and then put it into practice where you live and lead.

The world does not need more spectators. It needs more men and women willing to stand, to guard, to walk beside, and to protect. It needs more of us willing to carry the code.

—*Michael Davenport*

Foreword

Some leaders talk about courage; others write about integrity. Michael Davenport lives them both.

I personally know this because Michael once stood between me and the darkest moment of my life.

When the weight of the world pressed in, when the shadows threatened to win, he was there. Not just as a crisis negotiator, but as a warrior for my soul. He reminded me that the fight was worth it, that my family still needed me, and that even in the deepest valley, light could break through. That is who Michael Davenport is, and that is the code he carries.

This book is not simply about leadership; it is about life—everyone's life. It is a call to arms for every man and woman who has ever been entrusted with the responsibility of leading others.

Through the Warrior-Guardian-Shepherd-Protector, Michael shares lessons not just from the battlefield of tactics, but from the pressure testing of the human spirit.

Carry the Code will challenge you, inspire you, and call you higher. It will remind you that leadership is not about position or power, but about presence and sacrifice. It will press you to ask hard questions of yourself: Will I stand when others falter? Will I protect when others exploit? Will I lead with courage, compassion, and conviction when it matters most?

Michael Davenport does not offer empty words. His lessons were written in moments of crisis, refined by reflection, and proven in service.

This book is his gift to you—a guide, a compass, and a challenge to rise above.

If you are ready to lead with courage, live with conviction, and carry the code forward, then turn the page.

The journey begins now.

Rick Cockrell, Lieutenant – SWAT Commander
Texarkana Arkansas Police Department
ALERRT Active Attack Response Instructor
JPX Less-Lethal Master Instructor

CHAPTER 1

The Call to Courage

Guardian's maxim: "Silence is presence."

Every negotiator carries this maxim like a blade tucked beneath the armor. To the untrained, silence feels like failure—a void to be filled, an absence of progress. To the impatient, silence feels unbearable. But for the protector, silence is no void. It is a shield, a weapon, and a test of will.

We discovered this truth not in classrooms but in crucibles where words or their absence meant life or death. Early on, we treated silence as wasted time. We learned, painfully, that silence was often the hinge upon which survival turned. To endure it is discipline. To wield it is mastery.

The Battlefield of Silence

The command post, the central room where leaders, negotiators, and tactical teams coordinate during an incident, is its own battlefield.

Picture it: Radios crackling with fragments that never tell the whole story. A sniper whispering from the rooftop: "Movement at the window." A SWAT operator shifting behind his shield, sweat rolling down his temple as he waits for the order he hopes won't come. Commanders pace like caged animals, each glance at the clock striking like a hammer.

Outside the tape, families sob, the weight of their fear pushing through the thin walls of the trailer. Inside, the air hums with tension, as if the oxygen is charged with impatience. Every silence from the subject inside the barricade tightens the coil. Each pause on the line stretches until it feels like it could snap the room in two.

This is the battlefield of silence. No bullets fly, but the casualties can be permanent.

Weapons here are not rifles but words. And silence—disciplined, deliberate silence— becomes the heaviest weapon of all.

Biology as the True Enemy

The fight inside the command post is not against the suspect; it is against biology, the cortisol screaming in the bloodstream, and the adrenaline surging in waves. Against the human impulse to do something—anything—rather than endure the unbearable weight of stillness.

Impatience in the command post can be deadlier than the weapon inside the barricade. Every sigh from a commander, every whispered, "We need to move," presses against the negotiator like a vice. And yet this is where the protector stands firm.

We learned that silence is not absence but presence. To hold it is to master our own biology before we attempt to master another's. In martial arts, we bow before the strike. We breathe before the kata. Stillness is not weakness—it is declaration: I have mastered myself before I face you.

Negotiation demands the same.

Noise vs. Presence

Noise is easy. It feels powerful. Fill the room with commands, fill the air with threats, fill the silence with rehearsed reassurances. Rookies mistake noise for progress, and commanders mistake motion for momentum.

But noise accelerates chaos. Noise is gasoline poured on fear.

Silence is hard. It feels unbearable. It stretches patience, presses discipline, and demands courage without spectacle. But silence steadies storms, cools rage, and opens the door to dignity.

The talker fills the room with noise.

The protector fills the room with presence.

And on this battlefield, presence is what saves lives.

Case Reflection: The Silent Threshold

It was after midnight when the call dropped. A two-car garage on the edge of a quiet neighborhood, windows blacked out with trash bags, the door sealed tight against the world. Inside was a man who had lost nearly everything—his job, his family, his footing in life. On his lap lay a handgun, more companion than tool, the last object anchoring him in his despair.

We made contact. His voice hit the wire like broken glass—sharp bursts of anger, words spat into the night, fragments of shame and rage tangled together. He cursed himself, his family, and the world.

Then he stopped.

The silence that followed wasn't empty. It was heavy. It pressed into the command post like a storm front. Radios hissed with static. SWAT operators shifted their weight on the perimeter, the secure boundary officers establish to contain a scene, boots scraping against concrete. A commander leaned forward, eyes locked on the phone line as if he could force it alive again.

"Is he done?" one whispered.

"We need to move before he reloads," another muttered, the tension crackling in his voice.

The silence wasn't his problem. It was ours.

Every eye in the room turned toward us, the negotiators. The air seemed to hum with their impatience. Biology surged like a tide—cortisol, adrenaline, fear. The silence stretched. To the untrained, it screamed of failure. To the impatient, it felt like collapse.

But we had seen this silence before. It was not absence. It was biology cooling. His nervous system was fighting its own war. Adrenaline was burning itself out. Rage was giving way to exhaustion. If we carried the silence—if we stayed steady and refused to betray our own fear—biology would return him to us.

So we breathed with him—slow, measured, deliberate. Our cadence softened, our tone lowered, our words became sparse. Where he went silent, we stayed silent, tethered to him like climbers tied to the same rope. The urge to fill the void pressed hard against us, but we did not break.

Minutes dragged into hours. Radios clicked. Coffee went cold. At one point, a light flickered on inside the garage, then off again. The command post shifted in alarm, but the code held: The subject's tempo, not ours.

Finally, after the longest stretch of quiet that night, the voice returned. Thin. Fragile. Almost childlike.

"Are you still there?"

"Yes," we said. Calm. Certain. Steady.

"We're here to help you."

There was a pause—not empty, but alive. Then the groan of a garage door rising against rusted tracks. The subject stepped into the dawn, trembling hands open, the weapon abandoned behind him on a toolbox.

No shots. No eulogies.

He didn't surrender to us. He surrendered to the silence we refused to abandon.

Debrief

That night etched a permanent truth into our discipline: The silence was not what threatened him—it was what threatened us. The real battlefield was not the garage but the room filled with uniforms, impatience, and fear.

We learned to carry silence not as emptiness but as presence, not as a void but as medicine. It became ethos: Presence over performance, patience over pressure, life over haste.

Silence is the threshold every negotiator must cross. The untrained fear it. The protector masters it.

Case Reflection: When Silence Was Broken Too Soon

It was a one-story house with a porch to the left, blinds drawn tight, and a front room crowded with too many memories. Inside, a twenty-something man paced with a rifle, spiraling after a domestic argument that detonated into fear. He wasn't a villain; he was a storm in a small room.

We made contact quickly. His voice came out like sparks off a frayed wire—hot, repetitive, circling the same injuries. Then, as fast, it dropped into quiet. Not polite quiet. The kind that makes a command post lean forward and forget to breathe.

We all felt it: the threshold. Biology was trying to land the plane. His adrenaline was cycling down. The room needed to hold.

The rookie on the phone was sharp with good instincts, clean voice, and plenty of heart. He studied the doctrine—formal principles built from repeated lessons, not just personal opinion— shadowed calls, and ran drills until phrases felt like second nature. What he hadn't carried yet was silence. It was his first time in the big chair with a house surrounded and a rifle inside. He mistook the quiet for collapse and moved to fill it.

"Hey, I hear you . . . I'm listening . . . talk to me, okay? You're not alone," he said—soft, fast, stacking reassurance on reassurance, then questions on top of that. "Can you tell me where you are in the room? Are you by the window? Are you safe? I want to—"

We watched the line, heard the breaths on the far end change shape. The subject's exhale sharpened. The floor creaked. Then a voice, hard and wounded, ripped through the wire: "Shut up! You don't know me! You don't care!"

Something clattered. The rookie exhaled into the handset—too loud, too close—as a single deafening crack blew through the ceiling. Plaster fell. Outside, a neighbor screamed. Inside the command post, time folded into a silence no one wanted.

Containment held. No one moved on impulse. We tapped the tabletop twice—the signal to reset cadence. The secondary negotiator slid closer, and the team chief gave a small nod. The rookie's eyes were bright with shock and shame. He didn't need a lecture; he needed a shield. The Guardian part of the code took over. We covered him—absorbing the room's impatience, absorbing his own internal collapse—so the incident didn't swallow him and we didn't lose two people to panic.

"Stay with us," we whispered to him, not the line. "Hand it off clean."

He did. No flinch, no argument—discipline. We respected that.

The voice on the wire changed, lower and slower. "We're here," we said to the subject. Nothing more. The room breathed. We let the stillness return like the tide. Thirty seconds. A minute. Ninety seconds. It felt like forever; it was biology doing its work.

The subject's breathing turned ragged, then steadier. Words returned, less like shrapnel and more like a person: "I don't . . . I don't know what to do."

"You don't have to decide in a rush," we said. "We're not pushing you. No one here wants you hurt."

Silence again. Then a confession fell out in pieces—how the fight started, what he feared would happen if he put the rifle down, the humiliation he felt with half the neighborhood watching. We didn't solve any of it. We refused to run. We carried the silence like a stretcher until it could carry him.

He came out hours later, hands empty, eyes stunned by dawn. No one died that night. But we would be dishonest if we pretended there wasn't a cost. The shot was a message: The silence belonged to him, and we had stepped on it.

Debrief

We pulled chairs around the table and told the truth. The rookie had spoken from fear, not from doctrine. Fear of failing, doing nothing, or how he would look if the call ended in tragedy on his watch. Every negotiator has felt those shadows. The difference between a talker and a protector isn't that the fear disappears—it's that the protector refuses to obey it.

We wrote three lines into the log and then into training:

Silence is a trust, not a void. You didn't earn it; don't spend it.

Presence outranks performance. The room's heartbeat must slow before the subject's will.

Tempo belongs to the subject. Our job is to protect it from the room, the clock, and our ego.

We adjusted our reps. We added a "clock discipline" drill—rookies sit on a headset while a trainer simulates long, unbroken quiet. They are graded on breath control, posture, and restraint. We built a two-chair handoff—when silence fractures, the baton passes with one sentence and no commentary. We adopted nonverbal command post rules—two taps means slow, one palm down means hold, and a flat hand beside the ear means no more words.

The rookie asked for the next call. We gave it to him. He held his silence. He earned it the hard way—like everyone else who's ever worn the wire long enough to carry scars.

What the Scar Taught

Silence is not a spare tool; it is the operating system. It is where dignity returns, biology resets, and surrender is born without humiliation. Break it too soon and you don't lose a tactic—you break trust, spike adrenaline, and invite a shot through the ceiling, or worse.

And yet when the room groans, a chief breathes hard through his nose, or a camera light flicks on across the street, it will be the Warrior in you who must master the urge to swing. The Guardian in you must shield the room from its own timeline. The Shepherd in you must stay beside a hurting human without dragging him forward. The Protector in you must choose outcomes over optics every single time.

Maxim: Respect the silence you did not earn. It belongs to the person on the edge. We are there to carry it with them, not take it from them.

The night at the small house didn't end in eulogies, because the team remembered who we are when the first plan falters. We didn't pretend the shot hadn't happened; we learned from it. We didn't bury the rookie; we built him. That is what protectors do—with subjects, teammates, and themselves.

Doctrine of Silence: From Void to Medicine

Through scars and long nights, the craft distilled itself into a doctrine we now live by: Silence is never neutral. It is either poison or medicine, depending on how it is carried.

Two anchors of truth: Silence carried with discipline is medicine. It cools biology, restores dignity, and creates space for surrender. Silence mishandled is poison. Broken too soon, it reignites adrenaline, fractures trust, and puts lives at risk.

Rookies vs. Veterans

Rookies fear silence like drowning. They feel the weight of every pause as an accusation, so they fill the air with words to prove they're working. But the seasoned protector knows: Silence is not inactivity. It is active command of self. The true measure is not how fast we speak but how long we can hold.

Presence vs. Performance

Negotiators who endure become practitioners of presence. Their stillness steadies the room before it steadies the subject. When they speak, their words carry weight because silence has prepared the soil. Doctrine makes it clear: We do not perform calm—we deliver it. First inside ourselves, then through the wire.

Mini Scenes of Silence in Action

At Home: A Father and Son

A teenage boy slammed the door of his bedroom, angry at a world that seemed against him. The father's hand hovered at the knob, ready to burst in, lecture blazing. Instead, he leaned against the wall outside. Minutes passed. The storm inside quieted. When the door finally opened, the son muttered, "Thanks for giving me a minute." Silence had spoken louder than anger could.

On the Mat: The Bow Before the Strike

Martial arts teaches the same truth. Before sparring begins, there is a bow. In kata, there is the pause between movements. The silence is not weakness—it is declaration. I have mastered myself before I face you. Negotiators learn the same rhythm. The pause is the bow. It signals readiness, respect, and control.

In Business: The Boardroom

A CEO presented dire numbers, projecting collapse unless immediate cuts were made. The room erupted with suggestions, panic disguised as strategy. But one leader—quiet, still—waited. When the noise ebbed, he asked two questions: "What do we know, and what is fear?" The silence that followed stripped the noise away. They recalibrated, preserved jobs, and avoided a decision made for optics instead of outcome. Silence saved a business the way it saves a barricade.

On the Field: A Coach's Huddle

It was fourth down, the game on the line. Players looked to the sideline, expecting a torrent of commands. Instead, the coach called them in, took a knee, and said nothing. He breathed, counted three beats, then three more. By the time he spoke, the team had settled. They ran the play clean, not frantic. Silence steadied the field more than any speech could.

In Finance: A Credit Union Crisis

A federal credit union faced an exam that threatened its standing. Tension ran high and staff pressed for rapid fixes. Instead of chasing every noise, leadership protected the silence—separating signal from optics, calm from panic. When the examiners arrived, the institution wasn't frantic; it was steady. Five-star ratings weren't earned through frantic sprints but through disciplined silence when others demanded chaos.

Ethos Embodied in Silence

Warrior: Strength under control. The warrior does not swing at shadows. He holds the strike until it matters.

Guardian: Shield against impatience. The guardian absorbs the command post's pressure so the subject isn't crushed by it.

Shepherd: Ministry of presence. The shepherd walks beside, carrying the silence so the lost do not walk it alone.

Protector: Outcome over optics. The protector remembers the world may demand spectacle, but silence preserves life.

This ethos transforms silence from absence into doctrine. Without ethos, silence collapses into awkward voids. With ethos, silence becomes medicine carried with courage.

Reader Application: Silence Beyond the Command Post

- *Parents:* The pause before responding prevents words that scar. The silence that sits beside a hurting child says more than explanations ever could.

- *Leaders:* When optics demand speed, silence gives room for wisdom. The best decisions often come not from the loudest room but from the quietest reflection.

- *Coaches:* Players don't always need more words—they need space to breathe. Silence after failure creates resilience; silence before the play creates focus.

- *Spouses:* In arguments, silence is not withdrawal when carried with presence. It is the reset button that allows love to return before pride destroys.

- *Communities:* In times of conflict, silence is often the last courtesy people afford one another. When given, it is the soil where trust begins to grow again.

Maxims of Silence

"Respect the silence you did not earn. It belongs to the subject; we are stewards, not owners."

"If words can wound, silence can heal."

"Speed belongs to chaos. Stillness belongs to the protector."

Silence heals.

Protector's Practice: Field Drills for Silence

Doctrine is not complete until it is lived. In negotiation, silence is not a theory to be admired; it is a discipline to be rehearsed until it becomes reflex. Words may inspire, but practice builds muscle memory. And in the moment of crisis, it is not what you remember—it is what you become that decides outcomes.

The drills we teach negotiators can also be lived by parents, coaches, leaders, and anyone who carries responsibility for others. These practices take silence from abstract concept to daily habit.

Drill: Breath Cadence Under Stress

In negotiation, the wire transmits more than words. It carries breath. The subject hears what the body reveals before the brain has shaped a sentence.

So we train breath as a weapon. Under pressure, we slow it. We speak in measured cadence. We let the silence between sentences stretch like rungs on a ladder, each pause something to hold on to.

How to Practice

In your next heated conversation—with a colleague, spouse, or even a stranger on the road—notice your breath.

Deliberately slow it. Use a four-second cadence. Breathe in . . . Hold. Breathe out . . . Hold.

Match your words to your breathing, not your adrenaline.

You will feel control return. More importantly, others will feel it too. Calm is contagious.

Drill: Signal vs. Noise

Negotiators live and die by this distinction. Signal is the small shift that reveals change—tone softening, cadence slowing, a repeated phrase that points to deeper fear. Noise is the chaos around it— shouting commanders, clicking cameras, the hum of politics.

Leaders in every domain fail not from lack of skill but from chasing noise instead of reading signal.

How to Practice

After your next conflict—large or small—write down what was signal and what was noise.

Signal: words or actions that indicated change or risk.

Noise: distractions, posturing, ego, fear.

The practice rewires your perception. Soon, even in the storm, you will hear the note that matters.

Drill: Patience as Tactic

The rookie's greatest enemy is the urge to answer too quickly, prove value, and show that they are working. But we do not prove discipline with speed; we prove it with restraint.

How to Practice

The next time you feel compelled to fire off a rapid response—an email, a retort, a text—wait sixty seconds longer than your impulse demands.

Breathe. Count the silence. Let your biology settle.

Notice how often your response shifts, softens, or improves after the pause.

Patience is not delay. Patience is tactic.

Drill: Division of Burden

The maxim is clear: Any problem divided by two is half. Silence is one way we divide the burden. By carrying the weight of stillness for another, we lessen their load.

How to Practice

Share a decision, fear, or frustration you normally carry alone with a trusted ally.

Don't rush to solutions. Sit in the silence together.

Observe how the weight lessens, not because the problem is solved but because it is shared.

Negotiation is never a solo act. It is the art of bearing weight together.

Drill: Ethos Check

Doctrine without ethos collapses under pressure. Silence without character becomes avoidance. So we train ourselves to reflect not only on tactics but on identity.

How to Practice

At the end of a hard day, ask yourself:

Did I act as a Warrior, mastering my own biology before facing others?

Did I act as a Guardian, absorbing pressure so others could function?

Did I act as a Shepherd, refusing to abandon those who faltered?

Did I act as a Protector, valuing outcomes over optics and life over applause?

This reflective drill ensures that silence is not something we use but something we are.

Why We Train This Way

Extraordinary acts of negotiation are built on ordinary disciplines mastered. Silence is only a weapon for those who have practiced it. Calm only holds under fire if it has been rehearsed in daily storms.

We cannot wait until the barricade, the boardroom, or the field to test ourselves. We practice in traffic jams, in staff meetings, in family arguments. We practice so that when the storm breaks, silence is no longer theory—it is muscle memory.

The protector does not wait for crisis to begin living the code. He lives it now, in the ordinary, so that when the extraordinary comes, he is already steady.

Closing Call: The Creed of Silence

Every chapter of this craft ends where it began: with silence. Not the silence of absence but the silence of presence. The silence carried by protectors who refuse to rush, abandon, and mistake noise for progress.

We learned the cost of impatience in blood. We learned the power of silence in scars. We learned that carrying quiet is harder than pulling a trigger—but infinitely more powerful when lives hang in the balance.

The ethos of silence is not decoration; it is the compass.

The Warrior teaches us that courage is not volume but discipline under fire.

The Guardian teaches us that pressure will break a room unless someone carries it.

The Shepherd teaches us that dignity is restored not through speeches but through presence.

The Protector teaches us that optics are noise, but life is signal.

Silence is the thread that binds them all.

The Protector's Creed of Silence

We say it to rookies when the silence burns in their chest. We whisper it to each other in the command post when commanders pace like caged lions. We carry it like a prayer when the night stretches long and the phone line goes dead.

Win arguments.

We are here to preserve life.

Perform calm.

We are here to deliver calm.

Prove value.

We are here to add value.

We are here to protect.

We are warriors who master ourselves before facing others.

We are guardians who carry the room's fear so the subject is not crushed by it.

We are shepherds who refuse to abandon the broken in their darkest hour.

We are protectors who measure success not in headlines but in breaths still drawn.

Silence heals.

Silence is presence.

Silence is not delay. Silence is discipline.

Carrying Silence Beyond Crisis

The creed is not for the wire. It is for the kitchen table, the boardroom, the locker room.

A mother chooses not to shout but to sit, letting her child's sobs run their course.

A CEO pauses before cutting jobs, separating signal from noise.

A coach holds the huddle in quiet before calling the play, letting the players breathe.

A husband or wife breathes before speaking, choosing presence over pride.

In each case, silence saves something fragile: trust, dignity, connection, life.

This is why we train. This is why we practice. Because one day, the silence we have rehearsed in ordinary storms will decide an extraordinary outcome.

A Final Word to the Reader

Silence will test you. It will feel like failure. It will press against your chest and demand you fill it with words. The crowd will roar for action, the clock will scream for speed, your own fear will demand noise.

But if you hold—if you breathe—if you carry the silence with discipline—you will change the room. You will steady the storm. You will give someone the space to survive.

The creed is not ours. It is yours. It belongs to every leader, parent, coach, or protector who refuses to mistake noise for strength.

"Respect the silence you did not earn. Carry it with discipline until it becomes medicine."

Closing Cadence

We are warriors who do not confuse volume with strength.

We are guardians who hold the line when fear demands spectacle.

We are shepherds who refuse to abandon the lost in the darkest hour.

We are protectors who measure success not by applause but by breaths still drawn.

This is the creed of silence.

This is the weight we carry.

And from this page forward, it is not I.

It is we.

It is you and me—*we*—who are charged with carrying the Code forward.

CHAPTER 2

Warrior Ethos

Warrior's maxim: "Any problem divided by two is half. We are here to help you."

This is the starting point of every negotiation. One side buckles beneath the weight of fear, rage, or despair; the other side steadies it. We step into the chaos not to dominate but to divide the burden—to shoulder enough of the pressure so others can breathe, think, and choose life.

The maxim is simple, but its truth is profound. Crisis is never meant to be carried alone. When the negotiator takes the weight, the subject is no longer isolated in their panic. Even in silence, even in resistance, they now know: Someone is present, steady, and refusing to let go.

This is not a tactic. It is a posture. It is the posture of the protector.

A Battlefield Without Bullets

The command post is its own battlefield. Radios hiss with fragments of information, SWAT operators stand ready with shields and rifles, leaders demand updates, and every second ticks like a countdown. Tension presses down like a storm cloud.

On this battlefield, weapons are words. Silence is a tactic. Patience is a shield. The negotiator's presence steadies the room and shapes the tempo of the incident. Where others see delay as weakness, we see it as strategy. Where others measure strength by firepower, we measure it by control.

Here, the fight is not against a barricaded door but against fear, impulse, and chaos. Every decision carries weight—not just for the subject inside but for the team outside, the community watching, and the legacy left behind. This is combat without gunfire, and yet its consequences can be just as permanent.

Case Reflection: The Cost of Impatience

In the early days, before doctrine, we lived and died by instinct. One call still echoes: a barricade where voices shouted over one another, a suspect spiraled, and the entry came too fast.

Shots rang out. A hostage was wounded. The suspect was killed. The debrief was short and brutal: "We had no patience. We had no plan."

That night taught us time is not weakness; time is survival. It was the seed of what became the Time Revolution—the recognition that discipline often means doing less, not more.

We began to understand crisis work is less about speed and more about stamina. The suspect may be burning hot, the command post boiling over, the media howling—but if we hold steady, adrenaline breaks. Rage cannot sprint forever. Despair eventually slows. Time levels the field.

From that failure was born our first principle: Sometimes the most decisive action you can take is to wait.

Reader Application: Division of Burden in Every Battlefield

Spouses are an essential part of this readership as well—the fourth audience—because they carry the burden of service alongside the warrior and often feel its cost first.

A parent loses composure and creates distance where connection was needed.

A leader under pressure makes a hasty decision for optics, trading trust for relief.

A coach pushes too hard and breaks the very team they hoped to strengthen.

In every arena, impatience creates casualties. Time—steady, disciplined time—restores clarity, protects relationships, and creates the chance for dignity to return.

Maxim: "Time is not the enemy. It is the ally of the protector."

From Force to Precision Influence

In the early days, crisis response was dominated by force—commands barked through bullhorns, threats of tactical entry, and ultimatums delivered with volume rather than persuasion. The idea was simple: Overwhelm the subject until they broke.

But force rarely produced surrender. More often, it produced resistance, panic, and violence. Every shouted threat hardened resolve. Every ultimatum narrowed options. Each attempt to coerce drove subjects further into defiance.

The turning point came when we shifted from force to precision influence. Instead of battering doors with demands, we opened them with dialogue. Instead of stripping away dignity, we restored it. Instead of leaving subjects with ultimatums, we gave them choices.

Negotiation became less about dominance and more about precision. Words were sharpened like tools, applied with care, designed to build rapport and preserve options. The protector's mission was no longer to crush resistance, but to guide it toward surrender through presence, patience, and influence.

Parents discover shouting may silence a child, but it never wins their heart.

Leaders learn coercion breeds compliance, not loyalty.

Coaches see that fear sparks effort, but encouragement inspires growth.

Maxim: "Force provokes resistance. Influence builds cooperation."

The Four Revolutions That Made Us

Every profession is shaped by turning points—moments when old ways failed so badly that change became unavoidable. Crisis negotiation was no different.

In its early years, we learned our lessons the hard way: in the aftermath of shattered standoffs, wounded innocents, and lives cut short.

From those failures came revolutions. Each one reshaped how we approached crisis. Each one turned instinct into discipline and guesswork into doctrine. They were not born in classrooms but in the crucible of real incidents where failure cost lives.

These four revolutions—Time, Psychology, Integration, and Professionalization—transformed negotiation from improvisation into a profession built on precision, patience, and protector ethos. Negotiators and SWAT working as one unified team instead of separate groups.

The Time Revolution

The first scar taught us the power of time. What once was seen as delay, we came to see as discipline. Time is not neutral; it bends human behavior. Rage cannot sprint forever. Adrenaline fades. Despair, no matter how dark, eventually slows.

If we hold steady, the storm always breaks.

This revolution demanded a shift in mindset. Command posts had to unlearn the belief that speed equals strength. Tactical teams had to embrace waiting as part of the mission. Negotiators had to master silence and presence, carrying the unbearable weight of inaction while the world screamed for action.

The Time Revolution was not passive. It was a deliberate, disciplined slowing of the tempo—buying seconds, then minutes, then hours until clarity could emerge.

Speed belongs to chaos, but time belongs to the protector.

Parents, tempted to snap in frustration, find that waiting cools tempers more than shouting.

Leaders, pressured by deadlines, discover that restraint saves organizations from costly mistakes.

Coaches, caught in the heat of competition, learn that holding steady often wins more than panicked changes.

Maxim: "Speed belongs to chaos. Time belongs to the protector."

The Psychology Revolution: Biology Informs Tactics

The second revolution came when we began to study not only the suspect's mind but the body that carried it.

We stopped arguing with emotion and started reading it. Fight–flight–freeze, tunnel vision, shame spirals—these weren't quirks; they were predictable conditions.

A raging father threatening his family wasn't "irrational." He was hijacked by chemicals. A suicidal veteran who repeated the same sentence wasn't "ignoring us." He was locked in a stress loop.

By learning to see biology, we stopped being frustrated and started being strategic.

Fight: We slowed our tone, lowered our volume, gave space.

Flight: We promised safety, reinforced control, slowed the exits.

Freeze: We used silence, patience, and gentle prompts to reawaken thought.

Every response became less about debate and more about treatment.

This shift was radical. Before, we thought success depended on finding the right words. Now we knew success depended on regulating biology—through cadence, pacing, silence, and tone.

We discovered that our voice could act like a metronome for another human being's nervous system. When we were steady, they steadied. When we raced, they raced. This realization transformed negotiation from "good talking" into applied psychology under fire.

Parents see children mirror their tone: Calm steadies, anger escalates.

Leaders recognize that when they carry panic into the room, the team multiplies it; when they carry steadiness, the team absorbs it.

Coaches find that cadence and calm regulate performance better than shouting ever could.

Maxim: "We do not rush people back to logic. We protect them until their biology lets them return."

The Integration Revolution: Two Sides of the Same Shield

For years, SWAT and negotiators eyed each other with suspicion. One side saw words as delay. The other saw guns as impatience. Lives were lost in the gap.

Integration changed everything. Containment bought us time. Tactical presence reduced chaos. Negotiation leveraged both to move a human being toward surrender.

The rifle and the voice learned to breathe together. When snipers spotted movement at a window, they didn't just call it in; they asked how that intel could shape dialogue. When negotiators heard a shift in tone, they didn't just log it; they briefed tactical so posture could adjust.

The result was fusion. The team became one shield with two sides, indivisible.

Integration also reshaped morale. Tactical teams no longer felt sidelined, waiting endlessly while "the talkers" stalled. Negotiators no longer felt like the soft option about to be overrun. Both realized they were vital—and together they formed a system that could flex without breaking.

This was the Integration Revolution: the recognition that success does not come from rivalry between tools but unity of purpose.

Integration is not just a tactical principle; it is a leadership principle.

Parents must integrate firmness with compassion.

Leaders must integrate vision with execution.

Coaches must integrate discipline with encouragement.

Strength without empathy fractures. Empathy without strength collapses. Integration fuses both into a shield strong enough to protect.

Maxim: "The voice and the rifle are not adversaries; they are brothers in the same mission."

The Professionalization Revolution: From Good Instincts to Good Doctrine

In the early years, the "best negotiator" was often the most charismatic officer on shift—the natural talker who could charm, persuade, or improvise under pressure. Sometimes they worked miracles. Sometimes they failed catastrophically. Success depended on personality, not discipline.

That changed when we began to turn stories into doctrine.

After-action reviews became lessons.

Lessons became principles.

Principles became training.

We built checklists. We trained logging officers. We taught silence as a skill, not an accident. We built pipelines to produce negotiators, not just hope for them.

The Professionalization Revolution gave the craft longevity. No longer was success dependent on chance or personality. It became replicable. Any trained negotiator, equipped with discipline and ethos, could step in and deliver.

This also elevated credibility inside the command post. Where negotiators were once brushed aside as "opinion," they now carried doctrine—tested, taught, repeatable. It wasn't "what Mike thinks." It was "what the discipline requires."

The craft matured—from personality to profession, from hope to reliability, from "pray the right person is on duty tonight" to "every trained protector can deliver."

The same shift is needed in every domain.

Parents must pass down principles, not just personal habits.

Leaders must build systems, not just rely on charisma.

Coaches must leave legacies of training that outlast their presence.

Personality inspires. Doctrine endures.

Maxim: "Legacy is not personality. Legacy is doctrine passed down intact."

Case Reflection: The Integration Breakthrough

The first time we truly fused with SWAT, the difference was undeniable. A barricaded suspect had fired two shots out a window. Tension soared. Entry was requested.

But this time, negotiation and tactical were not in competition. We were one shield.

We briefed the team: "His threats are loud, but his cadence is softening. He mentioned his daughter twice. He's time-sensitive but not resolved to die. Hold perimeter."

For hours, SWAT held. We slowed our voices, mirrored his breathing, and offered dignity. At dawn, he stepped out unarmed.

No shots fired. No injuries. No funerals. The revolution had arrived.

What Changed, and What Didn't

The terrain of crisis work keeps expanding: phone calls to text, face-to-face to livestream, barricades to cyber hostages. We now share airspace with drones and dashboards that claim to read stress in syllables. We use the tools, but we do not worship them.

Technology sharpens steel; judgment wields it.

What has not changed is the center of gravity: a human being in crisis, and a protector on the other end of the line who refuses to treat that person as a problem to be solved rather than a life to be stewarded.

No matter how advanced the gear, it is still the tone in a negotiator's voice, the timing of silence, and the ethos in our hearts that tip the balance. Tools support; ethos decides.

Case Reflection: The Silent Surrender

A man locked himself in a garage after losing everything—job, family, hope. He spoke in bursts, then dropped into long silences. Commanders grew restless. Entry was debated.

But we knew silence wasn't absence; it was biology cooling. So we stayed. We carried the silence with him. Hours passed.

Finally, a quiet voice: "Are you still there?"

"Yes," we answered. "We're here to help you."

Moments later, he laid the gun down and walked out. His surrender was not to us, but to the silence we shared.

That day, the shepherd's duty was fulfilled: presence over performance, patience over pressure.

Parents who sit in silence with hurting children often give them courage to speak.

Leaders who allow space in hard conversations often earn more trust than those who rush to answers.

Coaches who hold stillness in the huddle often steady a team more than words ever could.

Maxim: "Silence is not absence. Silence is presence."

Doctrine We Live By

Through scars and lessons, the craft distilled itself into doctrines that could be passed down—not theories but battle-tested principles forged in fire.

Contain, Stabilize, Influence

Contain the scene to stop new harm.

Stabilize the biology with tone, pacing, and silence.

Influence behavior by offering choices that preserve dignity.

The Four Gates to Surrender

Safety: "No one is rushing you."

Dignity: "You can resolve this as the one in control."

Connection: "You are not alone in this."

Future: "There is a tomorrow we can get to if we slow down together."

Command Post Discipline

Separate signal (changes that alter risk) from noise (pressure, optics, politics).

Translate emotion into intel and intel into action.

Speak truth to authority—without ego and without fear.

Doctrine became our compass. With it, we no longer guessed at the next step. We had a path—forged by experience, tested in failure, and written in lives.

"Any problem divided by two is half."

We divide the problem the moment the subject realizes we are carrying it with them. We divide it again when the command post lets our cadence set the tempo instead of fear. We divide it again when the team breathes together—not as factions but as one shield.

Negotiation is not a solo act. It is the art of bearing weight together. Each moment we stand with the subject, steady the room, and convince tactical to hold, the burden grows lighter.

Maxims like this are not just words; they are anchors. Negotiators repeat them in the dead of night, when fatigue erodes judgment and pressure screams for action. They are shorthand for discipline—distilled wisdom grasped in a breath.

What We Tell New Negotiators (and Ourselves on Hard Nights)

Every rookie begins with the same fears: What if I say the wrong thing? What if I freeze? What if I fail?

The truth is you will. We all have. Perfection is not attainable. What matters is recovery—the ability to return to discipline and keep showing up with integrity.

What we remind them—and ourselves—when nights grow long:

- We are not here to win arguments. We are here to preserve life.
- We are not here to perform calm. We are here to deliver calm.
- We are not here to prove value. We are here to add value.
- We are not here to trick anyone. Influence without integrity breaks trust—and people.

The rookie half-believes until they live it. Then words become survival. Veterans repeat them not because they forget, but because under stress, memory fades. Doctrine restores clarity when fatigue and politics cloud the air.

The Value of Saying Less

One of the hardest lessons for new negotiators to learn is restraint. They want to fill every silence, correct every contradiction, steer every conversation. But negotiation is not performance. It is presence.

We teach them to count silently before responding, embrace pauses not as voids but as tools, and remember that silence is medicine.

Parents who pause before responding prevent words they'll regret.

Leaders who listen longer than they speak earn trust that lectures never achieve.

Coaches who allow silence after failure give players room to reset instead of react.

Maxim: "Silence is not weakness. Silence is medicine."

The Ethos That Guides Every Decision

The craft of negotiation is not simply about tactics; it is anchored in an ethos. Without ethos, skills become hollow tricks. With it, presence becomes doctrine embodied.

Warrior: Courage without ego, strength under control, action governed by purpose.

The warrior stands firm not because he seeks battle but because he has mastered himself. The negotiator as warrior refuses to let fear, anger, or pride dictate decisions. Strength under control is the essence of courage.

Guardian: A shield between chaos and the innocent, carrying weight others never see.

The guardian absorbs the anxiety of the command post so others can function. He stands between rash action and disastrous consequence, willing to bear criticism so that lives may be preserved.

Shepherd: Presence that refuses to abandon, guidance that restores dignity and choice.

The shepherd does not drag the lost; he walks beside them. In crisis, people feel stripped of dignity. The shepherd restores it—by offering options, granting time, and affirming that surrender does not equal defeat.

Protector: The unifying purpose of life over optics, outcomes over pride, legacy over applause.

The protector measures success not in medals or headlines but in breaths still drawn. Protectors know that true victory is quiet—a mother reunited with her child, an officer who doesn't have to fire, a subject who chooses life over death.

This ethos is more than description. It is the compass that guides every decision when pressure mounts and optics scream. Without it, even sharp tactics collapse under ego. With it, we hold the line with clarity, courage, and purpose.

Ethos in Action

This ethos is not decoration. It is doctrine. When timelines compress, optics scream, and political heat rises, ethos decides what we do next.

It is not uncommon for a commander, mayor, or governor to demand action. In those moments, doctrine alone is not enough. Checklists cannot answer politics. Procedures cannot silence pressure.

What holds the line is ethos.

It is ethos that gives us the courage to say: "We will hold. Lives matter more than optics."

Without ethos, even the best tactics are brittle, bending to fear and ego. With ethos, negotiators absorb storms without breaking. Ethos transforms doctrine from procedure into principle—from words on paper into courage in practice.

Parents feel pressure when outsiders judge their patience.

Leaders feel it when shareholders demand shortcuts.

Coaches feel it when crowds roar for quick results.

In those moments, tactics alone will not hold. Ethos does.

Maxim: "Doctrine guides us. Ethos anchors us."

Living the Ethos

We remind ourselves of the ethos daily.

We are warriors who do not confuse volume with strength.

We are guardians who hold the line when fear demands spectacle.

We are shepherds who refuse to abandon the lost in the darkest hour.

We are protectors who measure success not by applause but by breath still drawn in a chest that might have been stilled.

These are not slogans for posters. They are survival codes for negotiators who carry the burden of lives in the balance.

The ethos is what allows us to withstand criticism, endure pressure, and make unpopular choices in service of higher outcomes. It is not simply what we do—it is who we are.

Doctrine is not complete until it is lived. To understand crisis negotiation, one must train not only in the command post but in daily life. The habits we practice in ordinary moments become the disciplines that save lives in extraordinary ones.

Leaders fail when they chase noise instead of acting on signal. Protectors learn to tell the difference.

Why We Train This Way

These practices may seem small, even ordinary. But every extraordinary act of negotiation is built on ordinary disciplines mastered.

Silence is a weapon only for those who have practiced it. Calm only holds under fire if it has been rehearsed in daily storms.

We cannot wait for a barricaded gunman or a suicidal veteran to practice restraint. We practice in traffic, in meetings, in family conflicts. We practice so that when the storm breaks, patience is no longer theory—it is muscle memory.

Closing Call

We stand where generations of protectors taught us to stand—at the edge of harm with courage under control.

We are warriors who do not confuse volume with strength.

We are guardians who hold the line when fear demands spectacle.

We are shepherds who refuse to abandon the lost in the darkest hour.

This is the evolution of crisis negotiation:

- From force first to precision influence
- From lone heroes to fused teams
- From quick tempers to disciplined calm
- From accidents of success to a replicable craft

And from this page forward, the Code is no longer mine alone. It is yours. It is ours. Together, we carry it forward.

CHAPTER 3

Doctrine of the Warrior

The room was thick with tension. A young man sat barricaded in his apartment, blinds closed, phone clutched in his hand like the only tether between life and death. His voice shook with rage one moment and collapsed into sobs the next. SWAT operators crouched behind shields in the hallway. Radios hissed. A sergeant whispered the question no one wanted to say aloud: "How long before we go in?"

Everyone wanted movement. Everyone wanted resolution. But the negotiator on the line knew the truth—there are no shortcuts to change. You can't drag someone to surrender. You can't shout them into trust. You can't demand transformation. Change is a staircase, and every step matters. Miss one, and the whole structure collapses.

That staircase was given a name: the Behavioral Change Stairway Model (BCSM)—the FBI's five-step framework for moving someone from chaos to cooperation. Born from the FBI's Crisis Negotiation Unit, it gave us not just tactics but a map of how human beings shift from chaos to clarity. It showed us that the road to surrender isn't built on clever arguments or sheer willpower—it's built on presence, connection, and discipline, step by step.

The steps are simple to describe, but profound in practice:

- Active listening
- Empathy
- Rapport
- Influence
- Behavioral change

On paper, it looks like theory. In life, it is a lifeline. When followed with discipline, it carries people from the edge of violence back to the possibility of tomorrow. When ignored, shortcuts trigger panic, resistance, or tragedy.

We did not invent this stairway, but we carried it into the crises. We climbed it with lives on the line, often under the glare of politics, pressure, and impatience. We learned that every step is not just technique—it is ethos.

Listening is the discipline of the Warrior: controlling ourselves before trying to control the room.

Empathy is the compassion of the Guardian: absorbing pain without letting it crush us.

Rapport is the presence of the Shepherd: walking beside another until trust takes root.

Influence is the patience of the Protector: guiding without coercion, offering choices instead of ultimatums.

Behavioral change is the fruit of all four combined: a moment where chaos bends, and life is preserved.

The man in the apartment that night did not walk out because of force. He walked out because each step was honored. He was listened to until his words slowed. He was understood until his anger softened. He felt connection until he trusted. He was influenced by options, not commands. And finally, he chose change—not because we forced him, but because we carried him up the stairway until he could walk the last steps himself.

Active Listening: The Warrior's First Step

The first step on the Stairway looks deceptively simple: Listen. But listening under fire is not passive; it is discipline at the edge of chaos.

Case Reflection: The Barricaded Father

It was past midnight when the call came. A father had locked himself in a bedroom with a pistol after an argument with his wife. His voice thundered at first—accusations, shame, threats. Then, in waves, he grew quieter, like a man drowning under his own breath.

Our rookie negotiator wanted to reassure him immediately, argue away the fear, and speak calm into the chaos. But the veteran on the line raised a hand. "Wait. Don't fix. Listen."

So they did. They let him rant. They let him repeat. They caught the small fractures in his voice, the way it caught when he mentioned his daughter's name, the silence that stretched when he admitted he "wasn't sure anyone cared anymore."

Instead of filling the air with promises or counterpoints, they mirrored his words back gently:

"You're feeling abandoned."

"It sounds like tonight broke something that was already fragile."

"You're carrying more weight than you can hold."

And the man responded—not with escalation but with something closer to recognition. For the first time, he wasn't being argued with. He was being heard. The pistol eventually came down, not because we persuaded him with logic, but because he realized he was not alone in the storm.

Doctrine of Active Listening

Active listening is not waiting to talk. It is not holding your breath until you can insert your argument. It is not passivity. It is combat discipline with words.

The Warrior embodies this step because listening demands restraint under fire. Anyone can shout. Anyone can argue. But it takes a warrior's control to remain silent long enough to actually hear.

The doctrine rests on a few pillars:

Mirroring: Repeat key words to show presence and invite elaboration.

Labeling: Name emotions out loud: "It sounds like you feel trapped."

Minimal Encouragers: Small cues—"mm-hmm," "go on"—that let the other know you are there without hijacking the pace.

Silence: Holding the gap long enough for truth to emerge.

Active listening is the foundation of every other step. Without it, empathy is guesswork, rapport is counterfeit, influence is manipulation, and change is impossible.

Reader Application: Listening Under Fire

Active listening is not reserved for barricades. It is a discipline that transforms every arena where chaos presses in.

- *Parents:* A child storms in from school, shouting about unfair treatment. The impulse is to correct or explain. Instead, listen—mirror their words, label the emotion, and watch the storm calm without a single lecture.

- *Leaders:* In a boardroom, a team member resists a new plan. Instead of debating, ask, "It sounds like you're worried about trust. Can you say more?" Listening doesn't concede authority—it earns it.

- *Coaches:* An athlete makes excuses after failure. Instead of cutting them off, let them run until the words thin out. Then, repeat back what matters. The locker room hears presence, not condemnation.

- *Spouses:* Arguments collapse when one partner listens past the words to the emotion beneath. "It sounds like you felt dismissed" can cool a fight faster than any defense.

In every field, active listening is the warrior's stance—still, focused, waiting for the moment to act with precision rather than impulse.

Maxim: "Listening is not waiting to talk. It is the warrior's control under fire."

Empathy: The Guardian's Shield

If active listening opens the door, empathy is what walks through it. To hear words is one thing. To feel the weight behind them—and to let the speaker know you feel it—is another. Empathy is not weakness. It is the Guardian's shield: the discipline of absorbing pain without letting it destroy you and acknowledging another's burden so they can believe it is survivable.

Case Reflection: The Veteran in the Basement

He was a decorated combat veteran, alone in his basement, rifle across his knees. Years of trauma, isolation, and guilt had hardened into despair. When the call came, he told us straight: "I've got nothing left. Don't waste your time."

We listened. He repeated the same sentences like grooves in a broken record: "I failed my family. I failed my men." Hours went by, his voice circling the same words. The rookie grew restless—"He's not hearing us." But the lead negotiator leaned closer to the wire. "No. He needs to know we're hearing him."

So the team shifted. Instead of offering solutions, they named the pain.

"You've carried weight most men never will."

"It sounds like you're drowning in guilt, even after serving with honor."

"You're not talking to strangers—you're talking to protectors who understand what it means to carry scars."

The veteran didn't surrender to arguments. He surrendered to empathy. Hours later, when he emerged, rifle lowered, he said the words we never forget: "You actually understood me. No one else does."

Doctrine of Empathy

Empathy is not agreement. It does not mean we endorse harmful actions or justify violence. It means we see the person beneath the chaos.

The Guardian embodies this step because empathy is about carrying weight. The Guardian absorbs the anxiety of the command post, the fear of the family outside, the despair of the subject inside. It is not pity. It is disciplined recognition.

Pillars of Empathy in Negotiation

Emotion Recognition: Move beyond facts to feelings. What drives the words? Anger, shame, fear, grief?

Verbal Acknowledgment: Speak it aloud. "You sound exhausted," or "That feels like betrayal."

Humanization: Call the subject by name. Recognize their history. Restore dignity.

Consistency: Empathy collapses if it is performative. It must be steady, even when tested by rage.

Without empathy, listening is hollow. With it, rapport becomes possible.

Empathy is often confused with softness. In truth, it is strength: the ability to hold another's burden without losing your own footing.

- *Parents:* When a teenager screams, "You don't understand me," empathy answers not with rebuttal but with recognition: "It feels like I don't get it. Help me see." The argument loses oxygen.

- *Leaders:* When a team resists change, empathy reframes the moment. "You're worried this will make your work harder. That makes sense." Trust begins where empathy is shown.

- *Coaches:* An athlete breaks down after failure. Instead of analysis first, empathy goes deeper: "You poured yourself into this, and it hurts." Empathy doesn't excuse failure—it creates ground for growth.

- *Spouses:* In marriage, empathy is often the bridge between pride and peace. A simple, "I see you're exhausted, and it's wearing on you," can shift an argument into connection.

Empathy does not solve the problem immediately. But it steadies the field so that solutions can emerge.

Maxim: "Empathy is not agreement. It is the Guardian's shield—absorbing pain so trust can be born."

Rapport: The Shepherd's Bridge

If listening steadies the storm and empathy absorbs its weight, rapport is what builds the bridge across it. Rapport is not charm or flattery. It is the slow work of convincing another human being that they are safe enough to take a step toward us. It is the Shepherd's gift: presence that refuses to abandon and guidance that restores dignity and choice.

Case Reflection: The Hostage Taker and the Daughter's Photo

It was a standoff in a small duplex. The man inside had taken his girlfriend hostage. He shouted threats into the phone, alternating between blaming her and blaming the world.

The breakthrough came not through argument, but through connection. One negotiator noticed a detail buried in the chaos: The man had mentioned his daughter, briefly, almost as an aside. The team shifted.

We asked about her. At first, he resisted. Then, slowly, he spoke— about her age, her smile, and missing her birthday last month. Hours passed, and the daughter became the bridge. The girlfriend's name faded from his rage, replaced by stories of playgrounds and bedtime routines.

At one point, he sent a photo through the door—a crayon drawing his daughter had made. That moment was the turning point. For the first time, he was not shouting. He was remembering that he was more than his rage.

He eventually released his girlfriend unharmed and surrendered. Not because he was coerced, but because rapport reminded him he was still a father—and fathers choose life for their children.

Doctrine of Rapport

Rapport is not manipulation. It is recognition. It does not mean we become best friends with the subject. It means we create a human-to-human connection strong enough to outlast the chaos. When asked by the media if the suspect was "a bad guy," the negotiator's response was "I don't know if he's a good guy, bad guy, or any other kind of guy. What I do know is that he's a human being in crisis and needs our help!"

The Shepherd embodies this step because rapport is about walking alongside another—steady, patient, unwilling to let them walk alone.

Pillars of Rapport in Negotiation

Find the Anchor: A name, family member, or memory—something human to connect to.

Consistency of Presence: Rapport collapses if we break cadence, change tone, or betray trust.

Respect Small Openings: When the subject shares, however little, we honor it. Every detail is a foothold.

Dignity: Rapport is impossible if we strip away control. We give choices, not ultimatums.

Rapport is fragile but powerful. Once formed, it becomes the bridge that allows influence to travel.

Rapport is often mistaken for charisma. In truth, it is the discipline of presence. It is not about being liked—it is about being trusted.

- *Parents:* A child may resist lectures but will respond when they feel safe. Sitting on the floor to hear them and listening without rushing builds the bridge for guidance.

- *Leaders:* Teams follow leaders they trust, not just those they fear. Rapport is built by honoring small wins, remembering details of people's lives, and showing consistency under pressure.

- *Coaches:* Athletes run through walls, not just for strategy but for a coach who remembers their name, their struggle, and their worth.

- *Spouses:* Marriages survive not on constant agreement but on the bridge of rapport—small acts of presence that remind each partner, "I see you, I choose you, even in conflict."

Rapport does not mean weakness. It means strength anchored in connection. It is what allows influence to move without resistance.

Maxim: "Rapport is not charm. It is the Shepherd's bridge—presence that restores dignity and opens the way to trust."

Influence: The Protector's Guidance

Rapport opens the bridge, but influence is the path that crosses it. Influence is not coercion, manipulation, or trickery. It is the art of guiding another human being toward a decision they can own with dignity. The Protector embodies this step because influence requires patience, steadiness, and the courage to value life over ego.

Case Reflection: The Suicidal Teen and the Options on the Table

The subject was a teenager perched on the edge of a parking garage, threatening to jump. The crowd below grew restless. Officers tensed, fearing a sudden movement.

The negotiator didn't shout commands. He didn't lecture about consequences. Instead, he offered choices.

"You can stay sitting there while we talk."

"You can come down one level so we're closer."

"Or you can keep breathing and just tell me about what got you here."

Each option preserved dignity. Each choice gave control back to someone who felt stripped of it. Slowly, the teen shifted from silence to small answers. He agreed to move closer to the negotiator. Then, finally, he allowed himself to be guided down.

What worked was not authority—it was influence. By offering paths instead of ultimatums, the negotiator turned paralysis into motion. The teen lived because he felt he had chosen life, not surrendered it.

Doctrine of Influence

Influence in negotiation is not about dominance. It is about creating conditions where another person can make the safer choice themselves.

Pillars of Influence in Negotiation

Choice Architecture: Present options that preserve dignity. Never "Do this or else." Always "Here are paths, and you control which one you take."

Framing: Position surrender not as defeat but as survival, as a return to something worth living for.

Cadence of Patience: Influence collapses if rushed. Time is what makes choice possible.

Consistency with Rapport: Influence must grow naturally from trust. Without rapport, influence feels like manipulation.

The Protector embodies influence because it is about guarding outcomes, not ego. We protect life, not pride.

Influence belongs not only in crisis but in every realm where we guide others. The same principles work in homes, offices, and fields.

- *Parents:* Instead of barking commands, offer structured choices: "You can finish homework now or after dinner. You decide." The child learns responsibility, not resentment.

- *Leaders:* Influence comes when employees feel ownership. "You can approach the project with option A or option B— what do you see as best?" buys commitment where orders buy compliance.

- *Coaches:* Athletes resist being treated like robots. Influence is built when a coach frames choices: "You can attack with speed or patience—either way, trust your training."

- *Spouses:* Influence preserves dignity in conflict: "We can keep discussing this tonight, or pause, breathe, and pick it up tomorrow. Which feels right to you?"

In each case, influence succeeds not by overpowering but by guiding toward outcomes that preserve both life and dignity.

Maxim: "Influence is not control. It is the Protector's guidance— offering choices that preserve dignity and lead to survival."

Behavioral Change: The Summit of the Stairway

Active listening steadies the noise. Empathy absorbs the weight. Rapport builds the bridge. Influence opens the path. But all of these are means, not ends. The end is behavioral change—a subject choosing life, surrender, or safety where destruction once loomed.

Change cannot be forced. It cannot be demanded. True change is voluntary. It is the final step of the Stairway, built on the foundation of every step before it.

Case Reflection: The Gunman Who Walked Out Alive

It was a small-town bank, the kind with tellers who knew every customer by name. A desperate man had entered with a shotgun, taken hostages, and demanded money. For hours, he raged, insisting he had nothing left to lose.

But the negotiators climbed the Stairway with him.

Listening: They caught his real fear—that his family would see him as a failure.

Empathy: They named it: "You're carrying shame that feels heavier than this gun."

Rapport: They asked about his son and the fishing trips they used to take. The gunman softened when he spoke of him.

Influence: They framed surrender not as defeat but as protection. "You can walk out today as the father who chose life over headlines. That's a story your son can live with."

Hours later, the door opened. He stepped out, gun lowered, hands raised. The hostages emerged unharmed.

The behavioral change was not an accident. It was not luck. It was the product of every step, honored with discipline.

Doctrine of Behavioral Change

Behavioral change is not about us. It is about the subject choosing a future that seemed impossible when the incident began.

The Protector embodies this final step because it requires us to release ego. We do not measure success in applause but in survival. We are not the hero of their story—they are.

Pillars of Behavioral Change in Negotiation

Ownership: The subject must feel the decision is theirs. Anything coerced will collapse under pressure.

Alignment: The change must align with their values—family, dignity, identity. We point toward those anchors.

Timing: Change emerges only when biology cools and trust has been built. Rushing this step shatters the whole stairway.

Dignity in Surrender: We frame surrender not as humiliation but as survival with honor intact.

Behavioral change is the fruit, not the push.

Behavioral change is not limited to hostage scenes. The same stairway leads to transformation in everyday life.

- *Parents:* You cannot force maturity. But if you listen, empathize, and build rapport, influence guides your child to change behavior on their own. A teen apologizing without being ordered is true change.

- *Leaders:* Mandates produce compliance. Stairway leadership produces commitment. When employees feel heard, valued, and guided, they choose better performance rather than being pushed into it.

- *Coaches:* Yelling may produce effort for a moment, but it is influence rooted in rapport that produces lasting change. Athletes run harder when they choose to, not when they are threatened.

- *Spouses:* Lasting change in relationships comes not from ultimatums but from the slow climb: listening, empathy, rapport, and influence. Change that is chosen lasts. Change that is coerced breaks.

In every arena, behavioral change is the summit. It proves that presence, patience, and protection carry more weight than force.

Maxim: "Change cannot be forced. It must be chosen. The Stairway is the Protector's gift—guiding others until they can choose life themselves."

A Full Stairway in Action: The Warehouse Standoff

Not every incident fits neatly into one step of the Stairway. Most demand all five, stacked carefully, tested under fire. One such moment came during a warehouse standoff that could have ended in blood.

The Setup

A man in his forties, recently laid off, had barricaded himself inside a warehouse with his supervisor held at gunpoint. He'd been spiraling for months—financial stress, marriage crumbling, a sense that the world had discarded him. That night, his despair hardened into violence.

Tactical units surrounded the building. The media swarmed. The mayor called, demanding resolution before dawn. Pressure at the command post mounted like a storm cloud.

Inside, the man shouted through the phone: "I'm not going back to jail! Nobody cares if I live or die!" His voice ricocheted between fury and despair, a live wire that could snap in any direction.

Step One: Active Listening

The negotiator did not argue. He let the man vent. He mirrored words back—"You feel discarded," "You think no one cares"—until the rage began to steady. Each echo reminded the man he was heard, not ignored. Silence stretched. The storm began to lose oxygen.

Step Two: Empathy

Hours into the night, the subject repeated the same line: "I'm worthless." Instead of refuting it, the negotiator acknowledged it. "You've given years to a company that let you go. That pain is real." The man broke down crying. For the first time, the gun loosened in his grip.

Step Three: Rapport

The team searched for anchors. A detail emerged: He mentioned his teenage son. The negotiator leaned into it. "Tell me about him. What's he like?" Slowly, the man opened up—stories of football games, laughter, regrets about missed birthdays. The son became the bridge. Each word about him chipped away at despair.

Step Four: Influence

With rapport secured, influence began. The negotiator framed choices that preserved dignity.

"You can keep holding the gun, and we'll stay with you."

"You can let your supervisor walk out and show your son that even at your lowest, you chose life."

Every option left him with control. Each one gave him dignity.

Step Five: Behavioral Change

At dawn, the door opened. The supervisor stumbled out, shaken but alive. Minutes later, the subject followed, hands trembling, tears streaking his face. The rifle was left on the floor.

The command post exhaled. The mayor was satisfied. But more importantly, a father chose life instead of a legacy of violence.

Doctrine in Action

This incident embodied why the Stairway matters. None of the steps alone would have been enough.

Listening cooled rage.

Empathy broke isolation.

Rapport built the bridge.

Influence framed choices.

Behavioral change preserved life.

The model is not theory—it is discipline under fire.

We may not barricade ourselves in warehouses, but crisis creeps into every life: in strained marriages, businesses collapsing, teams fracturing, and children spiraling. The same Stairway carries us through.

- *Parents:* When a teenager slams the door and declares, "I hate this family," the temptation is to correct. Instead, walk the Stairway: Listen to the storm, empathize with the loneliness, build rapport through shared ground, influence with choices, and wait for change that is chosen, not forced.

- *Leaders:* When employees resist change, the Stairway steadies the way forward. Listen without defensiveness, empathize with their fears, build rapport through shared vision, influence with clear options, and watch commitment emerge.

- *Coaches:* When an athlete collapses under pressure, don't rush to correction. The Stairway brings them back—presence, trust, dignity, then guidance.

Everywhere we lead, love, or coach, the Stairway is there. It is not just a negotiation model. It is a way of life.

Maxim: "The Stairway is not a theory. It is a path—one step at a time, carrying chaos toward life."

Protector's Practice: Climbing the Stairway in Daily Life

Doctrine is never complete until it is lived. The Behavioral Change Stairway is not only for crisis sites and command posts. It is a discipline that can be practiced in every arena of life, because conflict and chaos visit us all. The protector does not wait for the worst day to train. The protector practices in the ordinary so that excellence is a reflex when the storm breaks.

Drill: Listening Under Pressure

The next time you feel the urge to cut someone off—whether in a meeting, a family argument, or traffic—pause. Instead of answering, mirror their last phrase back. Watch what happens. Most people, when mirrored, reveal more than they intended. You will see how presence slows storms.

Drill: Empathy Naming

In your next conflict, try naming the other person's emotion out loud. "It sounds like you're frustrated." "It seems like you feel ignored." Watch how the energy shifts. Emotional labeling does not inflame it; it acknowledges it. This is empathy as a Guardian's shield.

Drill: Rapport Anchors

Build bridges before you need them. Pick one colleague, teammate, or family member and recall one detail they've shared—about a hobby, a child, or a recent struggle. Bring it up intentionally in your next conversation. Rapport is built not in grand speeches but in remembered humanity.

Drill: Influence Through Options

Instead of delivering an ultimatum, frame options. "You can finish this tonight, or we can regroup tomorrow." "You can choose path A or path B." Dignity lives in choice. Try it once this week, and notice how influence grows where coercion would have collapsed.

Drill: Supporting Change

When someone around you changes—even in small ways— acknowledge it. "I saw how you handled that better than last time." "I noticed you stayed calm." Change is fragile; support strengthens it. Practice noticing and reinforcing change daily.

Why Drills Matter

Crisis responses are forged from habits repeated until they are reflex. Silence only becomes a weapon if you've practiced it in traffic jams and tense dinners. Calm only holds under fire if you've rehearsed it under everyday stress. These small drills build muscle memory. And when the true storm arrives, you will not scramble for tactics—you will climb instinctively.

Reader Application: Lessons in Controlled Courage

The Stairway belongs in every realm of life.

- *Parents:* Listen past slammed doors, empathize with the frustration, build rapport through shared ground, guide with choices, and trust that change comes when dignity is preserved.
- *Leaders:* In boardrooms, the Stairway steadies decisions. Active listening cools debates. Empathy eases resistance.

Rapport builds trust. Influence aligns options. Change comes through commitment, not compliance.

- *Coaches:* In locker rooms, Stairway discipline turns defeat into resilience. Athletes who feel heard, understood, and guided do not just improve—they transform.

- *Spouses:* In marriages, the Stairway prevents small arguments from turning into barricades. Listening and empathy build bridges where pride would burn them.

Everyday life is a training ground for extraordinary moments.

Maxim: "Excellence in crisis is born from discipline in the ordinary. The Stairway must be climbed daily."

The Stairway Beyond Crisis

The Behavioral Change Stairway is more than a model for negotiators. It is a blueprint for protectors of every kind—warriors, guardians, shepherds, leaders, parents, coaches, and friends. Crisis does not only arrive with barricades and rifles. It arrives in boardrooms where trust fractures, in homes where families strain, in teams where failure weighs heavy, and in hearts that whisper despair.

The Stairway gives us a way forward when words fail and pressure suffocates.

Doctrine in Closing

Listening reminds us that silence steadies storms.

Empathy shows us that to carry weight is not to collapse but to protect.

Rapport builds bridges across chaos.

Influence guides without breaking dignity.

Behavioral Change is the summit—life chosen when despair once ruled.

These are not sterile steps. They are disciplines forged in blood, tested in fire, and proven in lives preserved. They remind us that protection is not dominance—it is presence.

Case Reflection: The Stairway in the Command Post

The command post during a critical incident is a furnace. Commanders, politicians, families, and media collide in demands for action. The noise threatens to drown out the mission.

But the Stairway has changed the culture of command posts across the world. Leaders now recognize that time is not weakness. Empathy is not softness. Rapport is not stalling. Influence is not manipulation. Behavioral change is not surrender—it is victory.

One veteran commander summed it up best after a long night where a barricaded man finally surrendered without bloodshed: "We didn't win by force. We won by discipline."

Each of us will face moments where someone around us spirals into chaos:

A colleague in despair, threatening to quit.

A child breaking under pressure, declaring, "I can't do this."

A spouse overwhelmed by loss.

A team fractured by failure.

In those moments, the Stairway is not a negotiation tactic. It is a life tactic. Listen with discipline. Empathize with courage. Build rapport with presence. Influence with dignity. Support the change when it comes.

You may not be holding a phone to a barricaded suspect, but you may be holding the emotional line for someone you love. The stakes are just as real.

Living the Ethos

The Stairway aligns seamlessly with the ethos we carry.

The Warrior listens under fire, holding stillness like a weapon.

The Guardian empathizes, absorbing pain without breaking.

The Shepherd builds rapport, refusing to abandon those in darkness.

The Protector influences and guides toward survival, guarding life over pride.

When practiced daily, the Stairway is not steps on a chart. It is character in motion. It is ethos lived out under stress.

Closing Call

The Stairway begins with listening and ends with life. It is a path anyone can climb—negotiators, leaders, parents, coaches, and protectors in every sphere.

We stand as heirs to those who taught us these steps in fire. Their discipline preserved lives. Their ethos forged a craft. Their legacy is now ours to carry.

The code demands we keep climbing, in crises large and small. And it demands that we teach others to climb, too.

Because at the end of every stairway stands a choice. Despair or dignity. Death or life. Chaos or calm.

Maxim: "The Stairway is more than steps. It is a way of living, a way of leading, a way of protecting. And its summit is always life."

CHAPTER 4

Chickasha Barricade (Flagship AAR)

This After-Action Report is a structured debrief capturing what happened and what was learned.

Faith, trust, and proof of life in a barricaded hostage crisis.

Opening Maxim: "Rapport built on authenticity and anchored in trust can carry people through the darkest barricades."

Sunday mornings in small-town Oklahoma usually follow a steady rhythm. Church bells ring, front porches creak as neighbors wave, and the smell of bacon and coffee drifts across quiet streets. But on May 23, 2021, in Chickasha, the stillness was broken by a call that no one wanted to receive.

At 9:33 a.m., our team was requested for mutual aid. The report was grim: A seventy-one-year-old man had struck his wife with a metal pipe, tied her to a chair inside their home, and barricaded himself in. He was on the phone with police, ranting about government surveillance, cameras hidden in his house, and a demand for live television coverage. His wife's condition was unknown. Every minute of delay could mean further injury or death.

We moved quickly. Authorization was secured through our chain of command, and our two-deputy team rolled Code 3—emergency lights and sirens activated toward Chickasha, coordinating details en route. While the drive lasted less than an hour, the weight of the call settled heavy. Hostage situations are never routine. Each one is unique, unpredictable, and fragile.

Upon arrival, around 10:30 a.m., staging had already been established by Chickasha PD. Commanders, tactical officers, and medical support were in place. We were greeted by local leadership and immediately briefed with an LCAN (Location, Condition, Actions, Needs) report. The suspect had been in contact with negotiators since early morning but refused all appeals. His wife was still inside, still bound, and still in danger.

The scene carried the kind of tension you can feel in the air. Patrol officers kept their eyes on the residence. Tactical containment was set. Medical personnel stood by, ready for either rescue or tragedy. Every person on the ground understood what was at stake: a woman's life, a man's descent into paranoia, and the possibility of violence exploding without warning.

For us as negotiators, the work began before the first call was made. We needed to integrate into a scene that was already moving, to build trust with local command, and to begin shaping a strategy that could carry this to resolution. But even before we reached the suspect, another critical step unfolded—one that came not from inside the barricaded house but from the family gathered outside it.

When we arrived at staging, the suspect's adult children were already there. Their faces carried the strain of a long, fearful morning. Thomas, the son, stepped forward, his voice tense but steady. He told us about his father—a godly man, married to his mother for more than forty years, now spiraling into paranoia. He described his father's embarrassment over what had happened and his disbelief that the man he knew could be capable of such violence.

Robert's words weren't just about facts; they were about fear and faith. He was trying to reconcile who his father had been with the crisis unfolding before him. Then he said something that stopped us. He told us he trusted our team because of the way the lead negotiator carried himself. He noticed how he moved with calm purpose, spoke openly, and used his hands naturally as he talked. That presence—simple, human, authentic—gave Thomas confidence that we could communicate effectively with his father and bring both parents out alive.

Presence is easy to overlook in negotiation training. We drill words, strategies, active listening skills, and tactical coordination. But here, before a word was even spoken to the suspect, our presence was already shaping outcomes. To Thomas, we weren't just officers in tactical gear. We were steady, composed, and approachable—and that made the difference in whether he believed resolution was possible.

Then Thomas did something else. He asked if he and his family could pray over us. We gathered together in the staging area—negotiators, family members, and command—and Thomas prayed aloud. He asked God to guide us, give us the words that would land, and help us save his parents' lives. It was not a tactical maneuver, but it became a spiritual anchor. That prayer didn't change the plan, but it changed the moment. It reminded everyone present—family and officers alike—of the gravity of what we were trying to do.

With the family's faith echoing in our ears and their trust laid on our shoulders, we turned to the next step: making direct contact with the suspect.

Direct contact with the suspect began shortly after staging was complete. Using a mobile phone, we established an open line. His voice came across strained but deliberate—a mixture of anger, paranoia, and rehearsed control. He wanted to talk, but on his terms.

From the start, it was clear he was operating from a distorted reality. He spoke of government plots, cameras hidden in his home, and agents monitoring his every move. He insisted that unless the media covered his story, he would not release his wife or come out. The paranoia was thick, but within it, we looked for strands of logic and anchors we could use to build rapport.

Our first objective was not to argue or confront. It was to connect, keep him talking, and find openings that might shift the conversation. Early on, we emphasized respect, patience, and listening. He responded to being heard, even if he remained suspicious.

Proof of Life became our immediate priority. We needed to know his wife was still alive, still conscious, and still capable of communication. At first, he resisted. He deflected, insisting we take his word that she was fine. But persistence mattered. Eventually, he allowed her to speak briefly over the phone.

Her voice was trembling, weak but clear. She confirmed she had been tied to a chair since the assault and that she was in pain. She mentioned her legs hurt from being restrained and, in that moment, gave us a critical detail: He had just untied her legs. That was more than compassion—it was a signal. She was alive, responsive, and capable of giving information. It also gave us a probable location—a chair in the living room, later confirmed by her son. That detail was passed to the tactical team immediately.

Securing Proof of Life changed the tone of the mission. It validated our efforts, gave hope to the family, and reinforced our leverage with the suspect. With her voice echoing in our minds, the negotiation shifted from uncertainty to possibility.

Once Proof of Life was secured, the suspect returned to his demands. They came in waves, repeated and reshaped as the hours went on. His central focus was exposure: He wanted the world to know what was happening. He demanded a direct phone line to television reporters, live coverage of his story, and a scrolling banner across the news feed announcing his crisis. He insisted the police search his computers for hidden surveillance programs and spy cameras.

Each demand was more than words—it was a window into his mindset. He needed recognition, validation, and control. Denying him outright risked escalation, but granting him unrestricted access to the media was unacceptable. The challenge was to balance dignity with safety.

Our negotiation strategy leaned into controlled concessions. We acknowledged his concerns without promising the impossible. We redirected the energy of his demands into safer alternatives. The idea of a media ticker—a scrolling ribbon at the bottom of a live broadcast—emerged as a compromise. It would give him the validation of public recognition without ceding control to him.

The coordination was delicate. We engaged with a local news director, explaining the gravity of the crisis and requesting their cooperation. They agreed to broadcast the scroll, but only with precise timing. That timing became part of the negotiation. We told the suspect that if he honored his commitments, he would see the banner run live across his television.

Throughout these exchanges, we continued to reinforce respect and steady dialogue. We reminded him that we were listening, we were working to meet him halfway, and that his cooperation was essential to a safe outcome. The more he talked, the more manageable his paranoia became.

This approach did more than buy time. It built a sense of progression. The suspect began to see steps being taken, however small, toward meeting his needs. Each step pulled him closer to surrender—not because he lost control, but because he believed he was part of the process.

As the hours stretched on, we explored the use of third-party intermediaries—those trusted voices who might influence the suspect when law enforcement alone could not. Family was the obvious first choice. His son, Thomas, was willing, steady, and deeply invested. His daughter, however, was overcome with emotion. Using her risked inflaming the suspect's shame or guilt, so we set that option aside.

Next, a family friend emerged: an attorney named Diane. She knew the suspect and his wife but had no direct stake in the conflict. Vetting confirmed she was reliable, rational, and willing to help. We arranged a three-way call with her, the suspect, and our negotiator. Diane spoke calmly, assuring him that she understood his fears, but firmly redirected him back to our negotiation team. She reinforced the idea that the honorable path forward was cooperation and surrender.

The suspect responded to her in measured tones, circling back to his demands, but softening slightly with each exchange. His embarrassment at facing his children kept him from direct contact with them, but Diane's presence allowed him to hear a trusted civilian voice that carried weight without overwhelming emotion.

Meanwhile, we continued to apply steady pressure through dialogue. We reminded him that his wife was in pain and that every delay increased the harm she suffered. We framed surrender not as defeat, but as a way to prove he was still a husband and father capable of protecting his family. Each reminder was anchored in respect, but pointed toward resolution.

The strategy was working. With Diane reinforcing from one side and our negotiator guiding from the other, the suspect began to view surrender as a negotiated agreement rather than an imposed outcome. He was no longer simply barricading himself against the world; he was participating in a process that seemed, at least to him, honorable. That perception would be the bridge we needed.

With the attorney's reassurance and our consistent pressure, the suspect finally agreed to terms. He wanted his computers examined, the media ticker broadcast, and the chance to face reporters after surrender. We relayed these conditions to command. The police chief agreed to the inspection and approved the use of the news scroll, but speaking directly to the media would be postponed until after custody was secure.

Tactical staging was set. Containment remained tight, and the surrender element prepared to move forward once we gave the signal. The news station was cued, ready to roll the ticker across the bottom of live programming with a one-minute warning. Every moving part—media, negotiators, tactical teams—had to align.

At the appointed time, we contacted the suspect and told him to turn on Channel 5. Moments later, he saw the words scrolling across his screen. It was proof that we had kept our end of the bargain. For a heartbeat, he faltered. He wanted to renegotiate, insisting on speaking to reporters first. But we reminded him of his word, of the honorable path he had promised to walk. The weight of that reminder, paired with his need for credibility, pressed him forward.

Step by step, we guided him through the surrender protocol. Nothing in his hands. Move slowly. Follow the instructions of the officers waiting outside. He hesitated again, saying he needed to gather his computers and relieve himself before coming out. We allowed small delays, but we kept him moving toward the goal.

Finally, the front door opened. He stepped out onto the porch with a laptop bag, which he placed on the ground before raising his hands above his head. Tactical officers moved in quickly, securing him without injury.

Inside, his wife was untied and escorted out. She bore visible injuries—bruising around her face, swollen from the pipe strike—and the humiliation of being bound to a chair for nearly ten hours. Medical personnel rushed her to the hospital for care.

The suspect, weakened by diabetes and stress, was also transported for evaluation. Both were alive. For their family, and for us, that was enough.

Doctrine: Lessons from Chickasha

Every crisis teaches more than it resolves. The Chickasha barricade reminded us that success is never just about tactics or timing; it is about presence, patience, and purpose woven together in the heat of the moment. From that long day, several doctrinal anchors emerged—principles that carry beyond one incident and into the broader practice of negotiation and leadership.

Presence Precedes Words

Thomas's trust in us was built not on the promises we made but on the way we carried ourselves. Calm movements, open hands, steady tone—these communicated credibility before a single word reached his father. Leaders often underestimate the power of presence, but in high-stakes situations, people decide whether they will trust you long before they hear your arguments. Presence is the first negotiation.

Faith Can Anchor a Mission

The family's prayer in staging was not a tactical maneuver, but it had tactical effects. It unified the family, the team, and command in shared purpose. It reminded everyone of the stakes and added moral gravity to our mission. Leaders must recognize that faith, hope, and shared values are not weaknesses to be ignored; they are strengths that can fortify resolve under pressure.

Proof of Life Is a Priority

Until we heard the hostage's trembling voice, everything was assumption. Her words confirmed her condition, provided intel on her location, and gave us leverage with her captor. Proof of Life is more than a checkbox; it is the hinge on which both strategy and hope turn. Without it, negotiation risks becoming guesswork.

Media Must Be Managed, Not Feared

The suspect's obsession with media could have derailed the entire event. Instead, by channeling that demand into a controlled concession—the scrolling ticker—we provided recognition without ceding control. Leaders in every field face the same challenge: Noise from outside voices can destabilize progress if not managed. The lesson is simple—control the channel, or the channel will control you.

Third-Party Intermediaries Require Discernment

Family members and friends can be powerful assets in negotiation— or dangerous liabilities. The daughter's emotional state could have intensified her father's shame and instability, so we chose not to involve her. In contrast, the family friend, Diane, carried credibility, composure, and relational distance that made her a stabilizing influence. She was able to reinforce our direction without undermining it. The lesson is clear: Not every willing person is the right person. Leaders must carefully vet who speaks into the crisis, because the wrong voice at the wrong moment can undo hours of progress.

Medical Support Is Part of the Mission

Too often, leaders view medical support as secondary—something that comes after the "real work" is finished. In Chickasha, both the suspect and the hostage required immediate care. Diabetes and stress could have collapsed the suspect mid-surrender, while the hostage endured visible injuries and hidden trauma from being bound for nearly ten hours. Without integrated medical readiness, a "successful resolution" could have ended in tragedy within minutes. Doctrine demands that leaders think not only about resolving the crisis but also about sustaining life after the moment of surrender.

Patience Is a Weapon

At multiple points, the suspect stalled. He wanted to relieve himself, gather his computers, and delay just a little longer. It would have been easy to demand immediate compliance, to interpret hesitation as resistance. But patience bought us the outcome. Each small concession kept him moving forward while maintaining his perception of dignity. Patience is not weakness; it is controlled timing. It is the weapon that allows resolution to arrive intact rather than fractured.

The Chickasha barricade reaffirmed that negotiation doctrine is not abstract theory. It is lived discipline—presence that steadies, faith that anchors, proof that guides, media that is managed, intermediaries that are wisely chosen, medical support that is ready, and patience that holds the line.

Reader Application: Lessons in Controlled Courage

The Chickasha barricade was a crisis contained in one house, on one street, in one Oklahoma town. Yet the lessons it offered stretch far beyond law enforcement. Leadership is leadership, whether it is exercised in a negotiation with a barricaded suspect, a boardroom with competing executives, a locker room with restless athletes, or a kitchen table with family in conflict. The principles carry across.

Carry Yourself with Purpose

People are reading you before they are hearing you. Thomas trusted us because of how the negotiator carried himself—calm movements, natural gestures, steady tone. In any leadership role, your presence becomes the first message. If your body language shouts chaos, your words will be drowned out. Leaders must remember: Presence is the first negotiation, and credibility is established before the conversation even begins.

Honor Faith and Values

The prayer at staging anchored everyone present, not because it altered tactics, but because it reminded us of shared humanity and purpose. In leadership contexts outside law enforcement, values play the same role. Teams that feel anchored in something greater than the task at hand—whether it is faith, mission, or shared purpose—perform with greater unity and resilience. Wise leaders allow space for those anchors to surface.

Verify Reality Before Acting

Proof of Life in Chickasha parallels fact-checking in business or family leadership. Decisions made on assumption risk disaster. A leader who pauses to confirm truth, no matter how uncomfortable, makes choices that are steadier and more defensible.

Control External Noise

The suspect's obsession with media mirrors the distractions leaders face every day: rumors, critics, social media storms. If unmanaged, those voices can destabilize direction. Strong leaders channel noise into controlled outlets rather than allowing it to dictate the mission.

Choose Allies Carefully

Not every volunteer is the right partner. Leaders must discern who adds credibility and who subtracts it. Diane, the family friend, was a stabilizing voice; the daughter, though well-intentioned, would have magnified volatility. In your own team, discernment is as critical as enthusiasm.

Plan for the Aftermath

The hostage survived, but carried injuries and trauma. The suspect surrendered, but required medical care. Resolution was not the end. Leaders must prepare for what comes next: recovery, healing, and rebuilding trust.

The lessons from Chickasha do not belong only to negotiators. They belong to anyone who leads when the stakes are high and the margin for error is thin. Whether you are responsible for a company, a classroom, a church, or a family, the principles echo outward.

Business Leadership

A CEO guiding a company through crisis faces the same dynamics we did on that front porch. Investors, employees, and customers are watching not only what you say but how you say it. Calm presence builds trust. Hasty assumptions destroy it. Just as we sought Proof of Life before committing resources, business leaders must demand verified data before making decisions that affect livelihoods. Managing media parallels managing public perception—control the message or the message controls you.

Family Leadership

Parents lead their households the way negotiators lead crisis teams—with presence, patience, and values. When children see steadiness in a parent's eyes, they feel safe even in storms. When families anchor themselves in shared faith or principles, resilience grows. And just as we recognized the need for aftermath care for both suspect and hostage, families must attend to healing after conflict, not pretend it never happened.

Coaching and Mentorship

Athletic coaches and mentors often operate in moments that feel like small barricades: pressure to perform, tempers running hot, reputations on the line. Presence sets tone. Values anchor the team. Fact-checking prevents rash judgments about performance or conflict. Choosing the right team captain mirrors selecting the right third-party intermediary—credibility matters more than popularity.

Community and Civic Leadership

When communities face crisis—natural disasters, scandals, tragedies—leaders must balance noise from media, rumor, and politics. The Chickasha case showed that noise can be shaped into a tool rather than a threat. Leaders who can channel outside pressure into controlled concessions maintain stability when everything feels unstable.

The Chickasha barricade ended with life preserved, but scars remain. That is the nature of crisis. Victory is rarely clean. Yet in every scar, there is a story; in every story, there is doctrine. Leaders who carry those doctrines forward multiply their influence beyond the crisis.

Closing Compass: Epilogue and Ethos Connection

Every crisis has a way of teaching more than the immediate lesson. Chickasha was not just about securing a safe surrender or rescuing a hostage; it was about rediscovering what it means to lead under fire. The doctrine we carried out of that house was not new, but it was sharpened. Presence matters. Faith anchors. Proof protects. Patience wins.

Those principles do not belong only to negotiators or tactical teams. They belong to the Warrior ethos—the discipline to stand steady when others falter and remain purposeful when fear or anger threaten to scatter focus. The Warrior is not defined by aggression but by control. They know that force is an option, but restraint is the greater strength.

In Chickasha, further restraint was the real victory. Tactical officers were ready to breach if lives were threatened. Firearms were prepared, shields raised, medical teams staged. Yet the mission was resolved through words, not weapons. That is the paradox of the Warrior ethos: The ability to use force, held in reserve, empowers negotiation. It is not weakness to talk; it is strength to choose the harder path of patience when the easier path is violence.

The son's prayer in staging brought that reality into sharper focus. Warriors are not machines; they are men and women entrusted with lives, accountable to a higher calling. When the family prayed for us, it was a reminder that even in the tactical world, there is a spiritual dimension. Leadership is more than skill; it is stewardship.

Chickasha ended with scars, not perfection. The hostage was injured, humiliated, and traumatized. The suspect was taken to the hospital, facing charges and a broken family. Resolution in crisis rarely delivers tidy endings. But leadership is not about tidiness. It is about ensuring that life continues when death was an option. It is about pulling meaning out of chaos and forging doctrine from pain.

For us, Chickasha reaffirmed the Warrior ethos: courage under control, discipline under pressure, and presence that inspires trust. It taught that the strongest leaders are not those who shout the loudest but those who carry themselves with quiet authority, steady hands, and a purpose that others can believe in.

As we move deeper into the Warrior section of this book, Chickasha serves as the bridge—a story of faith, presence, and patience in action. It is the reminder that words, wielded with discipline, can be the most powerful weapons a Warrior carries.

CHAPTER 5

Warrior Lessons Carried Forward

Warrior's Maxim: "Strength without discipline is danger. Discipline without ethos is hollow. The Warrior carries both."

The Warrior Defined

The first face of our ethos is the Warrior. Not the caricature of aggression, not the brawler who mistakes noise for strength—but the disciplined fighter who holds their ground when chaos demands collapse. The Warrior is courage without ego, strength under control, action governed by purpose.

The Warrior negotiator does not raise their voice to match the subject's rage. They do not rush entry to satisfy command post fear. They stand steady. They absorb the tension without letting it leak into the team. They know that the loudest voice is rarely the strongest, and the truest strength is control.

Warriors live in every sphere of life: the parent who doesn't lash out in anger, the leader who doesn't buckle under pressure, the coach who steadies the locker room after a loss. Warriors are not defined by battle—they are defined by mastery of themselves.

The suspect was armed, pacing in the darkened hall of a run-down motel. He screamed into the phone, threatening to shoot through the walls if anyone moved closer. Tension bled through every radio call. Tactical stood ready. Commanders debated deadlines.

Then a negotiator stepped in—not with force but with the Warrior's ethos. He lowered his voice, slowing his words, deliberately calm. He refused to match the subject's volume. Silence filled the gaps where shouting once lived.

Minutes turned into hours. Slowly, the suspect's cadence shifted. His rage bled into exhaustion. His breathing steadied to match the negotiator's. At dawn, he walked out alive, hands empty.

No one called that negotiator a hero. But every officer there remembered: Strength was not found in noise. Strength was found in control. That is the Warrior's way.

The Warrior ethos in negotiation—and in life—follows three pillars:

Control of Self Before Control of Scene: If our biology spirals, we cannot steady anyone else. The Warrior masters their breathing, their cadence, their silence.

Strength in Restraint: To hold a position under pressure is harder than to rush forward. The Warrior knows that patience is often the fiercest form of courage.

Purpose Above Ego: Warriors act for mission, not applause. For life, not optics. Their courage is aimed, not flailing.

Reader Application: Presence Under Pressure

The Warrior ethos belongs outside of command posts. It belongs in every moment where fear or ego tempts us to lash out.

- *Parents:* A child yells in defiance. The Warrior parent does not meet noise with noise. They steady themselves first, speaking with control that cools the room.

- *Leaders:* A crisis threatens the organization. The Warrior leader resists panic. Instead of frantic emails and rash decisions, they act with discipline that protects long-term stability.

- *Coaches:* After a crushing defeat, the locker room boils. The Warrior coach does not scream. They steady their voice, teaching athletes that control wins more battles than chaos.

- *Spouses:* In conflict, the Warrior partner does not weaponize words. They choose silence, timing, and calm—protecting the relationship even when disagreement burns hot.

The Warrior is not always the loudest. More often, they are the quietest. Because real strength does not shout. It endures.

Maxim: "The loudest voice is rarely the strongest. True strength is control under fire."

The Guardian

"The Guardian is the shield—absorbing chaos so others can breathe."

The Guardian Defined

If the Warrior embodies control, the Guardian embodies protection. The Guardian stands between chaos and the innocent, carrying weight others never see. In the command post, the Guardian negotiator absorbs panic so the team can function. In life, the Guardian leader shoulders criticism so the group can stay focused.

Guardians are rarely thanked. Their victories are invisible: the crisis that never escalated, the decision that saved time, the silence that steadied the room. Their strength is measured not in applause but in the lives and trust they preserve.

Where the Warrior masters themself, the Guardian carries others. Both are essential.

It was a domestic barricade that had stretched into the night. The subject was erratic, the family terrified. Tension in the command post boiled. A commander snapped, "We need action now." A politician called in, pressing for a fast resolution before sunrise.

The negotiator on the line felt the pressure like a vise. But the Guardian stepped forward—not with force but with presence. Calmly, he told the room, "We will hold. Lives matter more than headlines."

He absorbed the frustration. He carried the weight of optics, politics, and fear. The command post steadied. Tactical held. The negotiator continued his slow cadence. Hours later, the subject surrendered without harm.

The Guardian's victory was not celebrated in press conferences. It was measured in the absence of funerals.

The Guardian's ethos rests on three disciplines.

Absorb Chaos: The Guardian carries stress so others can operate clearly. They do not leak anxiety into the team.

Speak Truth Without Ego: Guardians confront authority when needed, not for pride but for preservation. Their courage is quiet, grounded in protection.

Measure Success in Survival, Not Applause: Guardians know that true victory is often invisible—the disaster prevented, the harm avoided, the life preserved.

The Guardian ethos is universal. Every leader, parent, and coach will face moments where they must shield others from chaos.

- *Parents:* A child panics over a crisis at school. The Guardian parent absorbs their fear, speaks calm into the storm, and protects the family from spinning apart.

- *Leaders:* A CEO takes fire from shareholders. The Guardian leader carries the criticism, shielding employees so they can focus on the mission instead of drowning in fear.

- *Coaches:* A referee's bad call sparks outrage. The Guardian coach absorbs the team's fury, steadying them so they can finish the game with discipline.

- *Spouses:* In seasons of loss, the Guardian partner carries the weight of logistics, stress, and pain so their loved one can grieve without drowning.

Guardians make survival possible. They rarely get credit, but they always leave legacy.

Maxim: "Guardians measure victory in breaths preserved, not in medals won."

The Shepherd

"The Shepherd does not drag the lost. He walks beside them until they can walk again."

The Shepherd Defined

The Shepherd is presence without abandonment. Where the Warrior steadies and the Guardian shields, the Shepherd guides—slowly, patiently, restoring dignity to those stripped of it by crisis.

In negotiation, the Shepherd does not berate the subject into surrender. They do not force compliance. They walk with them—

minute by minute, breath by breath—until the weight of despair lightens enough for choice to reemerge.

In life, the Shepherd is the parent who sits in silence with a hurting child, the leader who refuses to cut off an employee in failure, the coach who guides a broken athlete back to confidence. Shepherds do not force movement. They create space for movement to happen.

A man had locked himself in his garage after losing everything—job, family, hope. He spoke in bursts, then fell into long silences. Commanders grew restless. Tactical teams debated entry.

But the Shepherd negotiator knew silence was not absence—it was biology cooling. He carried the silence with the man. He answered questions slowly, leaving space between every word. Hours passed in stillness.

Finally, a fragile voice asked, "Are you still there?"

"Yes," the Shepherd answered. "We're here to help you."

The man laid down his weapon and walked out alive. His surrender was not to a tactic. It was to presence—the Shepherd's refusal to abandon him in the dark.

The Shepherd ethos is built on three practices.

Presence Over Performance: The Shepherd is not there to impress. They are there to remain.

Dignity Restored: Surrender is never presented as defeat. It is framed as survival with honor. The Shepherd gives options that return agency to the lost.

Patience Over Pressure: Time is not wasted. Time is invested. The Shepherd understands that pressure fractures, while patience restores.

Every life has moments where someone near us spirals into despair. The Shepherd ethos gives us a way to walk with them.

- *Parents:* A teenager overwhelmed by failure does not need lectures. They need presence. Sitting quietly on the edge of the bed may guide them further than any words.

- *Leaders:* An employee who falters is not dead weight. The Shepherd leader restores their dignity with options, not ultimatums.

- *Coaches:* After a crushing mistake, athletes often feel stripped of worth. The Shepherd coach affirms their value, guiding them toward growth instead of discarding them.

- *Spouses:* In seasons of grief, Shepherd partners do not rush healing. They walk slowly, shoulder to shoulder, until strength returns.

The Shepherd ethos transforms desperation into hope, not by dragging but by walking alongside.

Maxim: "Presence is the Shepherd's power. Dignity is his gift. Patience is his weapon."

The Protector

"The Protector chooses life over optics, outcomes over pride, legacy over applause."

The Protector Defined

The Protector is the unifying purpose of the code. Where the Warrior steadies themselves, the Guardian shields others, and the Shepherd restores dignity, the Protector binds them all together. Their measure of success is not medals, headlines, or applause. Their measure is breath—the quiet victory of a life still drawn when it could have been lost.

The Protector is not swayed by politics. They are not seduced by spectacle. They are not driven by ego. They know that every choice carries legacy. The true measure of leadership, parenting, coaching, and command is not how loudly the world claps but how faithfully lives are preserved.

The standoff had stretched through the night. The subject was armed and volatile. Tactical was on edge. Commanders were exhausted. Then the phone rang in the command post—it was the mayor. His voice was sharp: "We can't let this drag on. Make it end now."

The Protector negotiator absorbed the pressure. He did not yield to optics or ego. He leaned into ethos. "Sir," he answered, calm and steady, "we will hold. Lives matter more than headlines."

The room tensed, but the decision stood. Hours later, the subject surrendered. No one died. No one was maimed. The mayor's frustration faded in the daylight, replaced by gratitude.

The Protector had not won applause. He had preserved life. That is the victory that endures.

The Protector's ethos can be distilled into three disciplines.

Life Over Optics: Protectors never trade survival for public approval.

Outcomes Over Pride: Protectors care less about credit and more about preservation. They can be criticized in the moment if it means lives endure afterward.

Legacy Over Applause: Protectors are measured not by what is said about them today but by the quiet victories that echo tomorrow.

The Protector ethos transcends the command post. It belongs wherever decisions shape futures.

- *Parents:* Sometimes the Protector parent lets a child be angry with them if it means setting a boundary that keeps them safe. Protection matters more than approval.

- *Leaders:* A Protector leader chooses unpopular strategies if they preserve the organization long term. They measure success by sustainability, not quarterly applause.

- *Coaches:* The Protector coach refuses to risk an injured athlete just to win a game. Victory is not worth legacy sacrificed.

- *Spouses:* A Protector spouse may take criticism for insisting on rest, medical care, or difficult choices—but love protects first, defends second, and explains later.

Protection is rarely celebrated in the moment, but it always leaves a mark that lasts.

Maxim: "True victory is quiet: a breath still drawn, a life still lived."

Ethos in Fusion

"Strength alone breaks. Shield alone bends. Guidance alone falters. Only together do we endure."

The Fusion of Roles

The Warrior, Guardian, Shepherd, and Protector are not four separate codes. They are four faces of a single ethos. Each role sharpens the others. Each without the others collapses under stress.

A Warrior without Guardian discipline becomes reckless—mistaking ego for courage.

A Guardian without Warrior strength becomes paralyzed—absorbing chaos without standing firm.

A Shepherd without Warrior grit or Protector resolve risks enabling despair instead of guiding to survival.

A Protector without the patience of a Shepherd or the shield of a Guardian risks trading preservation for optics.

The code demands fusion. The negotiator, the leader, the parent, the coach—none can thrive by living in only one face. They must draw on all four.

A subject had barricaded himself inside a suburban home with his children. Hours turned to days. Media vans lined the street. Neighbors watched from porches. Political pressure grew.

In the command post, the team held the ethos together.

Warrior: Negotiators controlled their breathing and cadence, refusing to mirror the subject's volatility.

Guardian: They absorbed political and tactical pressure, shielding the team from rash decisions.

Shepherd: They refused to abandon the subject in despair, offering dignity, choices, and presence.

Protector: They reminded leaders that optics mattered less than survival.

At dawn on the third day, the subject surrendered. The children ran out alive. The news vans packed up. The neighborhood returned to silence.

The world would never know how many times the ethos nearly cracked under pressure. But the team knew. And they knew the code had held.

The ethos, fused, creates a system of survival.

Control: Warrior mastery steadies biology and presence.

Shield: Guardian absorption protects the team and the subject.

Guidance: Shepherd presence restores dignity and choice.

Purpose: Protector focus keeps mission above ego or optics.

This is not theory. It is discipline forged in the crucible of lives preserved.

The fusion belongs in every sphere of life.

- *Parents:* The Warrior controls anger. The Guardian shields the family from outside chaos. The Shepherd sits in the silence of a hurting child. The Protector makes decisions that value safety over short-term approval.

- *Leaders:* The Warrior resists panic. The Guardian absorbs pressure from shareholders or politics. The Shepherd guides employees through failure with dignity. The Protector ensures legacy choices outweigh ego-driven ones.

- *Coaches:* The Warrior brings control after defeat. The Guardian shields the team from unfair criticism. The Shepherd restores dignity to broken players. The Protector ensures that health and growth come before trophies.

- *Spouses:* The Warrior steadies conflict with calm. The Guardian absorbs stress when life overwhelms. The Shepherd refuses to abandon during loss. The Protector makes hard choices that preserve the future over comfort in the moment.

Individually, the roles inspire. Together, they transform.

Maxim: "The code is not four paths—it is one shield, one guide, one purpose: protection."

Ethos in Leadership

"Leadership is not command. Leadership is presence, protection, and purpose under fire."

The Command Post as a Leadership Lab

The command post during a critical incident is the harshest leadership lab on earth. Radios crackle with half-truths. Tactical teams press for action. Families cry for resolution. Politicians demand optics. Every decision carries the weight of lives.

It is here, in this trial, that the ethos reveals its true power. Leaders who act as Warriors, Guardians, Shepherds, and Protectors do more than manage—they preserve. They prove that leadership is not about being the loudest voice but about being the clearest compass.

During one protracted standoff, a governor called the command post directly. His words were blunt: "You need to take action before this makes us look weak."

The negotiator leading the team—anchored in ethos—replied with calm clarity: "Sir, optics do not bury children. Bullets do. We will hold."

The room fell silent. The governor, bristling, relented. Hours later, the subject surrendered alive.

That was leadership in ethos—absorbing political fire, steadying the team, shielding the mission. Not the easy path. The right one.

The ethos becomes a compass for leadership in every domain.

The Warrior Leader steadies their team's biology. Calm is contagious. When the leader's cadence slows, so does the room.

The Guardian Leader shields subordinates from destructive pressure—absorbing stress from above so the mission continues below.

The Shepherd Leader restores dignity and value to people when failure strikes, walking with them instead of discarding them.

The Protector Leader measures success in long-term survival, not short-term applause.

Leadership is not titles. It is the daily choice to embody ethos under fire.

Every reader leads someone: a family, a business, a classroom, a team. The ethos applies universally.

- *Parents:* Warrior parents steady themselves before disciplining. Guardian parents shield children from adult fears they cannot carry. Shepherd parents guide through failures without shaming. Protector parents make unpopular choices if they preserve safety and future.

- *Executives:* Warrior executives resist panic in markets. Guardian executives absorb shareholder pressure to shield employees. Shepherd executives restore dignity when teams fail. Protector executives measure decisions by sustainability, not quarterly applause.

- *Coaches:* Warrior coaches steady a team after loss. Guardian coaches shield athletes from critics. Shepherd coaches restore dignity to broken players. Protector coaches prioritize health and future over trophies.

- *Community Leaders:* Warrior community leaders resist inflammatory rhetoric. Guardian leaders shield the vulnerable. Shepherd leaders guide neighbors with dignity. Protector leaders preserve legacies beyond headlines.

The ethos is not for specialists. It is for anyone who carries the weight of others.

Why Ethos in Leadership Resonates

In a world of noise—where headlines scream, shareholders pressure, families fracture—the ethos gives leaders a compass. It reminds them:

Volume is not strength, presence is.

Optics are not victory, survival is.

Approval is not leadership, protection is.

The ethos transforms leadership from performance into protection, from image into impact, and from noise into legacy.

Maxim: "Leadership is not proven in applause. It is proven in lives preserved."

Ethos in Everyday Life

"The Code is not a tactic for emergencies. It is a way of living every day."

Beyond the Command Post

The ethos was forged in the heat of critical incidents, but its power does not end at the edge of a barricade. It belongs in kitchens and offices, locker rooms and living rooms, in traffic jams and family dinners. The Warrior, Guardian, Shepherd, and Protector are not only roles in crisis—they are ways of being human.

Everyday life presents its own battles. Tempers flare. Deadlines close in. Families strain. Teams fracture. None of these situations will make the news, but all of them demand presence, discipline, and protection.

One negotiator once told of a lesson not learned in a standoff but at home. His teenage daughter stormed away from the dinner table, furious over rules she thought were unfair. His instinct was to follow, raise his voice, demand respect.

But ethos whispered otherwise. The Warrior steadied his tone. The Guardian absorbed the family's frustration without escalating it. The Shepherd gave her space, showing presence without pressure. The Protector reminded him that the goal was not to win the argument but to preserve relationship and trust.

Hours later, his daughter reappeared, calmer. They spoke—not in anger, but in dignity. No barricade. No negotiator's phone. Just a father choosing ethos at home.

The ethos guides ordinary conflicts with extraordinary clarity.

Warrior Discipline: Control your biology first—steady breathing, calm cadence, deliberate words.

Guardian Shield: Absorb chaos from the environment so others don't have to carry it.

Shepherd Guidance: Walk with others in failure or despair, restoring dignity instead of stripping it.

Protector Purpose: Keep long-term relationships and legacies above short-term ego or approval.

The code transforms arguments into dialogue, failures into lessons, and conflicts into connections.

- *Parents:* The Warrior steadies frustration in the face of tantrums. The Guardian shields children from fears they cannot process. The Shepherd restores dignity after mistakes. The Protector ensures that safety and trust are never traded for temporary relief.

- *Spouses:* The Warrior resists weaponizing words. The Guardian absorbs life's stress to protect the relationship. The Shepherd sits in silence during grief. The Protector makes hard calls for the sake of the family's future.

- *Friends:* The Warrior listens more than he speaks. The Guardian defends a friend's reputation when others attack. The Shepherd stays present during seasons of struggle. The Protector ensures loyalty remains unbroken.

- *Colleagues:* The Warrior resists office panic. The Guardian shields teams from unnecessary stress. The Shepherd guides peers with patience. The Protector ensures mission trumps politics.

Ethos turns everyday encounters into opportunities to protect, preserve, and strengthen.

Why This Matters

Crisis is not reserved for hostages and rifles. It is present in every strained conversation, broken relationship, and critical decision under pressure. The same ethos that preserves life in a command post can preserve trust at a dinner table, credibility in a boardroom, and loyalty in a locker room.

When we live the ethos daily, we prepare for the storms that matter most—the storms that come without warning and test not our tactics but our character.

Maxim: "Ethos is not for the rare crisis. It is for every moment that tests who we are."

Living the Code Daily

"Discipline in small things becomes strength in great things."

Doctrine without practice is fragile. The ethos must be lived, not just admired. The command post drills we taught negotiators—

steady breathing, silence, separating signal from noise—were not designed only for crisis. They were designed for daily life. Because the person who practices patience in traffic, restraint in arguments, and calm in meetings is the same person who can hold the line.

One rookie negotiator confessed after his first call that he had filled every silence with words, desperate to "fix" the subject. The incident ended without tragedy, but the lesson was clear: He had exhausted himself, created pressure, and nearly fractured the dialogue.

The veteran mentor told him: "You can't carry the burden for them. You carry it with them. That's how they survive—and how you do too."

The rookie learned the Code not through theory, but through exhaustion and reflection. From that day, he practiced silence in daily life. He waited in traffic without rage. He paused before replying in arguments. He learned patience in the small things, so he could preserve life in the great things.

- *Parents:* Practice patience when your child is frustrated. Do not always correct. Sometimes presence speaks louder than words.

- *Leaders:* In meetings, identify signal and noise before responding. Carry the team's burden by absorbing stress instead of projecting it.

- *Coaches:* Teach athletes that control is strength. Run drills that test patience under pressure—because self-mastery wins more games than emotion.

- *Spouses:* Slow breathing and silence in conflict changes outcomes more than rapid-fire arguments. Choose ethos in the smallest disagreements so it is ready when the biggest storms arrive.

Why We Train This Way

The ethos is not learned in a crisis. It is lived long before. By the time a negotiator picks up the phone, a parent faces rebellion, or a leader must make a defining call, the body and mind must already know the discipline. Muscle memory is built in daily practice.

The storms of life do not announce themselves. They arrive suddenly. If we have trained, we will hold. If not, we will fracture.

Maxim: "We do not rise to the crisis. We fall to the level of our training. Ethos is our daily training."

Closing Call: Carrying the Ethos Forward

"Clearly, it is *we* who are charged with carrying the Code forward."

The Creed of the Four Faces

We have walked through the four faces of ethos: the Warrior, who steadies himself. The Guardian, who shields others. The Shepherd, who restores dignity. The Protector, who measures victory not in applause but in lives preserved.

Individually, each face carries strength. Together, they form the Code—a way of being that survives pressure, preserves life, and creates legacy.

The command post taught us that no *one* face can stand alone. Courage without shield fractures. Protection without patience buckles. Guidance without purpose drifts. Fusion is survival.

One negotiator, reflecting after retirement, was asked what his greatest victory had been. He paused, then said, "The victories you've never heard about."

No press release. No headline. Just families reunited quietly. Officers who didn't have to fire. Subjects who chose life in silence.

That is the power of ethos. The world rarely sees it, but those preserved by it never forget.

When ethos guides us, the legacy is larger than any single decision.

Strength Under Control: Warriors remind us that presence outlasts panic.

Protection Over Applause: Guardians show us that shielding others is more valuable than credit.

Dignity Restored: Shepherds prove that guiding with patience changes outcomes more than pressure ever could.

Life Above Optics: Protectors anchor us in the truth that preservation outweighs politics.

This doctrine is not about moments of glory. It is about moments of survival.

The call is bigger than crisis negotiation. The Code belongs in:

Homes: Families steadied by Warrior patience, Guardian presence, Shepherd dignity, and Protector vision.

Workplaces: Leaders who absorb stress, restore dignity, and act for legacy rather than optics.

Teams: Coaches who teach discipline as strength, not rage. Who shield, guide, and preserve their players.

Communities: Neighbors who stand for each other, not just with noise but with presence.

Wherever people falter under the weight of life, the Code restores, steadies, and preserves.

The Legacy We Choose

The storms of life will come—unexpected, unrelenting, unforgiving. Titles will fade. Applause will vanish. Optics will blur. What will remain is whether we stood as Warriors, Guardians, Shepherds, and Protectors.

What will endure is whether someone draws breath tomorrow because we refused to break today.

The Creed

We are Warriors who do not confuse volume with strength.

We are Guardians who hold the line when fear demands spectacle.

We are Shepherds who refuse to abandon the lost in the darkest hour.

We are Protectors who measure success not in applause but in survival.

This is not decoration. It is not theory. It is our Code.

The Call Forward

The Code is not ours alone. It belongs to those we train, those we lead, those who will come after us.

We do not carry it for fame. We do not carry it for approval. We carry it because life, dignity, and legacy demand it.

Final Maxim: "The storms will come. The question is not if we face them—but whether we stand as protectors when they do."

CHAPTER 6

The Guardian Ethos

Guardian's Maxim: "Every word is a weapon. Every silence is a shield. Every cadence is a choice."

The Foundation of Communication

In every crisis, communication is the battlefield. It may look like a living room, a garage, a phone line, or a command post—but make no mistake, words and silences are the weapons and shields that decide survival.

We learned early that talking is not the same as communicating. Talking fills space. Communicating changes biology. It steadies the nervous system. It widens the tunnel of vision. It restores choice when panic has narrowed it to one desperate option.

In the command post, the wrong word can fracture trust. The wrong tone can escalate despair. The wrong cadence can accelerate biology toward violence. But the right word, the right silence, the right cadence—can open a door, slow a hand, steady a breath, and buy time that changes everything.

Case Reflection: The Barricade and the Bullhorn

Years ago, before doctrine, negotiators relied on bullhorns. The subject inside shouted in rage. Officers outside shouted louder. Threats were exchanged. The standoff spiraled.

Then one negotiator tried something different. He lowered his voice. He slowed his cadence. He let silence do the heavy lifting.

The shift was profound. The subject mirrored the calm. Rage cooled. Hours later, he walked out alive.

That night marked a turning point: Communication was not about volume. It was about cadence. Not about overpowering but about influencing. The battlefield had changed forever.

Doctrine of Communication

The ethos of communication rests on three pillars.

Cadence: Speech rhythm regulates biology. A steady cadence slows panic. A racing cadence accelerates it.

Silence: Pauses are not voids. They are medicine. Silence gives biology time to reset and dignity time to return.

Tone: More than words, tone transmits presence. Calm tones create trust. Harsh tones fracture it.

Words, silence, cadence, and tone are not accidents. They are chosen weapons and shields on the battlefield of communication.

Reader Application: Communication as Survival

Crisis communication rules apply in daily life.

- *Parents:* A calm cadence cools a child's anger. Silence allows emotions to settle before wisdom enters. Tone conveys presence more than lectures ever could.

- *Leaders:* Teams mirror the leader's tone and pace. Calm breeds clarity. Panic breeds chaos.

- *Coaches:* Athletes hear the rhythm of a coach's words as much as the content. Silence after a mistake often teaches more than shouting.

- *Spouses:* Tone and presence speak louder than arguments. A calm cadence in conflict preserves dignity and opens the door to resolution.

Communication is not performance. It is survival.

Maxim: "Words may open doors. Cadence decides if they stay open."

Active Listening and Empathy

"We cannot influence what we do not first understand."

Active Listening Defined

The first weapon of communication is not speech—it is listening. Negotiators learned that survival depends not on what we say first but on what we hear. Active listening is more than waiting for a pause to reply. It is immersion in the other person's world.

Active listening means hearing beneath the words. It is noticing cadence, silence, tone, and emotion. It is reflecting back not only what was said but what was felt. It is acknowledging the storm inside another human being without trying to erase it.

Case Reflection: The Echo Technique

A suicidal subject once repeated the same sentence for hours: "It's over. It's over. It's over." Early negotiators would have argued, corrected, or reasoned. But the negotiator on scene chose empathy instead.

He repeated back softly, "It feels like it's over."

The subject froze. For the first time, someone had mirrored his pain instead of fighting it. Hours later, after more patient reflection, the man walked out alive.

That incident became a textbook case: the moment we stopped arguing with words and started listening to wounds.

Empathy Defined

If active listening is the doorway, empathy is the step inside. Empathy is not agreement. It is alignment. It is the ability to stand in another person's shoes long enough for them to know they are not alone.

Empathy does not excuse. It does not condone. It connects. And connection creates the trust on which influence is built.

Negotiators learned: Until the subject feels heard, nothing else matters.

Doctrine of Listening and Empathy

Listen First: No advice, no persuasion, no correction until the other person knows they have been heard.

Reflect Emotion: Mirror feelings, not just facts. "You're furious" carries more power than "You're saying you're angry."

Validate Experience: Acknowledge that what they feel is real to them. Survival begins with dignity restored.

Patience in Silence: Resist the urge to fill every pause. Silence allows emotions to cool and meaning to emerge.

- *Parents:* When a child shouts, "You don't understand me," resist correction. Listen. Reflect the feeling: "You feel unseen." That reflection builds trust where lectures fracture it.

- *Leaders:* In meetings, repeat key emotions back: "You're frustrated because deadlines were unrealistic." That acknowledgment creates loyalty.

- *Coaches:* When athletes vent, mirror their frustration without judgment. "You feel like you let the team down." Naming the pain helps them move past it.

- *Spouses:* In conflict, reflect emotions before arguing facts. "You feel ignored." Connection builds when presence comes before persuasion.

In every sphere, active listening and empathy move people further than arguments ever could.

Case Reflection: The Father and the Rage

A father barricaded himself in his house, threatening his family. His voice shook with rage. Early responders labeled him irrational. But negotiators trained in empathy understood biology was at work—fight/flight chemicals flooding his body.

Instead of arguing, they validated: "You're furious. You feel cornered. No one's rushing you."

Slowly, rage cooled. His breathing slowed. His voice dropped. Hours later, he released his children unharmed.

The difference was not superior logic. It was superior listening.

Maxim: "Listening is not weakness. It is the first strike of influence."

Building Rapport and Trust

"Trust is the bridge that carries influence."

From Listening to Rapport

Active listening and empathy are the foundation, but they are not the destination. The goal is rapport—connection strong enough to carry influence across the divide. Without rapport, negotiations fracture. With it, even the most desperate subjects can begin to see alternatives.

Rapport is not manipulation. It is not flattery. It is the disciplined practice of respect. Respect for the other person's humanity and their pain, even if their actions are dangerous or destructive.

Negotiators learned: Rapport begins when the subject realizes they are not talking to an adversary but to a presence willing to bear weight with them.

Case Reflection: The Garage Door Conversation

One subject sat behind a closed garage door, shotgun across his lap. Hours of threats and silence had worn thin. Negotiators tried a different approach: They stopped the questions and began small talk.

They asked about his dog, truck, and favorite sports team. Slowly, the subject opened the door—first a crack, then halfway, then fully. By dawn, he had laid the shotgun aside and surrendered.

The turning point was not clever persuasion. It was connection. Rapport through shared humanity.

Doctrine of Rapport

Start with Humanity: Talk about family, work, memories—anything that reminds the subject that they are more than their crisis.

Find Common Ground: Shared experiences create bridges where arguments cannot.

Consistency Builds Credibility: Do what you say, say what you mean, and mean what you say! Broken promises fracture trust instantly.

Rapport is earned, not demanded. It cannot be forced. It grows with time, patience, and presence.

Trust as the Anchor

Rapport creates the bridge, but trust secures it. Without trust, every word is suspect. With trust, even silence carries weight.

Trust is built in moments of discipline:

Keeping promises, even small ones.

Staying calm when others lose control.

Listening without rushing to judge.

Showing consistency hour after hour.

Negotiators became experts not at winning arguments but at earning trust through presence, patience, and integrity.

- *Parents:* Trust is built not by perfect lectures but by consistent presence. When a parent listens, shows up, and keeps promises, rapport flourishes.

- *Leaders:* Employees don't follow titles—they follow trust. Leaders who show consistency, admit mistakes, and carry weight for their teams earn loyalty.

- *Coaches:* Athletes give their best not for fear but for trust. Rapport allows coaches to influence performance without coercion.

- *Spouses:* Trust grows when words match actions, empathy precedes correction, and promises are kept.

Rapport and trust are the currency of influence in every relationship. Without them, no doctrine matters. With them, almost anything becomes possible.

Case Reflection: The Threat That Softened

In one case, a subject repeatedly threatened suicide while waving a pistol. Every time negotiators pressed him with demands, he resisted. But when they spoke about his daughter—her school, her smile, her future—his tone shifted.

Rapport had opened a door. Trust walked him across. Hours later, the pistol was on the ground. He was alive.

The doctrine was clear: Trust does not erase pain, but it creates the space where life can be chosen over death.

Maxim: "Rapport is not a trick. It is the bridge built by respect, steadied by consistency, and crossed by trust."

Influence and the Shift Toward Change

"Influence is earned, not imposed. Change is invited, not forced."

From Rapport to Influence

Once rapport and trust are built, the negotiator gains the ability to influence—not by overpowering but by guiding. Influence in crisis is not about logic or threats. It is about creating space for dignity and choice. When people feel respected and connected, they can begin to see alternatives.

Negotiators learned: Influence is not control. It is stewardship. It is carrying the weight long enough for the subject to glimpse another path—and choosing it voluntarily.

The Behavioral Change Stairway Model (BCSM) is a framework that is still used worldwide:

Active Listening: Genuinely hearing the other person's words, feelings, and meaning.

Empathy: Demonstrating understanding of their emotional world.

Rapport: Building connection and trust on that foundation.

Influence: Using rapport to introduce new perspectives, options, and choices.

Behavioral Change: Supporting voluntary decisions that move toward safety and life.

The model is not theory. It is doctrine lived in the moment of crisis. It captures what protectors have always practiced: influence built step by step, never skipped, never rushed.

Case Reflection: The Hotel Balcony

A subject threatened to jump from a hotel balcony. Officers arrived with commands: "Don't do it!" The subject edged closer.

A negotiator intervened. He began with listening: "You feel like no one cares."

Then empathy: "It must feel unbearable."

Then rapport: "Tell me about your brother—you mentioned he checks in on you."

As trust grew, influence emerged: "What if we let him be the one who comes to meet you at the hospital instead of the coroner?"

Hours later, the subject stepped back over the rail.

That was the Stairway in action. Step by step. No shortcuts.

Doctrine of Influence

Never Skip Steps: Jumping from listening to persuasion fractures trust.

Offer Choices, Not Ultimatums: Influence thrives when dignity is preserved.

Guide, Don't Push: The protector's task is to illuminate options, not force decisions.

Support Change: Once movement begins, reinforce it—every positive step is progress.

Influence is less about power and more about presence. Presence that steadies, guides, and supports change without stripping away dignity.

- *Parents:* Listen first. Empathize with frustration. Build rapport through shared activities. Then influence behavior by offering choices instead of commands. Change follows trust, not orders.

- *Leaders:* Hear your employees. Empathize with their challenges. Build rapport through presence. Influence by aligning vision with their values. Change becomes voluntary, not coerced.

- *Coaches:* Listen to athletes' frustrations. Empathize with setbacks. Build rapport through consistency. Influence by offering better strategies. Performance shifts because they trust you, not because they fear you.

- *Spouses:* Hear the hurt. Validate it. Build rapport with patience. Influence decisions through shared dignity. Change arises through trust, not domination.

The Stairway is not just for crisis. It is for every relationship where trust is the bridge to change.

Why This Matters

Negotiators discovered what leaders, parents, and coaches often forget: Real change cannot be commanded. It must be chosen. Influence without empathy fractures. Influence without rapport collapses. Influence without listening is manipulation.

But when each step is followed, change becomes durable. It becomes anchored in trust, not fear.

Maxim: "Change that is forced is fragile. Change that is chosen endures."

Behavioral Change in Action

"Change is the summit, but the climb is step by step."

When Change Happens

Behavioral change is the moment of breakthrough—the instant when a subject lays down a weapon, steps back from the ledge, or releases a hostage. To the outside world, it looks sudden. But negotiators know it is the fruit of every step before it: listening, empathy, rapport, and influence.

Change is not magic. It is earned through presence, patience, and persistence. It is the natural outcome of trust carefully built and choices patiently offered.

Case Reflection: The Silent Exit

A man locked himself in a darkened house after losing his job and family. Hours passed in silence. Negotiators listened, empathized, and reflected. Slowly, he spoke—haltingly at first, then more openly.

As rapport grew, they offered choices: medical care instead of arrest, dignity instead of shame.

At dawn, he opened the door and walked out unarmed. No dramatic speech. No grand surrender. Just quiet movement toward life.

That is behavioral change. It rarely looks cinematic. It looks like survival.

Doctrine of Behavioral Change

Support Small Steps: Change often begins with small concessions—a hostage released, a window opened, a voice softened. Celebrate them. Each step is progress.

Preserve Dignity: Never strip away the subject's control. Change lasts when it is chosen freely.

Anchor New Direction: Reinforce positive choices with empathy and respect.

Stay Patient: Change is fragile. Do not rush to close the deal. Protect the momentum.

Change is not a finish line. It is a fragile bridge that must be walked carefully.

Case Reflection: The School Bus Incident

A man hijacked a school bus, panicked and armed. Negotiators built rapport through calm, cadence, and empathy. Hours later, they influenced him to let one child off the bus. Then another. Then half.

Finally, with dignity preserved, he stepped off himself, weapon down.

The breakthrough did not come all at once. It came in steps— each child released a sign of growing trust, each step a victory of the Stairway in motion.

The same steps that carry a subject from violence to surrender can carry us through ordinary conflicts.

- *Parents:* When a child resists homework, start with listening. Empathize with frustration. Build rapport through shared experience. Influence with options: "Would you rather start with math or reading?" Small steps change the outcome.

- *Leaders:* When a team resists change, listen first. Empathize with their fears. Build rapport by acknowledging challenges. Influence by offering choices. Change will follow more naturally than forced compliance.

- *Coaches:* When athletes resist discipline, walk the Stairway. Hear their complaints. Empathize with setbacks. Build rapport through consistency. Influence by presenting better strategies. Performance will shift voluntarily.

- *Spouses:* When conflict arises, do not leap to persuasion. Listen. Empathize. Build rapport through patience. Influence gently. Change will come through choice, not coercion.

The Stairway is not only for crisis—it is for life.

Change that emerges from trust and dignity lasts longer than change forced by fear or power. Subjects who surrender by choice are more likely to embrace help. Families who resolve conflict through empathy preserve connection. Teams that change through rapport strengthen loyalty.

The Stairway is not just a tool. It is a code for how protectors lead others toward a better path.

Maxim: "The measure of change is not noise or applause. It is the quiet step away from despair, toward life."

Communication Drills and Reader Practices

"Discipline in words begins with discipline in practice."

Why We Drill

Negotiators never wait until the crisis to practice communication. Silence, cadence, and empathy—these are not instincts. They are disciplines. And disciplines must be drilled until they become muscle memory.

Without practice, the Stairway collapses under pressure. With practice, the steps become reflex, guiding protectors in moments when adrenaline would otherwise erase judgment.

Protector's Practices for Readers

Active Listening Exercise

In your next conversation, repeat back the other person's words before adding your own. Use phrases like, "What I hear you saying is . . ." or "It sounds like you're feeling . . ." Practice reflecting emotions, not just facts.

Empathy Reflection

End one conversation today by naming the other person's emotion: "That sounds frustrating," or "You must feel proud." Observe how acknowledgment changes the tone of the interaction.

Rapport-Building Drill

Start a conversation by asking about something meaningful to the other person—their family, passions, or recent experiences. Watch how rapport shifts the atmosphere before any persuasion is attempted.

Influence with Options

Next time you need cooperation, offer choices instead of commands: "Would you prefer to do this first or later?" Influence is strongest when people feel dignity in their decisions.

Support Small Changes

When someone takes even a small positive step, acknowledge it. In negotiation, the release of one hostage signals progress. In life, one kind word, one concession, one pause matters. Reinforce it.

Case Reflection: Silence as Medicine

A negotiator once sat for hours with a subject who would not speak. Commanders grew restless. The urge to break silence was overwhelming. But the negotiator remembered: Silence is presence, not absence.

Finally, the subject whispered: "I thought you'd leave."

That was the turning point. Silence had proven commitment. The subject laid down his weapon hours later.

Drills in silence—counting slowly before responding, allowing pauses, practicing restraint—made that possible. Without practice, silence would have been broken by impulse. With practice, silence became medicine.

These drills are not for negotiators alone. They belong to every protector.

- *Parents:* Practice listening to your children without interruption. Reflect their emotions before offering correction.

- *Leaders:* In meetings, breathe before speaking. Reflect back the team's concerns before proposing solutions.

- *Coaches:* Drill athletes to pause before reacting to mistakes—teach patience in practice so it holds under pressure.

- *Spouses:* Practice slowing cadence in arguments. Offer options, not ultimatums. Empathy first, persuasion second.

Daily practice prepares protectors for storms. Ordinary conversations become training grounds for extraordinary crises.

The Stairway is not a concept to admire. It is a discipline to live. By practicing daily—breathing, listening, empathizing, building rapport, offering choices—we prepare for moments that decide survival, dignity, and legacy.

Without drills, we fracture under pressure. With drills, we steady others.

Maxim: "We do not rise to crisis. We fall to the level of our training. Practice is the stairway to survival."

The Fragility of Trust

"Trust takes hours to build and only seconds to break."

The Weight of Trust

Trust is the invisible currency of communication. Negotiators know that without it, the Stairway collapses. Listening, empathy, rapport—they are all fragile if trust is violated. Once broken, it is nearly impossible to restore amid crisis.

Trust is not declared. It is demonstrated. It is earned slowly through consistency and steadiness. It is lost instantly through deception, broken promises, or careless words.

Case Reflection: The Broken Promise

During one barricade, negotiators promised a subject that his surrender would allow him to see his daughter before being taken to jail. But when he surrendered, the tactical team—unaware of the promise—immediately cuffed and removed him.

The subject shouted, "You lied!" The damage was permanent. Future negotiations with that individual became impossible.

The lesson burned into doctrine: Never promise what you cannot guarantee. In the command post, words are contracts. Breaking them fractures trust not just for one incident but for years to come.

Doctrine of Fragile Trust

Say Less, Mean More: Never offer what cannot be delivered. Silence is safer than broken promises.

Consistency Builds Credibility: Trust grows when words match actions over time.

Integrity Outweighs Optics: Choosing honesty, even when unpopular, secures credibility.

Every Word Is a Contract: In crisis, even small statements carry immense weight.

Trust is not an accessory to influence—it is its foundation.

Case Reflection: The Radio Leak

On another call, a subject overheard a commander on an open radio channel saying, "We'll rush him if this drags."

The subject erupted: "You're lying! You're going to kill me!"

Negotiators had spent hours building rapport. In seconds, trust evaporated. The subject's behavior escalated dangerously, and though the incident ended without loss of life, the lesson was costly: Trust is fragile, and even indirect communication can shatter it.

- *Parents:* Children remember broken promises. When trust fractures, influence vanishes. Better to say "I'll try" than "I promise" if the outcome isn't certain.

- *Leaders:* Employees follow leaders they trust. One lie, one broken commitment, one manipulation can undo years of credibility.

- *Coaches:* Athletes will endure discipline and hardship if they trust the coach. If they suspect dishonesty, effort collapses.

- *Spouses:* Relationships thrive on trust. Small betrayals—promises not kept, words not backed by action—fracture bonds.

Trust is not just a leadership principle. It is a survival principle.

The fragility of trust reminds us: Communication is not just about words spoken but about integrity embodied. Negotiators who listen, empathize, and build rapport but then break trust are like builders who construct a bridge but saw through its supports.

Without trust, no maxim, doctrine, or creed will hold. With trust, even silence can carry the weight of influence.

Maxim: "In crisis and in life, trust is the only currency that never loses value—unless you spend it carelessly."

Command Post Discipline

"The calmest voice in the room sets the tempo of the crisis."

The Command Post as a Crucible

The command post is where crises are won or lost before a word ever reaches the subject. Radios buzz with fragments of information. Tactical leaders demand updates. Politicians call. Media vans set up outside. Every voice adds pressure, every second ticks like a fuse.

In this crucible, discipline is not just for negotiators—it is for everyone. The command post must filter signal from noise, protect trust, and steady the team. Without discipline, panic spreads. With discipline, the protector's cadence steadies the storm.

Case Reflection: The Noise of Politics

During one standoff, a governor's office called every thirty minutes demanding progress. The command post became frantic, rushing negotiators to "show movement."

The negotiator's team held the line: "We cannot measure success by optics. We measure success by breaths still drawn." Hours later, the subject surrendered alive.

Command post discipline had preserved the ethos. Politics demanded speed. Protectors demanded survival.

Doctrine of Command Post Discipline

Filter signal vs. noise.

Signal: changes in subject tone, cadence, behavior.

Noise: political pressure, optics, impatience.

Protectors must translate emotion into intelligence and intelligence into action.

Speak Truth to Authority: Even commanders under pressure must hear truth, not just what is convenient. Courage means saying, "Lives matter more than headlines."

Protect the Negotiator: The voice on the phone cannot be distracted by panic in the room. The command post shields them so their cadence remains steady.

Cadence Is Contagious: A frantic room creates frantic negotiation. A disciplined room steadies the call.

Case Reflection: The Scribe's Reminder

In one long negotiation, fatigue wore down the team. A young scribe tapped the maxim written on the board: "Time is not the enemy."

The reminder shifted the room. Commanders sat back. Tactical slowed their posture. Negotiators regained patience.

That small act of discipline—one written phrase, one reminder—kept the ethos intact when exhaustion tempted haste.

- *Parents:* The family home is its own command post. Children read the parents' tone more than their words. A calm parent sets the tempo. A frantic parent accelerates chaos.

- *Leaders:* The office under pressure becomes a command post. Employees mirror the leader's demeanor. If leaders panic, trust fractures. If they hold discipline, teams endure.

- *Coaches:* The sideline is a command post. Athletes absorb the coach's cadence. Panic spreads quickly. Calm preserves focus.

- *Spouses:* In conflict, the living room becomes a command post. The calmest voice in the room can de-escalate anger, protect dignity, and preserve trust.

Command post discipline is not just tactical—it is universal. Wherever pressure gathers, the protector's ethos steadies the field.

Why This Matters

The command post is a mirror of leadership. It reveals whether doctrine is truly embodied or just spoken. In the command post, protectors either hold ethos steady or allow it to fracture under optics and fear.

Discipline in the command post is discipline in life: Filter noise, speak truth, shield those on the front line, and remember that cadence is contagious.

Maxim: "Optics demand speed. Protectors demand survival."

The Protector's Communication Creed

"Communication is not performance. It is presence."

The Arc of Communication

We began this chapter on the battlefield of communication, where words are weapons, silence is a shield, and cadence decides survival. We walked the Stairway: listening, empathy, rapport, influence, and change. We drilled the habits that make presence a reflex under pressure. We warned of trust's fragility and commanded discipline in the crucible of the command post.

Every lesson converges on this creed: Communication is not what you say; it is what you carry.

The protector carries calm into chaos, patience into panic, and ethos into moments where fear screams for shortcuts.

Case Reflection: The Voice in the Dark

One negotiator sat in silence with a subject through the night. No clever persuasion. No magic phrase. Just presence—steady cadence, empathy reflected, silence honored.

By dawn, the subject whispered: "You never left me."

That was the creed embodied. Presence over performance. The subject surrendered not to words but to the discipline of being carried by another human being through the storm.

Doctrine of the Creed

Presence Over Performance: Words fail if presence collapses. Presence endures even when words are few.

Silence Is a Weapon: Use it not to punish but to heal. Let silence restore dignity and calm.

Trust Is Sacred: Every word is a contract. Protect it fiercely.

Cadence Controls Biology: Speak as if you are a metronome for life. Steady others by first steadying yourself.

Ethos Anchors All: Without warrior courage, guardian discipline, shepherd presence, and protector purpose, communication is just noise.

- *Parents:* When your child spirals, do not perform calm—deliver it. Your cadence steadies their biology. Your silence restores their dignity.

- *Leaders:* In crisis meetings, filter noise from signal. Speak truth to authority. Protect the trust of your team.

- *Coaches:* Teach athletes that performance begins with presence. Calm cadence on the sideline becomes discipline on the field.

- *Spouses:* In conflict, refuse to trade dignity for victory. Presence and empathy preserve connection when arguments would shatter it.

Every protector, in every arena, lives the creed not with slogans but with discipline.

Why This Matters

The creed distills everything negotiators learned through scars and survival: Communication is not decoration. It is doctrine embodied.

It is what turns doctrine into survival, ethos into courage, presence into influence. Without the creed, even skilled communicators fracture under pressure. With it, protectors anchor others through storms.

Closing Call

We end this chapter where we began: on the battlefield of communication. The terrain has changed—phone calls to text messages, bullhorns to livestreams, barricades to cyber—but the creed holds.

Words are weapons.

Silence is a shield.

Cadence is choice.

Trust is sacred.

Presence is everything.

Protectors carry these truths not just in crisis but in daily life.

Maxim: "Communication is not what we say. It is what we carry."

CHAPTER 7

Leadership Under Pressure

Guardian's Maxim: "Courage without control is recklessness. Strength without purpose is noise."

The Warrior Defined

When most people hear the word warrior, they imagine a fighter—muscle, weapons, aggression, force. In crisis work, that image is not only incomplete; it is dangerous.

The true warrior is not the loudest in the room, nor the first to act. The true warrior is the one who has mastered himself. A warrior's greatest weapon is not the rifle or the radio—it is discipline, strength under control, and courage without ego.

Negotiators discovered that the warrior ethos was as vital in the command post as on any battlefield. The warrior's role was not to dominate but to carry calm into chaos and steady others when fear screamed for action.

The Warrior in the Command Post

In the heat of a barricade or hostage call, emotions run high. Officers pace. Commanders demand progress. Media swarms. Tactical operators grip rifles, ready to act.

Amid the storm, the warrior is the one whose pulse stays steady. He is not seduced by optics. He does not confuse shouting with strength. He does not let impatience masquerade as courage.

The warrior's ethos allows the negotiator to say:

"We will wait, because waiting saves lives."

"We will hold, because rashness destroys."

"We will speak carefully, because every word is a weapon."

In this way, the warrior is not only a fighter. He is a protector.

One night, a suspect barricaded inside a house appeared at a window holding a rifle. Snipers called for authorization: "We have a shot."

The room erupted—"Take him!"

But the warrior's ethos held. The negotiator reported: "His voice is softening. He keeps mentioning his mother. He is not resolved to die tonight. Hold your fire."

For three more hours, negotiators steadied the line. At dawn, the suspect laid the rifle down and walked out alive.

Strength under control had preserved a life. Courage had not been the trigger pulled, but the trigger withheld.

Doctrine of the Warrior Ethos

Courage Without Ego: Courage is not about proving strength—it is about steadying fear without seeking applause.

Strength Under Control: The warrior resists the urge to act rashly. Control magnifies power; recklessness squanders it.

Purpose Over Optics: Decisions are guided by what preserves life, not what looks bold on the evening news.

Discipline in Chaos: When adrenaline surges, the warrior holds cadence steady.

The warrior ethos is not aggression—it is discipline applied under pressure.

Reader Application: Warrior in Everyday Life

- *Parents:* The warrior parent does not shout to prove strength. They hold firm boundaries calmly, showing children that discipline, not anger, is the real power.

- *Leaders:* The warrior leader does not confuse speed with courage. They make deliberate decisions, even when investors or bosses scream for shortcuts.

- *Coaches:* The warrior coach teaches athletes that control wins games—channeling fire into discipline rather than reckless fouls.

- *Spouses:* The warrior partner refuses to let pride or ego dictate words in conflict. They hold strength steady, protecting connection instead of "winning" the fight.

The warrior ethos is not confined to combat. It is a universal posture: courage without ego, strength under control.

Why This Matters

Without the warrior ethos, fear and ego drive decisions. Snipers fire too soon. Parents shout too quickly. Leaders act too rashly. Coaches push too hard. Spouses wound too deeply.

With the warrior ethos, protectors hold steady. They absorb fear without amplifying it. They carry strength not to show power but to preserve life.

Maxim: "The warrior is not the loudest voice in the room. The warrior is the steady presence that outlasts the storm."

Controlled Strength: Courage as Discipline, Not Impulse

"Strength without discipline destroys what it was meant to protect."

The Illusion of Strength

In crisis work, many mistake loudness for leadership and speed for courage. They equate boldness with bravery and confusion with chaos that must be crushed. But true warriors know this: Impulse is not courage.

The loudest voice may silence a room, but silence does not equal respect. The quickest action may seize headlines, but headlines do not equal survival. Real strength is measured not in noise or speed but in control.

Crisis taught us that the warrior's power lies in choosing restraint when ego demands reaction.

Case Reflection: The Hallway Standoff

A man armed with a handgun stood in a dim hallway of an apartment complex, shouting threats. Officers shouted back. Rifles trained on the doorway. The subject screamed that he was ready to die.

The impulse in the command post was to rush and silence the threat before it exploded. But the warrior ethos held: "Not yet. Hold the line."

Negotiators steadied cadence, reflected fear, and reminded the subject of his young son. Minutes stretched into hours. Finally, the man slid the gun onto the floor and surrendered.

Had impulse ruled, bullets would have flown. Instead, discipline carried the day.

Doctrine of Controlled Strength

Impulse Is the Enemy: Fear and ego drive haste. Haste drives mistakes.

Discipline Is the Weapon: Control is the warrior's shield—stronger than any rifle.

Courage Is Quiet: The bravest decisions are often those that never make the news.

Strength Protects, Not Destroys: True strength preserves dignity, even for those who threaten it.

The Cost of Impulse

Negotiators catalogued tragedies where impulse won:

A barricade rushed too soon, ending in crossfire.

A threat mocked instead of calmed, escalating into violence.

A leader chasing optics rather than outcomes, fracturing trust.

Each failure was a scar. Each scar taught the same lesson: Courage is not the absence of fear, but the mastery of it.

- *Parents:* The warrior parent resists the impulse to shout. They pause, breathe, and respond with steadiness, teaching children that love is firm, not frantic.

- *Leaders:* The warrior leader resists optics-driven decisions. They hold steady under pressure, choosing integrity over applause.

- *Coaches:* The warrior coach resists the urge to punish in anger. They discipline with purpose, not ego, guiding athletes toward growth.

- *Spouses:* The warrior partner resists the sharp retort. They choose patience, speaking with love even in conflict.

Controlled strength in daily life preserves relationships and builds trust that rashness would shatter.

Case Reflection: The Officer's Breath

One officer recalled the moment before a subject lowered his weapon: "I counted my breath instead of pulling my trigger. That gave him the time to make the right choice."

That was courage. Not the squeeze of a trigger but the mastery of fear in silence. Not impulse, but discipline.

In every arena, courage is tested not in explosions of action but in the restraint to act only when necessary.

Impulse is chaos.

Control is survival.

Discipline is courage embodied.

The protector's warrior ethos is not about proving strength but about carrying it wisely, even when every voice demands haste.

Maxim: "Courage is not the absence of fear. It is the refusal to let fear or ego dictate the next move."

Case Reflection: Ego vs. Ethos in the Command Post

"Ego shouts. Ethos steadies."

The Clash of Wills

Every command post carries two invisible forces: ego and ethos. Ego demands recognition. Ethos demands discipline. One pushes for control, credit, and speed. The other insists on patience, presence, and preservation of life.

When ego rules, fear and pride mix into a volatile fuel. Orders are barked to satisfy optics, not outcomes. Lives are risked to protect reputations, not people. When ethos rules, calm guides decisions. Lives are preserved, even when politics scream for action.

Case Reflection: The Competing Commanders

During a high-stakes barricade, two commanders clashed. One, driven by ego, pressed for tactical entry: "We need results now. The mayor is on the line."

The other, anchored in ethos, countered: "We don't gamble with lives for headlines. We hold."

Negotiators relayed that the subject's voice was slowing, his threats softening, his will eroding. But ego kept pressing: "This makes us look weak."

The ethos-driven commander held firm. Hours later, the subject surrendered alive.

In the debrief, the mayor congratulated the department for saving lives. The ego-driven commander was silent. The lesson was clear: Ethos may cost applause in the moment, but it secures outcomes that endure.

Doctrine of Ego vs. Ethos

Ego Protects Self. Ethos Protects Life. Ego asks, "How will this look?" Ethos asks, "Will they live?"

Ego Seeks Credit. Ethos Seeks Outcomes. Negotiation is never about recognition. It is about results.

Ego Reacts. Ethos Responds. Ego acts in fear. Ethos acts in discipline.

Ego Divides. Ethos Unites. Ego pits negotiators against tactical. Ethos fuses both into one shield.

The Subtlety of Ego

Ego is not always obvious. Sometimes it dresses itself as urgency: "We need to move now!" Sometimes it cloaks itself as strength: "We can't let him win."

But ethos unmasks it. Ethos says: "Strength is measured in lives saved, not risks taken." Ethos says: "Patience is not weakness. It is protection."

Reader Application: The Power of Steady Compassion

- *Parents:* Ego says, "My child embarrassed me, so I must react." Ethos says, "My child is hurting, so I must guide."

- *Leaders:* Ego says, "The board expects speed, so I will rush." Ethos says, "The team depends on me to protect integrity, so I will hold steady."

- *Coaches:* Ego says, "We can't lose face, so push harder." Ethos says, "We build for longevity, not headlines."

- *Spouses:* Ego says, "I must win this argument." Ethos says, "I must protect this relationship."

In every sphere, ego fractures trust. Ethos preserves it.

Case Reflection: The Rookie's Warning

In one incident, a rookie negotiator whispered to the commander: "Sir, if we go now, people will die."

Ego snapped back: "You're out of line."

But the ethos-driven leader silenced the ego: "Let him speak."

The rookie's assessment proved accurate. By holding the line, they avoided bloodshed. That moment taught the room: Wisdom is not about rank. It is about ethos embodied.

The battle between ego and ethos plays out in every crisis—and in every life. Ego fractures teams, clouds judgment, and destroys trust. Ethos preserves life, steadies chaos, and creates outcomes that endure beyond the headlines.

The warrior ethos demands we strip ego from decision-making. Not to diminish ourselves, but to preserve what matters most.

Maxim: "Ego seeks to win the moment. Ethos seeks to save the future."

The Pitfalls of Ego

"Ego blinds us. Ethos guides us."

The Trap of Pride

Crisis has a way of exposing what lies beneath the surface. Fear, fatigue, and frustration strip away the masks we wear. In those moments, ego tempts us to protect image over outcome. Pride whispers: "You must look strong." Fear whispers: "You cannot appear weak."

But the warrior ethos warns: Appearances are illusions. Lives are not. The moment ego takes the wheel, the protector's mission is compromised.

Case Reflection: The Optics-Driven Rush

In one standoff, the subject was barricaded in a small home. Negotiators reported he was cooling—his voice slowing, his threats easing. But a political figure at the scene pressed for immediate action: "We can't let the public think we're indecisive."

Ego pushed the room. Entry was ordered. Shots were fired. A hostage was injured. The subject was killed.

The after-action review was grim: "We didn't protect lives. We protected optics."

The cost of ego was measured in blood.

Doctrine of Ego's Pitfalls

Ego Rushes: It mistakes speed for strength.

Ego Competes: It pits team members against each other for recognition.

Ego Blames: When outcomes fail, ego shifts fault rather than taking responsibility.

Ego Fractures Trust: Once exposed, ego destroys credibility and influence.

Ethos Warns Us: Ego is not strength. It is weakness disguised.

Case Reflection: The Negotiator Who Mocked

During a negotiation, one officer ridiculed the subject to "break him down." Laughter in the command post seemed to validate the tactic. But the subject erupted, escalating to violence.

The lesson was written in doctrine: Mockery is ego in disguise. Influence is never gained through humiliation. The protector's ethos requires dignity, not derision.

- *Parents:* Ego says, "I must win this argument with my child." Ethos says, "I must protect this relationship, even in discipline."

- *Leaders:* Ego says, "We must appear strong to shareholders." Ethos says, "We must preserve integrity for long-term trust."

- *Coaches:* Ego says, "We must dominate at all costs." Ethos says, "We must grow athletes into disciplined, resilient people."

- *Spouses:* Ego says, "I must be right." Ethos says, "We must be whole."

Ego shouts. Ethos steadies. The difference is survival—of trust, dignity, and life.

The Subtle Pitfalls

Ego is not always loud. Sometimes it is subtle.

The quiet resentment when credit goes elsewhere.

The hidden urgency to act quickly so blame cannot stick.

The silent refusal to admit error.

Each is a fracture in the protector's shield. Each weakens the ethos.

Case Reflection: The "Strong" Commander

A commander once ordered negotiators to end dialogue after hours of progress: "He's playing us. End it. We'll take him."

The team resisted: "He's softening. We're close."

But the commander, unwilling to appear indecisive, pressed forward. The entry failed. Casualties mounted.

In the aftermath, one officer said quietly: "That wasn't strength. That was ego dressed as strength."

Ego destroys because it distorts. It makes speed look like courage, ridicule look like influence, and optics look like outcomes. But ego leaves scars—on lives, teams, and legacies.

The warrior ethos demands protectors strip ego from every decision. Courage without ego is not weakness—it is the highest form of strength.

Maxim: "Ego seeks victory for self. Ethos secures survival for all."

The Warrior's Discipline: Courage Under Control in Daily Practice

"Strength under control is the essence of courage."

The Warrior's Daily Battle

Courage under control is not tested only in standoffs, barricades, or command posts. It is tested in the unseen, ordinary moments of life. The warrior ethos is not a switch flipped in crisis; it is a discipline built daily in the choices we make when the world is not watching.

Every breath under pressure, every pause before words, every decision to wait rather than rush—these are the drills of the warrior's life. Negotiators discovered that their ability to perform under the most extreme conditions was forged not in the heat of the crisis but in the daily rehearsal of restraint.

Case Reflection: The Pause That Saved a Life

One negotiator recalled a call where a subject screamed threats for two hours straight. The command post wanted a rapid response. Instead, the negotiator paused. They breathed. They let silence work.

Eventually, the subject asked: "Why aren't you interrupting me?"

The negotiator replied: "Because I hear you."

Moments later, the subject's voice softened, and a pathway to surrender opened.

That pause was not an accident. It was discipline, rehearsed a thousand times before the call ever came.

Doctrine of the Warrior's Discipline

Breath Before Action: Breath steadies biology. Every action must begin with control of the self.

Silence as Strength: Silence is not weakness—it is presence that allows clarity to return.

Restraint as Power: Choosing not to act rashly is the truest demonstration of strength.

Cadence as Command: A steady voice sets the tempo of crisis, turning chaos into order.

- *Parents:* Courage under control is the pause before disciplining in anger, choosing to guide instead of wound.

- *Leaders:* Courage under control is resisting the pressure to act hastily for optics, choosing what preserves long-term trust.

- *Coaches:* Courage under control is teaching athletes that composure under pressure wins games more than raw aggression.

- *Spouses:* Courage under control is listening when pride wants to argue, protecting connection instead of proving victory.

The warrior's discipline is not about suppressing strength—it is about applying it precisely, at the right time, in the right way.

Case Reflection: The Breathing Drill

One SWAT negotiator recalled being taught a drill: "Before you key the mic, take one slow breath."

At first, it felt unnecessary. But under fire, that breath made the difference. Words came out steady, calm, and influential.

That one breath preserved composure in a room ready to erupt. That one breath carried lives to safety.

The Warrior's Drills

Count to Three: Before responding in conflict, silently count to three. Train patience into reflex.

Mirror Your Cadence: Practice speaking at a steady pace, even when interrupted or provoked.

Practice Restraint: Deliberately choose not to act on impulse in small matters.

Anchor with Maxims: Repeat truths in pressure: "Time is not the enemy. Silence is presence. Courage is control."

The warrior ethos is not revealed first in crisis—it is revealed in daily practice. Those who cannot control themselves in small conflicts will fracture under great ones. Those who master the daily disciplines of courage under control will stand steady when storms break.

Maxim: "The warrior does not conquer others first. The warrior conquers himself."

Case Reflection: The Warrior's Shield

"The warrior's shield is not to dominate but to protect."

The Call That Tested Unity

It was a winter night. A man barricaded himself in a rural farmhouse with his two young children. He had fired a single round into the ceiling and threatened that if anyone came closer, he would end it. The house was surrounded by deputies and tactical teams.

Inside the command post, fear and urgency collided. Some demanded immediate entry. Others urged patience. The negotiators pressed for time. SWAT prepared for breach. The fracture lines between teams were clear.

But then the warrior ethos showed itself. A negotiator and tactical commander stood together. One spoke of the subject's softening voice, his repeated mention of wanting his children safe. The other promised tactical containment and restraint: "We'll hold perimeter. No entry without your word."

In that moment, ethos overrode ego. The rifle and the voice fused into one shield. The children walked out alive at dawn. The subject followed hours later.

The warrior's shield was not a rifle or a radio. It was unity forged in courage under control.

Doctrine of the Warrior's Shield

Unity Preserves Life: Division between teams creates pressure that fractures patience. Unity buys time.

Courage Is Shared: When negotiators and tactical fuse ethos, the entire team steadies.

Strength Under Control Is Contagious: A steady negotiator calms a tactical operator; a disciplined operator protects a negotiator's work.

The Shield Is Ethos Embodied: Not hardware, not tactics, but a posture of protection that transcends tools.

The Enemy of Unity

Ego thrives in division. When negotiators and tactical compete, chaos wins. Ego whispers: "Your way is superior. Their way is weak."

But the warrior ethos silences that voice: "We are brothers on the same shield. The rifle and the voice breathe together."

This shield is not made of Kevlar. It is made of ethos—courage without ego, strength under control, unity in purpose.

- *Parents:* The shield is unity between father and mother. Children fracture when parents fight ego battles. They flourish when parents present a united ethos.

- *Leaders:* The shield is unity between vision and execution. Divided leadership breeds chaos. Unified leadership steadies organizations through storms.

- *Coaches:* The shield is unity between discipline and encouragement. Teams fracture when coaches compete with each other. They thrive when guidance is fused.

- *Spouses:* The shield is unity between love and respect. When ego divides, relationships collapse. When ethos fuses, marriages endure.

The warrior's shield is universal. In crisis or daily life, unity built on ethos preserves life and strengthens legacy.

Case Reflection: The Whispered Promise

During one prolonged call, a tactical operator whispered to the negotiator: "I'll hold my team and try to make command understand. You keep him talking."

That whispered promise was ethos embodied. It was the warrior's shield in action—strength under control, courage shared, life preserved.

The warrior's shield is not hardware. It is heart. It is ethos embodied in unity. It is courage under control, multiplied when protectors stand together.

Every protector—whether in law enforcement, family, leadership, or coaching—faces the temptation to divide. Ego pulls apart. Ethos fuses. The shield holds only when we choose unity over pride.

Maxim: "The rifle and the voice are not adversaries. They are brothers on the same shield."

The Warrior's Creed: Courage Under Control as Legacy

"The warrior's true victory is measured in lives preserved, not battles won."

The Warrior's Legacy

Every generation of negotiators, officers, leaders, and protectors leaves something behind. Some leave scars—rushed entries, fractured teams, decisions driven by ego. Others leave legacies— lives preserved, doctrines passed on, ethos carried forward.

The warrior's creed is simple: courage under control. This creed transforms fear into focus, ego into ethos, and chaos into clarity. It is the foundation on which protectors stand and the inheritance we hand to those who come after us.

Doctrine of the Warrior's Creed

Courage Under Control: Strength is nothing without restraint. The warrior does not confuse volume with power.

Discipline Before Action: Every decision begins with breath, cadence, and calm.

Unity Over Ego: The shield holds only when voices and rifles breathe together.

Ethos as Legacy: The creed is not theory—it is practice, discipline, and inheritance.

This creed is not ink on paper. It is lived doctrine, passed from protector to protector, leader to leader, parent to child.

Case Reflection: The Veteran's Words

A veteran negotiator, nearing retirement, was asked what he hoped his legacy would be. He answered quietly:

"That no one remembers my name, but everyone remembers the lives we saved because we had the courage to hold."

His words embodied the creed. The warrior does not seek applause. He seeks preservation of life.

- *Parents:* The warrior parent teaches discipline without cruelty, courage without intimidation. Children learn to trust strength that protects, not strength that wounds.

- *Leaders:* The warrior leader builds legacies that endure beyond quarterly results, shaping cultures where patience and integrity outlast politics.

- *Coaches:* The warrior coach instills composure in competition, reminding athletes that championships are built on discipline, not chaos.

- *Spouses:* The warrior partner anchors relationships in patience and presence, refusing to let pride dictate choices.

The creed is not limited to command posts. It is for every life, every leader, every protector.

Protector's Practice: Warrior Drills for Readers

Breath Before Action: Before making a decision under stress, take a single slow breath. Train your body to steady before you act.

Count the Cost: Ask, "Am I acting for optics or outcomes?" Choose outcomes.

Replace Ego with Ethos: When tempted to prove yourself, ask, "What preserves life, dignity, or trust?"

Hold Unity: In conflict, resist division. Choose the shield of unity over the fracture of pride.

Anchor in Creed: Repeat the maxim: "Strength under control is the essence of courage."

These drills embed the creed in daily life so that when storms break, courage under control is not theory—it is reflex.

Without the warrior's creed, teams fracture, families collapse, and leaders fail. With it, chaos is steadied, lives are preserved, and legacies endure.

The creed is more than a code for negotiators—it is a blueprint for protectors in every sphere.

The Warrior's Closing Call

We are not here to prove ourselves. We are here to protect. We are not here to dominate. We are here to steady.

We are warriors who do not confuse noise with strength.

We are guardians who absorb fear so others can breathe.

We are shepherds who walk beside the lost until dignity returns.

We are protectors who measure victory not by applause, but by breaths still drawn.

Final Maxim: "The warrior's creed is courage under control. This is our legacy, and it must outlive us."

Case Reflection: The Riverbend Call-Out

It was a Sunday morning when the phone buzzed: barricaded subject, armed, unstable, threatening suicide. By the time we pulled into staging at Riverbend High School, local police already had the perimeter locked down. Our role was clear—establish contact, slow the tempo, and work for a surrender.

The subject, thirty-five-year-old Mark Johnson, had drifted back into his father's life after years of absence. He brought with him alcohol, instability, and a pistol he'd already brandished while threatening to kill himself. His father, exhausted and afraid, sat with us at the negotiation post and sketched out the layout of the house. He warned that prescription narcotics were inside, that a pit bull was loose, and that his son was unraveling.

The strategy was straightforward: Make contact, listen, and let time do its work. Every training block we had ever delivered echoed the same principle—time, used wisely, is a weapon.

We dialed Mark's phone again and again—over sixty times from our devices, plus as many more through a borrowed phone. Sometimes he answered. Sometimes he didn't. When he did, his voice was quiet, distressed but never hostile. He promised he would come out, but always after "a minute" or "a few more minutes." Then he would hang up.

It would have been easy to force the issue. To let frustration or command pressure dictate tempo. But negotiation discipline means remembering that every second without violence is progress. Silence isn't failure; it's space for breathing. Space for survival.

We reminded him again and again: Put the firearm down, walk to the porch, hands visible, nothing in them. Each time, he said he needed "just a little longer." Each time, we honored it—until his very delays became the tool we used against his crisis.

When the Bearcat's PA system called his name, he finally answered again. We told him it was time. We had given him the minutes he asked for; now it was his turn to keep his word. Step out. Hands up. No weapons.

At 10:11 a.m., Mark Johnson stepped onto the porch, hands raised, empty. Officers moved in and took him safely into custody. Not a single round fired. Not a single life lost.

***

Lessons in the Code

Time is leverage. Used with discipline, it weakens panic and strengthens patience.

Respect earns credibility. Each time we honored his request for "a few more minutes," we built currency we could spend later.

Discipline holds the line. Frustration tempts negotiators to push; discipline reminds us that no one has ever bled to death from waiting.

Maxim: "Time is a weapon—if you have the discipline to use it."

CHAPTER 8

Ramirez Confession (Flagship AAR)

Opening Maxim: "When deception is the barricade, values become the key that unlocks truth."

Truth revealed through patience, persistence, and values.

Case Reflection: The Ramirez Confession

The call came on a humid Oklahoma afternoon in late summer. A church parsonage was on fire. When the flames were finally knocked down, firefighters discovered a body inside—the pastor, a man respected in his community. His throat had been slashed, his chest and back riddled with stab wounds. The house smelled of gasoline. What looked at first like an accidental blaze was quickly recognized as a fire meant to mask and cover up a gruesome murder.

Within hours, suspicion turned to a local man in his late thirties, whom we will call Ramirez. He had been seen near the property earlier in the day, and when officers contacted him, his arms and hands bore burns consistent with splashing fuel and igniting flames. He was transported to a hospital for treatment, then later taken into custody for questioning.

From the start, Ramirez had a story ready. He told detectives that masked men had forced him into the parsonage, that he was a victim, not the attacker. He insisted they had threatened his family and made him douse the house with gasoline. His account was elaborate, detailed enough to sound rehearsed, but just improbable enough to raise suspicion.

Investigators from the state bureau joined with local detectives, pressing Ramirez for hours. They circled back on inconsistencies, challenged timelines, and compared his words to the physical evidence. Still, he held to his story of faceless intruders. The interviews dragged on, tension thick in the air, frustration mounting on both sides of the table.

By the time our negotiation team was asked to step in, Ramirez was exhausted but still defiant. He leaned on his false story as a barricade, a way to shield himself from the crushing weight of truth. Detectives had facts. We needed something different. We needed a way to reach beyond his lies and touch the values he could not deny.

When I entered the room with another negotiator, I knew the challenge ahead. This was not about tactical concessions or stalling for time. It was about peeling back deception, layer by layer, until honesty surfaced. It was about showing Ramirez that dignity could still be found in truth—even if that truth condemned him.

The Wall of Lies

Ramirez leaned heavily on his story of masked men. He described them in vague but dramatic detail—tall, faceless intruders who forced their way into the parsonage and threatened his family's lives if he didn't comply. They supposedly handed him the gas can, ordered him to spread it, and forced him to strike the lighter. He insisted he was nothing more than a pawn in someone else's crime.

At first glance, the story carried enough color to seem possible. But the more he repeated it, the thinner it became. When pressed for specifics, his details shifted. The number of men changed.

Their voices changed. Their movements contradicted the physical evidence at the scene. Detectives challenged him, showing the inconsistencies, but Ramirez doubled down each time. Lies became his barricade, and he clung to them with desperate resolve.

The earlier interviews had taken the traditional approach: Confront the inconsistencies, press on the contradictions, and highlight the impossibility of his tale. But instead of breaking, Ramirez dug deeper. Each time the facts boxed him in, he lashed out with fresh embellishments. The detectives grew frustrated. Hours slipped by. Progress stalled.

By the time I entered the room, it was clear another path was needed. Beating Ramirez with facts had failed. He wasn't ready to surrender to evidence—but he might surrender to values.

I started not with the crime but with him. I asked about his family, his children, and the example a father sets when the weight of truth presses in. I shifted the frame from accusation to identity. "Good fathers," I said, "don't hide behind lies. Good men don't leave their children carrying shame. The truth is hard, but it's what your kids will remember."

Ramirez shifted uncomfortably, crossing and uncrossing his arms. He avoided my eyes, his earlier defiance fading into something more fragile. For the first time, the barricade wavered. This was not about evidence anymore. It was about the legacy of a man who still wanted to be seen as more than a killer. By appealing to that identity—husband, father, man of dignity—we began to reach past his lies and pull him closer to honesty.

Cracks in the Story

The shift was subtle at first. Ramirez leaned back in his chair, his earlier posture of defiance slipping away. His hands fidgeted on the table, tapping against the surface as if trying to drown out the silence. For hours, he had deflected with the story of masked men, but now, when I pressed him again about the example he was leaving for his children, the answer came slower.

"You don't understand," he muttered, his voice trailing off. "They made me . . ." His words stopped, hanging in the air. It wasn't the confident declaration of innocence we had heard earlier. It was the shaky voice of a man caught between his lie and the truth he was terrified to face.

I didn't rush to fill the silence. Silence, when wielded correctly, becomes its own tool. The weight of it forces a choice: Retreat into the safety of denial, or step into the risk of honesty. Ramirez shifted in his chair, rubbed his temples, and finally whispered, "I didn't want it to go that far."

It wasn't a confession, but it wasn't denial either. It was a crack. And cracks, when widened carefully, can bring down even the strongest barricade.

We pressed gently. Not with accusations, not with threats, but with questions about who he wanted to be remembered as. "When your children hear about this—when they see your name in the news—what do you want them to know? That you hid behind lies? Or that you had the strength to tell the truth?"

He lowered his head, his shoulders slumping. The bravado was gone. His story of masked men no longer held its edge. Instead, fragments began to emerge—a fight with the pastor, anger flaring, and a moment when control slipped away. He spoke in half sentences, broken and incomplete, but they pointed toward a reality he had worked so hard to bury.

We could feel the turning point. Ramirez was teetering between two worlds—the safety of his lies and the crushing relief of confession. All he needed was the push that would force him to finally step across.

The room was heavy with silence. Ramirez stared down at the table, his fingers tracing circles on the wood as though he could draw himself an escape. His voice trembled when he finally spoke, almost a whisper.

"I don't want my kids to hate me."

It was the clearest break yet—no denial, no blame on masked men, just fear of how his children would remember him. I leaned forward, lowering my tone so it was steady but firm. "They won't hate you for telling the truth. They'll hate the lies. The truth is the only way they'll ever see you as a man who still cared enough to be honest."

Ramirez lifted his eyes and met mine. For a moment, all the rehearsed stories, all the false bravado, drained away. His lips parted, and he said the words that changed everything:

"I killed him."

The barricade of lies collapsed in an instant. The story of masked intruders was gone. What remained was raw, unfiltered admission. My partner and I let the silence linger just long enough for the weight of those words to sink in, then guided him gently: "Tell us what happened."

The dam broke. Ramirez leaned forward, his hands trembling as he recounted the night. He described, in vivid detail, a confrontation with the pastor that turned into a heated argument and ultimately a violent, deadly encounter. He admitted striking him, stabbing him numerous times, and then with a slashing motion drawn left to right across his own throat advised he did that to make sure he was dead. His voice shook, but he didn't stop. The details spilled out, each one darker than the last.

Then came the fire. He explained how he grabbed a gas can, splashed fuel across the room, and lit it with a lighter. The flames caught faster than he expected, licking up the curtains, searing his hands and arms as he stumbled out of the house. He claimed he only wanted to destroy evidence, but his words betrayed the deeper truth: It was a desperate attempt to cover up a brutal killing.

When the confession ended, Ramirez slumped in his chair, sweat beading on his forehead, his eyes wet with tears. For hours, he had fought to hold on to lies. Now, the fight was over. He had spoken the truth—and in that truth came both condemnation and relief.

Securing the Truth

A spoken admission in a tense room has power, but it cannot remain just words drifting in the air. A confession must be anchored, secured, and preserved in a way that can withstand the courtroom and the scrutiny of justice. For Ramirez, that process began the moment he whispered, "I killed him."

We let the silence settle again, allowing the weight of his words to rest on him. Then we guided him forward. "You've done the hardest part," I said quietly. "Now you need to put it on record—for yourself, your family, and the truth."

Ramirez hesitated. His eyes darted toward the door, his body tense, as if he was considering retreat. This was the danger zone—the moment where a suspect can try to walk back what he has admitted. I steadied my voice, keeping it calm but firm. "You've already told us. You've said it. Don't bury the truth again. If you want your children to remember you as honest, this is where you prove it."

He nodded slowly, the defiance gone, replaced by resignation. We moved carefully into the process of documentation. First, he agreed to allow the session to be recorded. His voice, cracking but resolute, carried the same admissions he had spoken minutes earlier. Then came the written statement. We slid a notepad in front of him, placing a pen in his unsteady hand.

Writing slowed him down. Each word scratched onto the page was a weight he could not easily retract. At first, his sentences were short, choppy, almost reluctant. But as the ink flowed, so did the confession. He described the argument, the stabbing, the slashing of the throat, the fire set to erase the evidence. His handwriting trembled, but the details aligned with what he had already admitted aloud.

We did not celebrate. There was no fist-pumping, no outward show of victory. To do so would have shattered the fragile dignity that kept him writing. Instead, we treated him with measured respect, reminding him that taking responsibility was not weakness but strength—the final chance to show his children the truth about who he really was.

By the time Ramirez placed the pen down, the confession was no longer fragile. It was permanent. It was preserved in his own voice and his own hand, sealed into the record not as rumor or suspicion but as fact.

Doctrine: Lessons from Ramirez

The Ramirez case was not a barricade with rifles or a hostage held at gunpoint. It was a battle for truth inside an interview room. Yet the principles that carried the day were no different than those that resolve stand-offs and crises. This case showed us, once again, that when deception is the barricade, negotiation is still the weapon.

Deception Creates Its Own Barricade

Ramirez's story of masked intruders was not just a lie—it was a fortress he built to protect himself from the crushing reality of guilt. Detectives hammered at that fortress with evidence and contradictions, but each strike only made him reinforce the walls with more lies. The lesson is clear: The harder you push against a lie, the stronger the liar may cling to it. Breaking deception requires a different approach than brute confrontation.

Persistence Wears Down Defenses

Hours of repetition created exhaustion. Ramirez was tired from carrying the weight of a story that would not hold. Persistence was not about endless accusations—it was about consistency. We kept the dialogue going, circling back calmly, never letting him rest comfortably in denial. Time and patience created the cracks that evidence alone could not.

Values Become Leverage

The breakthrough came not when we shouted louder or piled more facts onto the table but when we spoke to who Ramirez still wanted to be: a father, husband, and a man his children could remember with some dignity. When guilt and shame battle against facts, facts often lose. But when guilt collides with values, truth has a chance to surface. Leaders must remember: People are more likely to change when their identity is appealed to, not just when their logic is challenged.

Negotiators Succeed Where Confrontation Fails

Detectives did not lack skill. They pressed evidence, challenged lies, and followed standard procedure. But negotiation added something else—patience, silence, empathy, and respect woven into persistence. Where direct confrontation failed, negotiation created space for Ramirez to let go of his lies and step into truth.

The doctrine is simple but vital: When deception is the barricade, negotiators don't storm the walls. They find the cracks, appeal to values, and wait for the moment when the wall collapses under its own weight.

Doctrine Continued: Timing Is Everything

Ramirez had already been interviewed for hours before we entered the room. Detectives had worn him down with questions, contradictions, and evidence. By the time we stepped in, the timing was right for a shift in strategy. If we had entered too early, his defenses would have been stronger. Too late, and fatigue might have pushed him into complete shutdown. Negotiation often hinges not only on what is said but on when it is said. Leaders must recognize the windows where change is possible—and be ready to act.

Silence Is a Weapon

When Ramirez faltered, it wasn't because of something we shouted. It was because we allowed silence to press against him. Silence forces people to hear their own words echo back. It strips away the comfort of noise and creates a vacuum that truth is drawn to fill. Many leaders fear silence, rushing to fill every gap. But in negotiation, silence can be louder than any argument.

Documentation Secures Victory

A spoken confession is fragile. Without careful recording and written statements, it risks being dismissed as hearsay or later retracted. Securing Ramirez's confession in his own handwriting and voice ensured that the truth he admitted could not easily be undone. The lesson extends beyond law enforcement: Victories are incomplete until they are recorded, preserved, and made part of the record. Leaders must always think about what comes after the breakthrough.

Preserve Dignity, Even in Guilt

Ramirez was guilty of a brutal, senseless murder. Yet treating him with respect was not about excusing his crime—it was about preserving the process. Humiliation closes doors; dignity keeps them open. By appealing to his identity as a father and allowing him to confess without ridicule, we gave him space to choose truth. Leaders must remember: Even when people fail, dignity can be the bridge that keeps progress possible.

The Ramirez confession reinforced a doctrine every negotiator must hold close: Facts alone rarely change people. Timing, silence, persistence, values, documentation, and dignity are the tools that do. A confession was not extracted that day—it was unlocked.

Reader Application: Breaking the Lie Barricade

The Ramirez confession was about homicide and arson, but its lessons extend far beyond the walls of an interview room. At its core, it was a story about deception, identity, and the struggle between lies and truth. Leaders in every arena—business, family, coaching, community—face those same dynamics. The tools may differ, but the principles remain.

When Lies Become Barricades

Every leader has faced it: an employee hiding mistakes, a child avoiding consequences, a teammate covering for poor performance. Lies are not only about avoiding accountability; they are walls people build to shield themselves from shame. The harder you batter those walls with accusations, the stronger the lies become. Leaders must learn to recognize when confrontation is reinforcing resistance rather than breaking it down.

The Power of Timing

There are moments when people are open to change and moments when they are not. Detectives hammered Ramirez with facts, but he wasn't ready. By the time we stepped in, his fatigue and contradictions had created the conditions for truth. Leaders, too, must learn to recognize windows of openness—the late-night conversation with a teenager, the quiet moment after a business failure, the pause after conflict when pride has finally cooled. Timing matters as much as words.

Appeal to Identity, Not Just Logic

Ramirez did not confess because the evidence trapped him. He confessed because we spoke to the kind of father and man he still wanted to be. Logic points out contradictions; identity points toward transformation. Leaders who appeal to values—who someone is, or who they want to become—unlock change that facts alone cannot.

Silence as Leadership

In a world addicted to noise, leaders rush to fill every pause with explanation or instruction. But silence carries weight. In the interview room, silence pressed harder than arguments. In leadership, silence gives others space to reflect, own their words, and move toward honesty.

Securing the Aftermath

Ramirez's confession had to be documented to hold. In leadership, breakthroughs must also be preserved—written down as commitments, captured as lessons, turned into systems. Otherwise, victories fade into memory and are lost.

The lesson is universal: When deception is the barricade, leaders must not batter the walls. They must find the cracks, wait for the moment, and appeal to values that make truth possible.

The Ramirez confession is a stark reminder that truth does not surface by accident—it must be cultivated. That principle extends far beyond criminal interviews. Whether leading a company, raising a family, or guiding a team, the same dynamics unfold in quieter ways.

Business Leadership

A manager dealing with an underperforming employee may find the truth buried under excuses: supply chain problems, miscommunication, other people's failures. Hammering those excuses with accusations rarely works. But appealing to professional pride—"You've always been someone who takes ownership. What changed?"—can break through denial. Silence after a pointed question can do more than a stack of reports. Just as Ramirez's story crumbled under values, so too can workplace deception collapse when identity is challenged with respect.

Family Leadership

Parents face this daily. A teenager sneaks out or hides poor grades. Facts may prove the lie, but confrontation often fuels rebellion. The turning point comes when parents speak to identity: "You're better than this. I know the kind of person you want to be." That appeal to character mirrors the way Ramirez was guided toward confession. It was not evidence that forced honesty; it was a reminder of who he still wanted to be.

Coaching and Mentorship

Athletes, like suspects, sometimes hide behind excuses—blaming refs, teammates, or bad luck. Confrontation has its place, but progress often comes when a coach appeals to pride: "You're the captain. Others follow you. Own this moment." By framing accountability as a path to dignity, coaches turn deception into development.

Community and Civic Leadership

When organizations face scandal, denial is often the first reaction. Leaders who confront only with facts may find walls rising higher. But those who speak to values—integrity, honor, service—create space for honesty. Communities, like individuals, respond to appeals that remind them of who they are meant to be.

Securing Progress

The confession was not complete until Ramirez wrote his words. In leadership, progress is not complete until commitments are captured. Families write agreements, businesses draft action plans, teams set clear goals. Truth spoken must become truth secured.

The doctrine holds steady: When deception stands in the way, leaders must move beyond confrontation to timing, silence, values, and documentation. These principles are not only for interview rooms—they are for every room where trust and truth matter.

Closing Compass

The Ramirez confession reminds us that not every barricade is built of brick, wood, or steel. Some are built of lies—layer upon layer of deception crafted to shield a guilty conscience from the weight of truth. Breaking those barricades requires more than facts and evidence. It requires persistence, patience, and an appeal to the values that still breathe beneath the surface of guilt.

This case was not about clever questioning or trickery. Detectives had already pressed the facts. The difference came when negotiation shifted the ground. By speaking to Ramirez as a father, by appealing to his desire to be remembered with dignity, we reached the one part of him that lies could not cover. Truth surfaced, not because we forced it, but because we gave him reason to claim it.

That is the Warrior ethos at work. Warriors do not always break doors with force. Sometimes they sit across a table and hold silence until the weight of it compels honesty. Sometimes they carry themselves with calm resolve so that others see truth reflected in their steadiness. And sometimes they appeal to the values that cannot be extinguished even in the darkest of circumstances.

For leaders in every arena, the lesson is clear: Facts matter, but values move people. Evidence proves, but identity transforms. Whether in a negotiation room, a boardroom, or a living room, the path to truth often runs through the heart before it reaches the mind.

Ramirez's confession did not bring back the life he took, nor did it heal the wounds left in the community. But it preserved the integrity of justice. It showed that even when lies stand tall, truth can still be drawn out when leaders have the patience to wait, the courage to press gently, and the wisdom to appeal to what matters most.

Epilogue and Ethos Connection

The Ramirez confession was more than an investigative milestone; it was a reminder of what it means to lead when the easy path is confrontation and the harder path is patience. It proved that the most powerful tools in a warrior's arsenal are not always weapons or evidence but presence, silence, and values spoken at the right time.

When Ramirez finally admitted, "I killed him," it was not just the end of a lie. It was the collapse of a barricade that words alone had built. His admission came not because he was cornered, but because he was given a way to step into truth without losing the last fragments of dignity he still carried. That is the paradox of strength in negotiation: To win, you must sometimes give the other side a reason to surrender with honor.

For leaders, this case is a call to look beyond the surface of resistance. Lies in a boardroom, excuses in a locker room, or denial in a family argument may look like defiance—but often, they are barricades built to protect fragile identity. Breaking them requires courage to sit in silence, discipline to persist without anger, and wisdom to speak to the deeper values that still live beneath the surface.

As we transition to the next chapter, the Ramirez confession stands as a bridge. It links the art of negotiation with the ethos of the warrior-leader: control under pressure, courage to press for truth, and presence that steadies those who falter. It reminds us that in every fight for honesty, the strongest leaders do not just expose lies—they cultivate the conditions where truth becomes the only path forward.

CHAPTER 9

Guardian Lessons Carried Forward

Guardian's Maxim: "The guardian absorbs weight others never see."

The Guardian's Role

If the warrior's ethos is courage under control, the guardian's ethos is protection under pressure. Where the warrior stands firm against fear and ego, the guardian steps forward to shoulder the weight of others—the unseen burden of chaos, politics, optics, and fear that can crush decision-making in crisis.

Every command post carries this weight. Leaders demand updates. Families demand answers. Media demand timelines. Politicians demand optics. Beneath all of it lies the life of a human being in crisis.

The guardian does not flinch. The guardian absorbs the weight, steadies the room, and creates space for others to function.

Case Reflection: The Command Post Storm

It was midnight when the storm broke. A barricaded subject had threatened to kill his wife. Tactical stood ready. Negotiators worked the line. And in the command post, the temperature rose with every passing hour.

The mayor wanted updates. The media circled outside. A commander pressed: "We look weak. End this."

But the guardian ethos prevailed. Negotiators bore the criticism. They absorbed the glare of leaders demanding action. They carried the weight so the tactical team could hold their perimeter and the negotiators on the line could work.

Hours later, the subject surrendered alive. The family was reunited. The command post quieted. The guardian had carried the weight until it passed.

Doctrine of the Guardian Ethos

The Guardian Absorbs Pressure: By carrying stress, the guardian frees others to function.

The Guardian Creates Space: Steadiness gives time for adrenaline to fade, dignity to return, and outcomes to shift.

The Guardian Holds the Line: When fear demands action for optics, the guardian insists on patience for life.

The Guardian Preserves Unity: By carrying criticism, the guardian prevents fractures within the team.

Reader Application: Living as a Guardian

- *Parents:* The guardian parent carries the anxiety of family storms, absorbing it so children feel safe.

- *Leaders:* The guardian leader absorbs organizational stress, shielding teams from political noise so they can perform.

- *Coaches:* The guardian coach absorbs the pressure of competition, freeing athletes to play with focus.

- *Spouses:* The guardian partner absorbs the weight of shared hardship, protecting the bond by carrying more when the other cannot.

The guardian's power is not in noise or visibility. It is in quiet strength—the ability to bear weight so others can breathe.

Case Reflection: The Rookie Who Panicked

During one incident, a rookie negotiator panicked when a commander shouted for results. His voice faltered on the line. The subject sensed weakness. The situation teetered.

The senior guardian stepped in—not with volume but with presence. He steadied the rookie, carried the commander's anger, and absorbed the subject's fury. Hours later, the rookie whispered: "I couldn't have done it without you."

That is the essence of the guardian ethos: carrying the weight until others can stand again.

Why This Matters

The world rarely notices guardians. They don't seek credit, headlines, or applause. Their victories are quiet. Their discipline is invisible. But without them, teams fracture, outcomes collapse, and lives are lost.

The guardian ethos is not about recognition. It is about carrying weight until storms pass and life is preserved.

Maxim: "The guardian is not the loudest voice. The guardian is the steady shield."

Doctrine of Bearing Weight

"The guardian carries what would crush others."

The Hidden Weight

In every crisis, there are two battles: the visible one at the scene and the invisible one inside the command post. The visible battle is raw—subjects in crisis, weapons, barricades, fear. The invisible battle is quieter but just as deadly—politics, optics, deadlines, and fear of appearing weak.

The negotiator who lives by the guardian ethos steps into this second battle. They bear the weight of leaders demanding speed, the media screaming for updates, and commanders tempted by ego. By absorbing this pressure, the guardian shields the team working the line, giving them room to breathe, listen, and influence.

Case Reflection: The Governor's Call

During one hostage crisis, the governor personally called the command post: "End this before morning. This makes us look weak."

Pressure spiked. Some wanted to comply. Optics seemed louder than lives. But the guardian stepped in: "Governor, our mission is not speed—it is survival. We will resolve this without funerals."

Hours passed. Negotiators held steady. The subject released the hostages, then surrendered alive.

In the debrief, the governor admitted: "I wanted action. You gave me results."

The guardian had carried the political weight until the crisis broke.

Doctrine of Bearing Weight

Absorbing Pressure Protects Performance: By taking criticism, guardians free operators and negotiators to stay steady.

Time Is Bought by Bearing: Every ounce of pressure absorbed translates into more time for the subject to cool.

The Shield Must Not Crack: If guardians yield to fear or ego, fractures ripple through the entire operation.

Quiet Strength Speaks Loudest: The guardian's influence often comes without raising their voice—it comes from refusing to bend under pressure.

- *Parents:* Guardianship is absorbing financial stress or external judgment so children can grow without carrying burdens they cannot yet bear.

- *Leaders:* Guardianship is absorbing criticism from shareholders or boards to protect the integrity of the team's work.

- *Coaches:* Guardianship is taking on the pressure of fans or boosters so athletes can focus on performance rather than politics.

- *Spouses:* Guardianship is carrying more when one partner is faltering, shielding them until they can recover strength.

Guardianship is rarely visible. Its value is not in recognition but in relief—the freedom it gives others to function.

Case Reflection: The Negotiator's Shield

One negotiator recalled a standoff where tactical grew restless: "He's playing us. Let's take him."

The guardian stepped in: "He's slowing. His threats are softening. Hold."

For hours, the guardian bore the brunt of tactical frustration. When the subject surrendered alive, the tactical commander pulled him aside and said: "I wanted to break. You kept us steady."

The guardian shielded the mission, not by volume but by endurance.

The Cost of Bearing

Carrying weight takes a toll. Guardians absorb criticism, frustration, and fear. They often walk away unnoticed, even blamed. But they accept the cost because they know the alternative is worse—fractured teams, rushed entries, funerals that could have been prevented.

The guardian ethos is sacrifice. It is willingness to be criticized to protect others. It is the discipline to stand silent when insulted, endure pressure when tempted to break, and choose survival over recognition.

The guardian ethos ensures that weight does not crush the wrong shoulders. If negotiators carry it, they fracture. If tactical carries it, they rush. The guardian absorbs it all—politics, optics, fear—so others can perform their mission with clarity.

Maxim: "The guardian does not pass on pressure. The guardian absorbs it."

The Guardian Steps In

The guardian did not flinch. He stepped into the storm, absorbing the noise, criticism, and impatience. He steadied the negotiator on the phone: "Stay your course. He's still talking. That's progress."

He steadied tactical: "Hold perimeter. No entry. Trust the dialogue."

He steadied the command staff: "Lives matter more than headlines. We will not trade blood for optics."

The storm raged, but the guardian bore it. Hours passed. The subject surrendered, laying down his weapon. No shots fired. No funerals.

The guardian carried the weight at the crossroads until survival was secured.

Doctrine at the Crossroads

Fear Demands Action: Fear shouts: "Do something now!" The guardian steadies.

Optics Demand Spectacle: Optics insist, "Look decisive." The guardian insists, "Be protective."

Life Demands Patience, Life Whispers: "Wait. Hold. Endure." The guardian listens.

The Guardian Decides: At the crossroads, it is guardianship that tips the scale toward preservation of life.

Case Reflection: The Rookie's Question

After the standoff ended, a rookie negotiator asked the guardian: "How did you stand against all that pressure?"

The guardian answered quietly: "Because I'd rather be hated for hours than attend funerals for years."

That one sentence became doctrine. Guardians accept criticism in the moment to prevent tragedy in the aftermath.

- *Parents:* At the crossroads of discipline and anger, guardians choose to carry frustration rather than unleash it on children.

- *Leaders:* At the crossroads of politics and integrity, guardians choose what preserves trust rather than what appeases optics.

- *Coaches:* At the crossroads of winning now or developing character, guardians choose to build people, not just scoreboards.

- *Spouses:* At the crossroads of pride and patience, guardians choose presence over victory, carrying tension until it eases.

Every life faces crossroads. Guardianship is the discipline to carry weight until dignity and survival can return.

The Cost of Standing Firm

After the duplex call, the guardian received little recognition. Commanders claimed credit. Politicians moved on. The news cycle shifted.

But the officers on the perimeter never forgot. The negotiator never forgot. The subject's family never forgot.

Guardians rarely earn applause. Their reward is quieter—the knowledge that lives were preserved because they chose to hold the line.

At every crossroads, ego and optics scream for action. Fear whispers that waiting is failure. But the guardian knows the truth: Patience is discipline, not weakness. Absorbing weight is strength, not surrender.

Without guardians, crossroads become collisions. With them, they become survivable.

Maxim: "The guardian chooses preservation over perception, every time."

The Guardian's Tools

"The guardian's strength is not in weapons but in the weight they are willing to carry."

The Invisible Arsenal

Unlike the warrior, whose shield is discipline under fire, the guardian wields a quieter arsenal. These tools cannot be strapped on or fired downrange. They are forged in patience, presence, and endurance. They are invisible to the crowd but decisive in the outcome.

The guardian's tools are not glamorous. They do not appear in headlines. But without them, command posts fracture, tactical teams rush, negotiators falter, and lives are lost.

Doctrine of the Guardian's Tools

Calm in the Room: The guardian controls their own biology first—slowing cadence, steadying tone, lowering volume. Calm is contagious.

Translation of Chaos: Guardians turn emotional noise into usable intel—"He isn't stalling; he's cooling."

Shielding Others: Guardians absorb the glare of leaders, politicians, or media so operators and negotiators can focus.

Refusing to Rush: Guardians stand against fear disguised as urgency, creating the space for dignity to return.

Sacrificing Ego: Guardians accept criticism, ridicule, even blame—knowing survival matters more than reputation.

Case Reflection: The Press Conference That Never Happened

During one high-profile call, the mayor demanded a press conference mid-standoff. Commanders considered pulling negotiators off the line to prepare talking points. The guardian intervened: "Our focus is saving lives, not saving face. The press can wait."

Negotiators stayed on the line. Hours later, the subject surrendered alive. There was no press conference, only a reunion between a father and his daughter.

The guardian had wielded their tools: calm, translation, shielding, and sacrifice. The cost was political criticism. The reward was life preserved.

The Power of Translation

One of the most overlooked guardian tools is translation. Emotions in the room—anger, fear, frustration—are often misread as intel. Guardians sift through the chaos, separate signal from noise, and give leaders clarity.

"His silence is not defiance; it is biology cooling."

"Her repetition is not manipulation; it is trauma looping."

"His anger is not escalation; it is exhaustion breaking through."

Translation reframes crisis. It prevents rash action. It restores perspective when adrenaline blinds decision-makers.

- *Parents:* Guardianship means calming yourself before calming your child. Translating tantrums as biology, not defiance.

- *Leaders:* Guardianship means absorbing the anxiety of the boardroom, translating noise into signal, and protecting your team's focus.

- *Coaches:* Guardianship means shielding athletes from outside critics, translating pressure into growth, not collapse.

- *Spouses:* Guardianship means steadying the home when fear or frustration enters, translating conflict into connection.

The guardian's tools are not for show. They are for survival—whether of a hostage, a family, a team, or a marriage.

Case Reflection: The Shielded Rookie

A young negotiator once froze when a commander snapped: "You're wasting time. Wrap it up." The guardian stepped in, absorbing the commander's fury: "That frustration is on me, not on him."

The rookie steadied. The subject kept talking. Hours later, the surrender was achieved.

The guardian's tool that day was sacrifice—accepting blame so another could succeed.

The guardian ethos depends on these tools. Without calm, chaos multiplies. Without translation, intel is lost. Without shielding, negotiators collapse under pressure. Without sacrifice, teams fracture.

These tools are invisible to the crowd but visible in the outcomes: lives preserved, funerals prevented, dignity restored.

Maxim: "The guardian's tools are unseen by the crowd but decisive in the outcome."

The Cost of Guardianship

"The guardian pays the price so others don't have to."

The Burden No One Sees

Guardianship is not free. Every ounce of pressure absorbed leaves a mark. Guardians take criticism that was not theirs, anger that was not earned, and weight that was not visible. They protect others but often go home carrying the storm inside themselves.

The public never sees it. The team rarely notices it. Even families may only glimpse the edges of it. But the guardian feels it—fatigue that lingers, sleepless nights replaying decisions, scars invisible but permanent.

Case Reflection: The Loneliness of Bearing

A negotiator once described the aftermath of a fourteen-hour standoff. The subject survived. The family was reunited. Tactical praised the outcome.

But in the debrief, the guardian was berated by a commander: "You dragged this out too long. You made us look weak."

The team moved on. The family healed. But the guardian carried those words like shrapnel. For months, he questioned whether patience was weakness. The scar was silent but real.

This is the cost of guardianship—loneliness, criticism, and scars carried in silence.

Doctrine of Cost

- *Guardians Absorb Criticism:* They choose to bear it so others can function.

- *Guardians Sacrifice Recognition:* They forfeit applause for survival.

- *Guardians Carry Invisible Scars:* The weight they bear leaves marks no one else sees.

- *Guardians Endure for Legacy:* They accept the cost because the alternative—lives lost—is too high.

The Enemy Within: Fatigue and Doubt

The greatest threat to guardianship is not external pressure but internal erosion. Fatigue whispers: "You can't carry this forever." Doubt whispers: "Maybe they were right. Maybe you are weak."

Without renewal, guardians collapse under the very weight they carry.

This is why doctrine, ethos, and maxims exist—not as decoration but as anchors to hold the guardian steady when fatigue and doubt attack.

- *Parents:* Guardianship means absorbing stress to protect children—but exhaustion is real. Parents must find renewal or risk breaking under the weight.

- *Leaders:* Guardianship means carrying criticism for the team—but doubt can corrode integrity if never replenished by conviction.

- *Coaches:* Guardianship means absorbing pressure from outside voices—but fatigue can lead to burnout if ethos is not practiced daily.

- *Spouses:* Guardianship means carrying more when the other falters—but only if renewal is sought together, not in silence.

Guardianship demands cost. Pretending it is free only guarantees collapse.

Case Reflection: The Silent Guardian

A veteran guardian retired after decades of service. At his ceremony, officers praised his steadiness, commanders praised his patience, and families thanked him for lives preserved.

But afterward, in private, he confessed: "The scars are heavy. I bore them so others wouldn't have to."

His legacy was survival. His cost was silent scars.

The cost of guardianship must be acknowledged, or guardians will break unseen. Leaders must recognize the weight their guardians carry. Families must see the toll. Teams must value the sacrifice.

Guardianship is noble, but it is not free. Its cost is borne quietly, often alone. But when it is carried with ethos, it becomes the price of survival.

Maxim: "The guardian accepts scars so others may live without them."

"The guardian's strength is proven not in moments of calm but in storms they absorb for others."

The Guardian Beyond the Command Post

Guardianship is not glamorous. It will not make headlines. But it is essential to the survival of families, organizations, and communities. Living as a guardian requires daily practice, because weight always finds its way into our lives.

Case Reflection: The Parent's Shield

A single mother worked three jobs to keep her children sheltered and fed. The kids never saw the bills she juggled, the tears she wiped away in private, or the doubt that haunted her in silence. They only saw the steadiness—the guardian who carried the weight so they could grow.

That is guardianship outside the command post: carrying storms so others can grow in peace.

Reader Drills for Living the Guardian Ethos

Breath Before Bearing: In your next conflict, pause before responding. Take one slow breath. Anchor your biology before absorbing the pressure of others. Guardianship begins with calm in yourself.

Translate the Noise: After your next heated moment, write down what was signal and what was noise. Signal is what truly mattered.

Noise is ego, fear, or optics. Guardianship means sifting through both to protect others from being crushed by the irrelevant.

Shield, Don't Spread: When criticized, resist the urge to pass it down to your children, team, or partner. Absorb it instead. Say, "I'll carry this one." That act of shielding steadies those around you.

Choose Legacy Over Optics: In your next hard choice, ask yourself: "Will this decision matter in ten years?" Guardianship chooses survival, trust, and dignity over short-term appearances.

Share the Burden: Guardianship is not about isolation. It is about carrying weight wisely. Share your own struggles with a trusted ally. Division of burden makes survival possible.

Case Reflection: The Leader Who Chose Legacy

A business leader once resisted pressure to slash corners for quarterly numbers. He bore criticism from shareholders. But years later, his organization stood tall because he had chosen integrity over optics. His legacy was preserved because he carried the burden others wanted to drop.

This is guardianship: choosing to carry weight in the present so the future remains intact. Don't sell tomorrow to finance today.

The Guardian's Creed for Daily Life

I will absorb pressure so others can function.

I will separate signal from noise.

I will shield others from criticism I can bear.

I will choose legacy over optics.

I will share my burden with trusted allies so I do not collapse.

The creed is not decoration. It is a daily practice that protects families, strengthens teams, and steadies communities.

Without guardians, storms destroy families, teams, and organizations. With them, storms pass, lives endure, and legacies survive.

Guardianship is not a call to carry everything—it is a call to carry wisely, with ethos and endurance.

Maxim: "Guardianship is not noticed in the moment, but its absence is felt forever."

The Guardian's Closing Call

"The guardian holds the line when others cannot."

The Quietest Protector

In the history of crisis work, some heroes are remembered for bold actions—the shot taken, the entry made, the words spoken in the right moment. But the guardian is often remembered only by those who lived because of them. Their victories are quieter, their legacies more hidden, but their impact is profound.

The guardian does not walk away with medals. They walk away with scars no one sees. They walk away criticized by some, forgotten by others, but remembered by the lives they preserved.

This is the cost, and this is the calling: to hold the line when others cannot, stand steady when storms rage, and absorb the weight no one else can carry.

Case Reflection: The Funeral That Never Happened

One guardian told this story years after retirement. A hostage situation spiraled, and commanders screamed for entry. The guardian resisted, absorbing the criticism, insisting on patience. Hours later, the subject surrendered.

Decades passed. The guardian grew older. And one day, a young man walked up to him at a grocery store and said: "You don't know me, but my mother told me I'm alive because of you. I was a child in that house."

That is guardianship: funerals that never happen, lives that continue because someone carried the weight.

Doctrine of the Closing Call

Guardianship Saves Quietly: The world rarely notices, but lives endure because of it.

Guardianship Demands Sacrifice: Scars, criticism, and silence are the cost.

Guardianship Builds Legacy: The future is shaped not by applause but by breaths preserved.

Guardianship Anchors the Ethos: Warrior fights, shepherd guides, protector unifies—but guardian carries the weight.

- *Parents:* Your guardianship may never be thanked, but children live stronger because of it.

- *Leaders:* Your guardianship may never make headlines, but organizations endure because of it.

- *Coaches:* Your guardianship may never earn applause, but athletes thrive because of it.

- *Spouses:* Your guardianship may never be recognized, but marriages survive because of it.

The measure of guardianship is not applause. It is survival.

The Guardian's Creed

We are guardians.

We absorb weight others cannot.

We shield others from storms.

We choose legacy over optics.

We measure success not by credit but by survival.

We carry scars so others do not have to.

We hold the line when others cannot.

This is not decoration. This is doctrine.

Closing Reflection

The warrior ethos steadies courage under fire. The guardian ethos absorbs pressure under storms. Together, they form the shield that allows shepherds to guide and protectors to unify.

But the guardian is unique. Their victories are invisible, their sacrifices unrecorded, their scars unnoticed. Yet without them, the craft collapses. Without them, lives are lost.

The guardian does not seek recognition. They seek survival—for others.

Closing Maxim: "The guardian will be forgotten by many, but remembered forever by those who lived because of them."

CHAPTER 10

The Shepherd Ethos:
Presence Over Performance

Shepherd's Maxim: "The shepherd does not drag the lost; he walks beside them."

The Shepherd's Role

If the warrior's ethos is courage and the guardian's ethos is weight-bearing, the shepherd's ethos is presence. The shepherd does not force. He does not command obedience. He walks alongside.

The shepherd ethos is about restoring dignity and choice to those who feel stripped of both. In crisis, people often feel reduced to their worst moment—a man threatening his family, a veteran on the brink, a mother barricaded in despair. The world sees danger. The shepherd sees a human being who has lost their way.

Where the warrior steadies courage and the guardian carries weight, the shepherd restores dignity. Their power is not in controlling others but in granting the time, space, and presence that allows others to reclaim control for themselves.

Case Reflection: The Longest Walk

One negotiator described sitting in silence with a suicidal veteran on the phone for nearly three hours. Words were scarce. Breath was shallow. Commanders grew restless. Tactical whispered: "He's wasting our time."

But the shepherd ethos prevailed. The negotiator stayed. No demands. No threats. No rush. Just presence. At one point, the veteran whispered: "Are you still there?"

"Yes," the negotiator replied. "We're here. We're walking with you."

Eventually, the man surrendered his weapon. Later, he said: "I thought I had no one left. But you stayed. That's what changed it."

That is the shepherd ethos in action—not dragging someone back but walking beside them until they could walk on their own.

Doctrine of the Shepherd Ethos

Presence Over Performance: It is not what you say, but that you stay.

Restoring Dignity: Choices and options are dignity restored.

Patience as Guidance: Time itself is a form of guidance—long enough for clarity to return.

Compassion Without Rescue: The shepherd does not rescue by force; they guide until the subject chooses their own way out.

Reader Application: Shepherding in Daily Life

- *Parents:* Shepherding is not dragging your children toward decisions but guiding them with presence and patience.
- *Leaders:* Shepherding is giving employees the dignity of choice rather than forcing outcomes for optics.

- *Coaches:* Shepherding is walking alongside athletes in defeat, teaching resilience rather than demanding perfection.

- *Spouses:* Shepherding is presence during storms—not fixing immediately, but being steady until healing begins.

The shepherd ethos recognizes that no one finds their way back by being shoved. They find it because someone was willing to walk beside them until they remembered the road.

Why This Matters

Without shepherds, people in crisis feel abandoned, reduced to their failures. With shepherds, they feel seen, valued, and accompanied. The shepherd's ethos transforms despair into dignity—not through force but through presence.

Maxim: "The shepherd restores dignity not by dragging but by walking beside."

Case Reflection: The Abandoned Mother

"Presence is not passive. It is the strongest form of guidance."

The Call That Broke the Room

It was late in the evening when the call came: A mother had barricaded herself in her home with her two children. Her husband had left weeks earlier, her job was gone, and eviction loomed. When police arrived, she screamed from the window: "You've taken everything. You won't take my kids!"

Inside the command post, pressure mounted. Tactical wanted to act quickly—"We can't let the children stay in there all night." Commanders debated. The air was thick with urgency.

But the shepherd ethos whispered another truth: Survival comes not from force but from presence.

The Shepherd Steps In

A negotiator connected with the woman on the phone. Instead of countering her rage, he acknowledged it: "You've been abandoned. You've been carrying this alone. We see you."

For hours, the negotiator did not lecture or argue. He did not rush toward resolution. He simply stayed. He reminded her she was not alone, her pain was real, and her children deserved tomorrow with their mother still alive.

Slowly, her tone shifted. Rage softened into tears. Defiance bent into exhaustion. Presence carried her through the breaking point.

By dawn, she stepped outside with her children. No one was harmed. Dignity was restored—not by force but by shepherding presence.

Doctrine of Shepherding Presence

Acknowledgment Precedes Change: People cannot move forward until they feel seen where they stand.

Stability Is Contagious: The shepherd's calm cadence steadies even the most volatile storms.

Patience Restores Dignity: Waiting is not weakness—it is the soil where dignity grows back.

Presence Opens Doors: Where ultimatums slam doors shut, presence leaves them open.

Case Reflection: The Rookie's Misstep

A rookie once interrupted a similar call, urging: "Think about what you're doing! Don't you care about your kids?"

The subject's rage exploded. Connection shattered. The situation nearly unraveled.

Afterward, the shepherd explained: "She didn't need judgment. She needed presence. If you stand with her, she will walk out with dignity. If you push her, she will collapse under shame."

That correction transformed the rookie. From then on, he learned to walk beside rather than drag.

- *Parents:* When children feel abandoned or misunderstood, shepherding presence means listening first, guiding second.

- *Leaders:* When employees falter, shepherding presence means standing with them until they rediscover dignity.

- *Coaches:* When teams lose, shepherding presence means walking them through the loss, not berating them in it.

- *Spouses:* When partners feel unseen, shepherding presence means steady companionship—not fixing, not forcing, simply staying.

Presence is a discipline. It requires silencing ego, resisting the urge to fix, and enduring discomfort. But it is presence that restores dignity when nothing else can.

The Cost of Presence

The shepherd pays a price for presence. Hours of silence drain energy. Bearing another's despair weighs heavily. Recognition is rare, criticism frequent. Commanders may call it stalling, families may call it weakness.

But the shepherd knows the truth: Presence is not weakness. It is the strongest form of guidance.

The mother who walked out with her children did not surrender to threats. She surrendered to presence. That moment proved a truth written across decades of crisis work: When people feel abandoned, they don't need answers but companionship.

The shepherd ethos ensures that no one walks alone through despair.

Maxim: "The shepherd's gift is not solutions but presence that restores dignity."

Doctrine: Walking Beside, Not Dragging

"The shepherd does not command the lost to move. He walks until they can."

Doctrine of Walking Beside

The shepherd ethos is built on patience, dignity, and accompaniment. Unlike force or control, it does not demand immediate compliance. Instead, it grants enough stability for someone to rediscover their own strength.

Patience Is Guidance: Shepherds know people rarely change on command. They change when given time to breathe.

Dignity Is Influence: Shepherds restore agency by offering choices, not ultimatums.

Presence Is Power: Shepherds know presence itself calms, steadies, and guides.

Compassion Is Discipline: Compassion without discipline becomes enabling. Discipline without compassion becomes tyranny. The shepherd balances both.

Walking beside is not weakness—it is the discipline of guiding without dragging.

Case Reflection: The Man in the Warehouse

A man threatened suicide in a warehouse after being fired from his job. Tactical wanted to breach. Supervisors wanted quick resolution.

The shepherd negotiator slowed everything down. Instead of pressing the man with solutions, he sat in silence and asked only one question: "What do you want me to know right now?"

The man began to talk. Rage turned to grief. Hours later, he surrendered quietly.

The lesson was clear: Dragging would have broken him. Walking beside allowed him to walk out on his own.

Doctrine in Leadership

Patience Before Action: Shepherd leaders wait before correcting, ensuring emotions cool first.

Restoring Agency: Shepherd leaders ask questions that return dignity: "What do you need to succeed?"

Presence Over Optics: Shepherd leaders show up in crises not to perform but to endure with their teams.

Shepherd leaders understand that rushing people may get compliance, but walking beside them builds loyalty, resilience, and trust.

- *Parents:* Walking beside means giving children the dignity of failure and the chance to rise again, rather than dragging them toward perfection.

- *Leaders:* Walking beside means standing with employees during failure, guiding them toward learning, not shame.

- *Coaches:* Walking beside means carrying losses with the team, turning them into growth rather than punishment.

- *Spouses:* Walking beside means presence during storms—choosing companionship over control.

Every person will face moments where the temptation is to drag others forward. The shepherd ethos asks a harder discipline: Walk beside instead.

Case Reflection: The Rookie Who Dragged

A rookie negotiator once barked commands at a suicidal subject: "Put it down! Don't be stupid!" The subject snapped: "You don't care about me. You just want me to comply."

Connection broke. Trust was lost.

Later, the shepherd explained: "When you drag, you shame. When you shame, you sever. When you sever, you lose."

The rookie learned. Next call, he tried presence. This time, the subject surrendered. The difference was not in technique but in posture.

Why Walking Beside Matters

Dragging reduces dignity. Walking beside restores it. Dragging creates resistance. Walking beside creates cooperation. Dragging satisfies ego. Walking beside preserves life.

The shepherd ethos ensures that people are not treated as problems to be solved but as humans to be guided.

Maxim: "Dragging breaks trust. Walking beside restores it."

Case Reflection: The Lost Officer

"The shepherd guides not only the lost in crisis but the weary within the flock."

The Officer on the Edge

Not all shepherding happens across a barricade. Sometimes it happens inside the team.

One night, after a grueling twelve-hour standoff, a young officer sat in the parking lot with his head in his hands. He had been on the perimeter, exhausted, and blamed himself for not spotting a subject's movement earlier. "If something had gone wrong, it would've been on me," he whispered.

Commanders moved on, paperwork loomed, but the officer stayed in the lot, crushed under a weight of guilt that wasn't his to carry.

The shepherd ethos answered—not through lecture, not through command, but through presence.

The Shepherd Steps In

A veteran negotiator walked out, sat beside him in silence, and waited. No lectures. No correction. Just presence. After a long pause, the veteran said: "We all carry ghosts. The question is—will you carry them alone, or let us walk with you?"

The young officer looked up, eyes wet. For the first time, the weight began to lift—not because of solutions but because of companionship.

That night, shepherding did not save a subject. It saved a teammate.

Doctrine of Shepherding Within the Team

Presence Protects the Protectors: Shepherding is not only outward—it strengthens the flock itself.

Dignity Restored Internally: Officers, leaders, or coaches need dignity just as much as those they serve.

Companionship Reduces Collapse: Shepherd presence prevents burnout and despair inside the team.

Ethos is Cyclical: To shepherd others, we must sometimes be shepherded ourselves.

Case Reflection: The Rookie's Collapse

A rookie once faltered after a failed negotiation. He broke down privately, convinced he had failed the craft. Another officer barked: "Toughen up or get out."

That response nearly drove him away.

But a shepherd stepped in. He listened. He reminded the rookie that failure was not the end but part of the craft. He walked beside him until strength returned. Years later, that rookie became a team leader—because someone shepherded him when he was lost.

- *Parents:* Shepherding your children also means shepherding each other as parents—walking beside, not blaming, when mistakes happen.

- *Leaders:* Shepherding means protecting your team from burnout by restoring dignity and value after failure.

- *Coaches:* Shepherding means guiding athletes through mistakes, turning errors into lessons rather than punishments.

- *Spouses:* Shepherding means carrying storms together—not letting one partner collapse in silence.

The shepherd ethos is not just for those outside the circle. It must be lived inside the circle, or the circle collapses.

The craft of negotiation—and life itself—depends on people who can shepherd not only strangers in crisis but teammates, families, and loved ones when they falter. Without shepherds, people collapse in silence. With shepherds, people rise again.

Closing Maxim: "Shepherds walk with the lost and with the weary who carry them."

Maxim: Restoring Dignity in Practice

"The shepherd restores dignity not by taking control but by returning it."

Doctrine of Restoring Dignity

The heart of the shepherd ethos is dignity. When crisis strips a person of choice, the shepherd returns it. When shame crushes, the shepherd restores worth. When despair isolates, the shepherd re-establishes connection.

- Choice Is Dignity: Offering options—even small ones—restores agency.
- Time Is Dignity: Patience itself communicates value.
- Presence Is Dignity: Staying communicates: "You are not abandoned."
- Compassion with Boundaries: True dignity balances empathy with accountability.

The shepherd does not seize control to "save." They give just enough stability for dignity to awaken, and then they walk beside until surrender is chosen.

Case Reflection: The Man with No Options

A suicidal subject once said: "I have no choices left." Commanders urged an ultimatum. The negotiator, instead, offered options: "You don't have to decide right now. You can put the gun down and step outside. You can stay inside and talk longer. Either way, we'll stay with you."

Moments later, the man set the gun aside. It wasn't surrender to authority—it was surrender to dignity.

Doctrine in Leadership and Life

- *Parents:* Shepherd dignity means allowing children to make choices, even imperfect ones, so they grow in strength.
- *Leaders:* Shepherd dignity means involving employees in solutions, not dictating answers.
- *Coaches:* Shepherd dignity means letting athletes own their recovery from mistakes.
- *Spouses:* Shepherd dignity means presence in conflict, offering options instead of ultimatums.

Dignity restored is influence multiplied.

Drill: The Option Test

Next time you face conflict, give the other person two meaningful options instead of an ultimatum. Notice how their posture changes when they feel they still have dignity.

Drill: The Patience Test

In your next disagreement, count silently to ten before speaking. Notice how patience shifts tone, restores calm, and opens dignity for both sides.

Case Reflection: The Coach Who Restored Dignity

A high school coach once faced a team crushed by a last-second loss. Instead of berating them, he restored dignity: "You fought to the end. That's who we are. Loss doesn't take that from us."

The players lifted their heads. Dignity restored became strength for the next game.

Drill: Presence in Practice

Sit in silence with someone who is hurting—not fixing, not advising, simply staying. Presence alone restores dignity.

Doctrine of Boundaries

Restoring dignity is not indulgence. It is not letting people avoid responsibility. It is giving them enough space to face reality with dignity intact. Shepherds guide; they do not excuse.

When people feel stripped of dignity, they spiral deeper into despair. When dignity is restored, people rediscover the will to live, lead, and rise.

The shepherd ethos is not about dragging or rescuing. It is about restoring dignity so people can walk out of crisis themselves.

Maxim: "Dignity restored is strength renewed."

The Shepherd's Practice: Field Drills for Readers

"The shepherd's strength is measured in the quiet choices that restore others."

Why We Train This Way

The shepherd ethos is not theory. It must be practiced daily—in the command post, the home, and the workplace. Ordinary habits prepare us for extraordinary moments.

Silence does not become a shield by accident. Patience does not endure under fire without rehearsal. Compassion does not balance with discipline unless trained.

Field drills for shepherds are not about technique alone. They are about shaping posture, presence, and discipline so that when storms break, ethos is not an idea but a reflex.

Field Drills for Living the Shepherd Ethos

The Listening Drill: In your next conversation, say less than half of what you want to say. Use questions to draw the other person out. Train yourself to hear what is beneath the words, not just the words themselves.

The Silence Drill: Practice holding silence. In meetings, family discussions, and arguments—count to ten before filling the gap. Learn that silence is not absence. It is medicine.

The Option Drill: Offer choices. When giving feedback or facing conflict, present at least two viable options. Options restore dignity. Dignity restores cooperation.

The Companion Drill: Sit with someone in struggle—not fixing, not advising, simply staying. Train yourself to endure discomfort without filling it with solutions. Presence itself is guidance.

The Patience Drill: Delay your immediate reaction—by a breath, a minute, or an hour. Notice how patience shifts outcomes. Make patience muscle memory.

Case Reflection: The Shepherd's Influence

A young officer once rushed into silence, filling it with nervous chatter. The subject grew restless, then defiant.

Later, the mentor corrected him: "Silence is not something you endure. It's something you carry."

The rookie began practicing silence in daily life—in traffic, family conflicts, and team huddles. Weeks later, on another crisis call, silence became his shield. The subject surrendered.

Presence practiced in ordinary storms became discipline in extraordinary storms.

Doctrine in Life

- *Parents:* Practice silence after your child's mistake. Let dignity re-emerge before you speak.

- *Leaders:* Practice listening more than directing. Let employees discover solutions with dignity.

- *Coaches:* Practice patience with failure. Let growth happen in the space between effort and correction.

- *Spouses:* Practice presence in conflict. Sometimes the greatest gift is staying without fixing.

The shepherd ethos is not a heroic act once in a lifetime. It is daily discipline, ordinary repetition, and quiet strength that becomes reflex when lives hang in the balance.

Case Reflection: The Spouse Who Shepherded

A husband described sitting silently with his wife after she lost her father. "I wanted to fix it, to find words. But instead, I stayed. Hours passed. She looked at me and said, 'You don't know how much it means that you're just here.'"

That is shepherd ethos in its purest form. Not fixing. Not dragging. Just walking beside.

In traffic, let silence be your teacher instead of anger.

In meetings, listen longer than you speak.

In family conflict, give options rather than ultimatums.

In friendships, stay when others would leave.

Each small act of practice builds the reflex of shepherding.

When the storm breaks—whether in a crisis scene or in a personal loss—your reflex will not be to drag or control. It will be to stay, wait, and walk beside. That reflex can mean the difference between despair and survival.

Maxim: "We do not shepherd once. We shepherd daily—until presence becomes reflex."

The Shepherd's Closing Call

"The shepherd's gift is presence, not performance."

The Quietest Ethos

The warrior ethos is seen in courage. The guardian ethos is felt in weight carried. But the shepherd ethos is often invisible. It does not look heroic to those outside the circle. It looks like waiting, listening, and walking beside.

The world often overlooks the shepherd. But lives saved in silence know the truth: Survival does not always come from boldness. Sometimes it comes from presence.

Case Reflection: The Child Who Slept Through the Night

One shepherd negotiator recalled that during a barricade, while adults shouted and tactical units pressed, a young child inside fell asleep. Hours later, when the child emerged, unharmed and unaware of the chaos, the negotiator realized the quiet power of shepherding.

"It struck me," he said, "that the greatest victory that night was a child who never knew how close death had come. He just slept. And he could sleep because we stayed."

That is the essence of the shepherd: presence that preserves innocence.

Doctrine of the Closing Call

Presence Is Guidance: Words may fail, but presence endures.

Dignity Is Restoration: Choices restore humanity.

Patience Is Power: Waiting steadies storms.

Walking Beside Builds Legacy: Survivors remember not the speeches but the presence that carried them.

- *Parents:* Your children will not remember every word you said, but they will remember that you stayed.

- *Leaders:* Your teams will not remember every directive, but they will remember if you walked beside them in hard times.

- *Coaches:* Your athletes will not remember every play you called, but they will remember if you stood steady after defeat.

- *Spouses:* Your partner will not remember every argument, but they will remember if you were present when they felt alone.

Presence, not performance, is the legacy of the shepherd.

The Shepherd's Creed

We are shepherds.

We walk beside the lost until they can walk again.

We restore dignity when despair strips it away.

We do not rush. We do not drag.

We wait. We guide. We stay.

We measure success not by applause but by survival, dignity restored, and lives that breathe another day.

Closing Reflection

The shepherd ethos completes the triad: Warriors bring courage, guardians carry weight, and shepherds restore dignity. Together, they form a shield strong enough to protect life under the heaviest of storms.

Without shepherds, the shield cracks. Without shepherds, people are reduced to their worst moment. With shepherds, people are restored to their humanity.

The shepherd is not the loudest, fastest, or most celebrated. But they are the ones whose presence allows the others to succeed. Without shepherds, there are no survivors.

"The shepherd restores dignity not by dragging but by walking beside—and staying until the lost remember the way home."

CHAPTER 11

Leadership Beyond the Tactical World

Shepherd's Maxim: "Presence protects more than performance ever will."

The Shepherd's Ethos

The shepherd is not the warrior charging into battle, nor the guardian raising the shield, nor the protector making the final call. The shepherd is quieter, gentler, but no less essential.

Where warriors master themselves, guardians steady chaos, and protectors measure legacy, shepherds embody presence. They remind us that people in crisis do not only need tactics; they need dignity. They do not only need someone to save them; they need someone to stay with them.

Negotiators came to learn that the shepherd's ethos was often the difference between words that were heard and words that were rejected. To sit in silence, walk beside someone in despair, and refuse to abandon them when everything in you screams for resolution— that is shepherding.

Doctrine Principle: The Three Commitments of the Shepherd

Commitment to Presence

The shepherd does not measure value in words spoken but in presence offered. Even silence can heal when it communicates: "You are not alone."

Commitment to Dignity

The shepherd restores choice where despair has stolen it. He offers small decisions—water, time, phrasing—that remind the subject they still matter.

Commitment to Patience

The shepherd does not rush a wounded mind back to health. They wait. They steady. They carry the weight of waiting so others can recover at their own pace.

Case Reflection: The Night in the Garage

A man who had lost everything locked himself in a garage with a weapon. He spoke in bursts, then sank into long silences. Commanders grew restless. Tactical debated entry.

But the negotiators chose the shepherd's path. They carried the silence with him. They bore the weight of waiting.

After hours, the man asked, almost in disbelief: "Are you still there?"

"Yes," the negotiators answered. "We are here to help you."

Moments later, he laid the gun down and walked out. His surrender was not to threats, persuasion, or even tactics. His surrender was to presence.

That is the power of the shepherd.

Reader Application: Shepherding Beyond Crisis

The shepherd's ethos is not confined to negotiation. It is a daily discipline, one that transforms families, organizations, and teams.

Parents shepherd when they sit with a hurting child in silence instead of rushing to fix the problem. Presence says more than advice ever could.

Leaders shepherd when they give employees space to grieve, recover, or process—choosing dignity over deadlines.

Coaches shepherd when they protect athletes' humanity over performance, teaching that character matters more than stats.

Spouses shepherd when they stay in hard conversations, refusing to walk away, even when the air feels heavy with silence.

Performance may win applause, but presence wins trust.

Case Reflection: The Coach Who Stayed

An athlete missed a critical shot in the final seconds of a championship. The locker room fell silent. Teammates whispered blame. Reporters circled outside.

The coach sat beside the player, saying nothing. He did not lecture, criticize, or console with empty words. He simply stayed.

Later, that player said: "What I remember most is not the shot I missed, but that my coach never left my side."

That is shepherding.

The shepherd's call is simple but costly: Stay. Stay when silence feels unbearable. Stay when patience feels endless. Stay when others demand speed.

Presence protects more than performance ever will.

The Shepherd's Burden

"The heaviest weight is not carried on your back but in your heart."

The Quietest Weight

The shepherd does not carry rifles or command posts. He carries something heavier—the weight of another person's despair.

Negotiators discovered this burden in the long hours of silence, in the trembling voices that whispered, "I can't do this anymore." The shepherd's task is not to erase despair but to stand under it, refusing to let it crush the one who carries it.

This is not glamorous. It does not make headlines. The shepherd's burden is invisible to those who do not stand in it. But for the one in crisis, that presence can mean the difference between life and death.

Doctrine Principle: Four Costs of Shepherding

The Cost of Patience

Hours of silence feel like torture in a world that worships speed. The shepherd accepts this cost, knowing silence steadies biology better than words ever could.

The Cost of Criticism

Others accuse the shepherd of wasting time, being too soft, or refusing to act. The shepherd absorbs criticism, knowing presence is often mistaken for weakness.

The Cost of Empathy

Empathy is not free. To sit in another's despair is to feel it. Shepherds carry sorrow that does not belong to them, and it leaves marks.

The Cost of Loneliness

The shepherd is often alone in the room. Others move on, demand action, or grow restless. The shepherd stays. Loneliness is the price of presence.

Case Reflection: The Mother Who Broke

A mother barricaded herself in a home after losing custody of her children. For twelve hours, she screamed, cried, and raged. Negotiators said little. They offered dignity where the system had stripped it.

At dawn, she whispered: "I don't want to do this anymore."

She surrendered peacefully. No one applauded. Most forgot the incident within days. But for that mother, someone had finally stayed long enough for despair to break.

That was shepherding.

The shepherd's burden belongs not just to negotiators but to every leader, parent, coach, and spouse willing to stand with another person in pain.

Parents carry the burden when they sit beside a child struggling with failure, listening more than fixing.

Leaders carry it when they protect employees' dignity after mistakes, even when pressure demands punishment.

Coaches carry it when they allow players to grieve losses before demanding resilience.

Spouses carry it when they stay present through conflict, bearing silence without retreat.

The burden of shepherding is emotional, not physical. But its weight is no less real.

Case Reflection: The Silent Pastor

A pastor once sat with a grieving family who had lost a child. He did not speak for hours. He simply stayed.

Years later, the family said: "We don't remember his words. We remember that he never left."

That is shepherding—bearing another's burden not by solving it but by staying under it with them.

Doctrine Principle: Burden Divided, Burden Halved

Shepherds embody the maxim: "Any problem divided by two is half." By simply staying, they cut despair in half. The person in crisis may still carry sorrow, but they no longer carry it alone.

The shepherd's burden is not to fix but to carry with.

The shepherd's burden is the heaviest weight: patience that feels endless, criticism that cuts deep, empathy that scars, and loneliness that isolates.

But protectors know this truth—presence lightens despair. And divided burdens, no matter how heavy, always become survivable.

The Shepherd's Gift

"We do not drag the broken; we walk beside them until they can walk again."

The Gift Hidden in Burden

For every ounce of burden the shepherd carries, there is an equal measure of gift given. The gift is not applause or recognition—those rarely come. The true gift of shepherding is restoration: of dignity, connection, and hope.

Negotiators learned this in the quiet aftermaths. Long after headlines faded and radios were silent, lives that had been spared carried forward. Families were reunited. Futures were preserved. People who were ready to die discovered they could live again.

The shepherd's gift is not visible in the moment. It is written in the ripple effects that outlast the crisis.

Doctrine Principle: Three Gifts of Shepherding

Restoring Dignity

The shepherd returns choice to those who feel stripped of it. Even small decisions—whether to speak now or later, whether to drink water, whether to open a door—become reminders: "You still matter. You still choose."

Rebuilding Connection

Crisis isolates. People in despair feel cut off from family, community, even humanity. The shepherd bridges that gap by saying with presence: "You are not alone."

Reawakening Hope

The shepherd plants seeds of tomorrow. By holding steady today, they remind the lost that despair is not forever, and that even in ashes, a future can rise.

Case Reflection: The Veteran's Tomorrow

A veteran barricaded himself after years of untreated trauma. He was convinced he had no future, no reason to live. Negotiators stayed with him, hour after hour, validating his pain, refusing to abandon him.

At dawn, he surrendered. Weeks later, he wrote a simple note: "Thank you for reminding me tomorrow still exists."

That was the shepherd's gift: not just preventing death but reopening the possibility of life.

The shepherd's gift is not confined to crisis. Anyone can give it.

Parents shepherd by restoring dignity to children after failure, reminding them that mistakes do not define worth.

Leaders shepherd by staying connected with employees during downturns, proving people matter more than numbers.

Coaches shepherd by affirming athletes after losses, showing them that character outweighs scoreboards.

Spouses shepherd by protecting trust through presence, giving hope when relationships feel strained.

The shepherd's gift is this: Wherever despair whispers, "You are alone," the shepherd's presence answers, "Not while I am here."

Case Reflection: The Teacher's Presence

A high school teacher noticed a quiet student withdrawing, skipping assignments, losing spark. Instead of lecturing, she began spending her lunch breaks sitting with him. Some days they spoke, other days they didn't.

Months later, the student said: "Those lunches reminded me someone cared. I started to believe I could make it."

That is shepherding. The gift was not in solving every problem but in staying.

Doctrine Principle: The Ripple Effect of Shepherding

The shepherd's gift rarely stops with the one person in crisis.

A child preserved grows up to raise their own family.

An employee protected carries trust into their next role.

An athlete shepherded becomes a mentor who passes on resilience.

A marriage preserved becomes the foundation for generations yet unborn.

The ripple effect means the shepherd's gift extends far beyond the moment, becoming legacy itself.

The shepherd's gift is restoration—of dignity, connection, and hope. It is a gift invisible to crowds but undeniable to those who receive it.

Protectors know this truth: The shepherd's greatest power is not to drag the broken but to walk beside them until they rise again.

"Presence is leadership's first responsibility."

The Transfer of Ethos

The shepherd's ethos did not remain confined to radios and standoffs. Over time, negotiators realized the same presence that steadied barricades could steady boardrooms, classrooms, and homes.

The code of the shepherd—presence, dignity, patience—was transferable. It was not dependent on a badge or a command post. It was dependent only on courage: the courage to stay when others flee, listen when others shout, and carry when others criticize.

Parenting with a Shepherd's Heart

Parents face their own standoffs: tantrums in the kitchen, rebellion in the teenage years, silence at the dinner table. The instinct is often to fix quickly, impose control, and fill silence with lectures.

But the shepherd-parent remembers that presence steadies more than correction.

Sitting beside a child in failure communicates, "You matter more than your mistake."

Listening without rushing to solve teaches, "Your voice is worth hearing."

Waiting instead of demanding shows, "We believe you can rise on your own."

Shepherding in parenting is not about preventing pain; it is about ensuring children never carry it alone.

Leading with a Shepherd's Compass

Leaders in business and organizations face crises every day: financial downturns, ethical failures, cultural fractures. Under pressure, leaders are tempted to accelerate decisions, chase optics, and demand performance at all costs.

But shepherd-leaders recognize that the first responsibility of leadership is presence. Employees who know they are not abandoned will follow leaders through storms. Trust is preserved not by speeches but by presence under pressure.

In downturns, shepherd-leaders sit with teams, explaining honestly, staying visible.

In conflict, they listen longer than they speak.

In uncertainty, they slow decisions enough to preserve dignity, not just numbers.

Shepherd-leadership may not always maximize speed, but it maximizes loyalty and resilience—which outlast every quarterly metric.

Coaching with a Shepherd's Ethos

On the field, crisis is measured in seconds, mistakes, and the weight of entire seasons. Coaches are often judged by wins, losses, and statistics. But athletes remember something different: whether their coach stayed with them in failure.

Shepherd-coaches do not confuse volume with strength. They steady players not by shouting, but by reminding them that performance is not identity.

After a missed shot, shepherd-coaches sit with silence instead of criticism.

After a loss, they allow grieving before demanding resilience.

After injury, they protect futures instead of sacrificing them for short-term victory.

Athletes who are shepherded carry that ethos into life— competing not only for trophies but for character.

Marriage and the Shepherd's Vow

In marriage, shepherding may be the most difficult and most necessary. Conflict, disappointment, and failure invite distance. The easy path is retreat, silence, or abandonment.

But shepherd-spouses choose presence. They stay in hard conversations, even when resolution feels far away. They protect trust not by winning arguments but by refusing to walk away.

Saying, "I'm not leaving, even in silence," communicates more than lectures ever could.

Choosing patience over pressure gives time for dignity to return.

Carrying burdens together divides their weight until they become survivable.

Marriage requires shepherding because life itself will present storms. The vow, at its heart, is this: "I will not abandon you."

Doctrine Principle: Presence as Daily Discipline

Shepherding is not about grand gestures. It is about daily choices:

To listen instead of lecture.

To stay instead of retreat.

To protect dignity instead of preserving ego.

Everyday shepherding transforms ordinary relationships into lifelines.

Shepherding beyond the command post means carrying presence into homes, workplaces, teams, and marriages.

The shepherd's maxim remains true: Presence is leadership's first responsibility. Everything else follows.

The Shepherd's Burden and Gift in Leadership

"The same presence that breaks you is the presence that builds others."

The Paradox of Shepherd Leadership

Every leader who chooses the shepherd's path accepts a paradox: Presence costs them dearly, but it restores others profoundly. The weight is heavy, yet the gift is priceless. The shepherd's role in leadership is both burden and gift, inseparably linked.

Negotiators discovered this paradox in the silence of standoffs. To stay with despair for hours drained them emotionally, yet it was precisely that endurance that gave the subject enough courage to surrender. The weight carried by the shepherd was transformed into hope carried by the subject.

Leadership in every arena mirrors this paradox.

The Burden Leaders Carry

Shepherd-leadership does not come free. It demands costs that few see.

The Cost of Patience: Slowing decisions when speed is demanded feels unbearable. Yet patience steadies.

The Cost of Criticism: Critics will label shepherd-leaders indecisive, soft, or weak. Yet dignity is restored only by those who resist optics.

The Cost of Empathy: Leaders who listen deeply absorb pain that is not theirs. It leaves marks but also builds trust.

The Cost of Loneliness: Staying when others retreat isolates leaders. Yet presence in loneliness becomes proof of commitment.

Burden is inevitable when leaders shepherd.

The Gift Leaders Give

The other side of burden is gift. Those who receive shepherd-leadership rarely forget it.

The Gift of Dignity: When leaders give space instead of shame, they restore worth to those who feel diminished.

The Gift of Connection: When leaders stay, they prove relationships matter more than optics.

The Gift of Hope: When leaders hold the line long enough, people discover that tomorrow still exists.

Shepherd-leadership does not eliminate pain, but it ensures pain is never carried alone. That is the gift.

Case Reflection: The CEO Who Chose Presence

During a financial crisis, a CEO faced pressure to slash jobs immediately. Advisors urged swift action. Investors demanded reassurance. The optics screamed for speed.

Instead, the CEO chose shepherding. He met with teams, listened to fears, explained the realities with transparency, and delayed cuts while exploring every alternative.

The burden was heavy: criticism from investors, sleepless nights, personal stress. Yet the gift was undeniable: trust soared, employees rallied, and when reductions finally came, they were fewer and carried with dignity.

Years later, employees still spoke of the CEO's presence, not his profits.

Leaders at every level must decide whether to accept both sides of the shepherd's paradox.

Parents carry the burden of waiting with their children through failure, but the gift is children who rise stronger.

Leaders carry criticism for delaying decisions, but the gift is organizations that trust their motives.

Coaches carry empathy for disappointed athletes, but the gift is players who remember their worth was never tied to a scoreboard.

Spouses carry the loneliness of sitting in silence during conflict, but the gift is marriages that endure storms.

The question is not whether shepherding has a cost. It is whether we are willing to pay it, knowing the gift is far greater.

Doctrine Principle: Burden Transformed into Gift

The burden and gift of shepherding are inseparable. Presence drains the leader, but it restores the one being led. Burden becomes gift through sacrifice.

This is the essence of shepherd-leadership: to accept the weight others cannot carry, so they may rise again.

The shepherd's burden is loneliness, criticism, and weight. The shepherd's gift is dignity, connection, and hope.

Leadership that shepherds transforms burden into gift. And in that transformation, futures are preserved.

The Shepherd's Legacy

"What endures is not what we say but who we refuse to leave behind."

The Quiet Power of Legacy

When negotiators looked back over years of calls, few remembered the words they used. What they remembered was the people who walked out alive because someone refused to abandon them.

That is the shepherd's legacy. It is not carved in medals, promotions, or headlines. It is carved in lives preserved, futures restored, and trust built quietly, one presence at a time.

The shepherd knows legacy is not about victory in the moment but about the ripple effects left behind.

Doctrine Principle: The Four Marks of a Shepherd's Legacy

Lives Preserved: Legacy is written in the breaths still drawn because someone stayed.

Futures Restored: The child reunited with a parent, the family held together, the career protected—these become monuments of shepherding.

Trust Built: Communities remember leaders who stayed present, not those who abandoned them.

Hope Renewed: The simple reminder that tomorrow still exists becomes a legacy that outlasts despair.

Case Reflection: The Forgotten Victory

In one incident, negotiators stayed with a suicidal man for ten hours. The press mocked them for delay. Commanders grew restless. The tactical team prepared for entry.

But the negotiators stayed.

The man eventually surrendered. Years later, his daughter wrote a letter: "Because you stayed, I still have my father. And my children will know their grandfather."

No one remembered the press release. Everyone remembered the presence. That was legacy.

Shepherding legacies are not built in crises alone. They are built in the daily choices of parents, leaders, coaches, and spouses.

Parents leave legacies not in perfect control but in the trust children carry into adulthood because they were never abandoned.

Leaders leave legacies not in quarterly numbers but in teams that endure because they knew they were valued more than results.

Coaches leave legacies not in trophies but in players who learned resilience, dignity, and presence.

Spouses leave legacies not in arguments won but in marriages that endured storms because presence was stronger than pride.

The shepherd's legacy is this: People remember less what we said, and more that we stayed.

Case Reflection: The Teacher's Enduring Impact

A teacher who shepherded struggling students rarely received recognition. Years later, dozens of students returned to thank her. Not one mentioned a lesson plan. Everyone mentioned her presence.

She had stayed. That was enough.

Doctrine Principle: Legacy as Compass

Shepherds measure decisions by their impact on tomorrow, not applause today. This is legacy as compass:

Does this preserve life?

Does this restore dignity?

Does this build trust?

Does this give hope?

When leaders answer yes, they are leaving a legacy that outlasts them.

The shepherd's legacy is not performance, but presence. Not optics, but outcomes. Not applause, but lives preserved.

Protectors know this truth: The most enduring legacies are built not by those who lead loudly but by those who quietly refuse to leave anyone behind.

Closing Charge

"Legacy is written by those who stay."

The Call to Live as Shepherds

The shepherd's way is not easy. It demands patience in a world of speed, presence in a world of distraction, and endurance in a world addicted to immediacy. Yet it is precisely this path that forges legacies worth leaving.

Negotiators carried this ethos into crisis situations, but the same call extends to every parent, leader, coach, and spouse. The shepherd's code is not reserved for radios and command posts. It is a code for life.

Doctrine Principle: The Shepherd's Daily Charge

Stay Present: Presence is the first gift and the last defense. Refuse to abandon.

Protect Dignity: Even when people fail, remind them that they still matter.

Endure Silence: Do not rush to fill the void; let patience heal.

Divide the Burden: Carry weight with others until it becomes survivable.

Plant Hope: Always leave people with the reminder that tomorrow still exists.

Case Reflection: The Quiet Victory

One negotiator reflected on a case where no one outside the command post ever knew what happened. A man on the brink of suicide laid down his weapon after eight hours of silence. No cameras were present. No news story followed.

But his life went on. He saw another sunrise. He reconnected with family. He lived.

That quiet victory is the essence of the shepherd's charge: to stay when no one applauds, carry when no one notices, and preserve what no one else sees.

The closing charge of this chapter is not to admire shepherding, but to embody it.

- *Parents:* Stay in the room when your child withdraws. Do not abandon them to silence. Your presence may be their lifeline.

- *Leaders:* Stay with your people when pressure mounts. Do not let fear of optics drive you from them. Trust is built when you stay.

- *Coaches:* Stay with your players when they fail. Do not let defeat drive you away. They will remember your presence long after they forget the score.

- *Spouses:* Stay in the hard moments. Do not retreat in conflict. The vow of marriage is shepherding at its core: "I will not leave you."

The code does not call for perfection. It calls for presence.

Case Reflection: The Father Who Stayed

A father once faced his teenage son's rebellion. Arguments failed. Boundaries crumbled. For weeks the son withdrew, testing the limits of rejection.

The father refused to leave. He sat on the porch night after night, waiting silently. Finally, the son asked, "Why are you still here?"

The father answered: "Because I love you more than I fear you."

That is shepherding. That is the charge.

Doctrine Principle: From Burden to Legacy

The shepherd's burden becomes the shepherd's gift. The shepherd's gift becomes the shepherd's legacy. And the shepherd's legacy becomes the charge for all of us.

This is the cycle:

Burden carried → Gift given

Gift given → Legacy left

Legacy left → Charge received

Every generation of shepherds lives this pattern so the next can continue it.

The shepherd's charge is not to fix every problem, win every argument, or carry every burden alone. The charge is simpler and harder: to stay.

Stay when silence is long. Stay when pressure is heavy. Stay when others retreat.

Legacy is written by those who stay.

Final Maxim: "What we carry together, we survive together. What we refuse to carry, we lose."

The Essence of the Shepherd's Code

Every chapter has carried us deeper into the ethos of the shepherd: presence, patience, dignity, endurance. But it is here, at the close, that all of it must be distilled into one truth.

The shepherd does not measure success by applause, optics, or speed. The shepherd measures success in lives preserved, dignity restored, and hope reawakened. This is the code. It is not theory. It is not abstract. It is a way of being.

The final maxim captures the heart of this ethos: Burdens divided become survivable. Burdens abandoned become fatal. The shepherd's charge is to ensure that no one carries despair alone.

Doctrine Principle: The Final Lens

When decisions grow cloudy, pressure mounts, and fear tempts retreat, the shepherd asks one question: "Am I carrying this with them or leaving them alone in it?"

That lens clarifies every action.

If you carry with, you preserve life.

If you abandon, you risk loss.

The shepherd's code is simple, but it is not easy. It demands courage not of the trigger but of the heart.

Case Reflection: The Forgotten Partner

In one incident, negotiators worked with a man on the brink of suicide. Hours passed. At times, silence dominated. At times, rage exploded. Through it all, the team refused to abandon him.

At dawn, he surrendered. Later, he admitted: "I thought everyone had left me. But you didn't."

That statement—"But you didn't"—is the final maxim embodied. Legacy is not in perfect words or flawless tactics. Legacy is in presence.

The final maxim is not for negotiators alone. It belongs to all of us.

- *Parents:* When your child feels crushed by failure, carry it with them. Do not abandon them to shame.

- *Leaders:* When your team fears collapse, carry the burden with them. Do not abandon them to optics.

- *Coaches:* When your players falter, carry their weight. Do not abandon them to defeat.

- *Spouses:* When conflict grows silent, stay. Carry the silence together. Do not abandon one another to loneliness.

The maxim is transferable because the human need for presence is universal. No one survives despair alone.

Doctrine Principle: Together We Endure

The shepherd's code leaves no one behind. Its wisdom is not complicated, but it is costly. It demands that we remain when retreat would be easier. It demands that we listen when silence would be safer. It demands that we divide burdens when self-preservation whispers to walk away.

But together we endure. Together we survive. Together we carry burdens until they become bearable.

Carrying the Code Forward

This is the final maxim and the final charge: We must carry the code forward.

Carry it in homes, where children learn that love stays.

Carry it in teams, where players discover that trust holds.

Carry it in workplaces, where employees know dignity matters more than optics.

Carry it in marriages, where presence outweighs pride.

Carry it in communities, where the vulnerable know they are never abandoned.

The shepherd's code is not meant to remain on these pages. It is meant to be lived.

Final Words

The shepherd's legacy is not finished in this chapter. It continues in you. In us.

The code is not mine to keep—it is ours to carry.

CHAPTER 12

Case Reflection:
The Choctaw Barricade

Flexibility, presence, and the art of controlled surrender

Opening Maxim: "Leaders who protect dignity open the doors that confrontation keeps closed."

Case Reflection: The Choctaw Barricade

The call came in just after noon on May 31, 2022. Dispatch relayed what every negotiator dreads hearing: a potential hostage situation involving children. Reports indicated that a woman had barricaded herself inside a home in Choctaw, Oklahoma, possibly armed, with two juveniles under her control. Text messages had suggested threats, and family members outside feared for the safety of the kids.

Our team was mobilized immediately. Staging was set at the Vo-Tech's Emergency Operations Center, a location that allowed tactical teams, medical, and negotiators to coordinate before pushing closer. The atmosphere was tense but focused. Two children—ages eleven and fourteen—were believed to be inside. If the reports were accurate, every minute carried risk.

When we arrived, command briefed with a standard "LCAN" size-up report: Location, Condition, Actions, Needs. The location was secure, with outer containment set. The condition, however, was murky. The subject—a woman we will call Jennifer—was inside the residence, emotionally charged, distrusting of her family and law enforcement, and reportedly resistant to releasing the children. She was said to have access to firearms, though none had yet been confirmed on scene. Her actions included refusing initial commands and venting anger through text. What command needed was clear: negotiation to resolve the barricade without harm to the children or subject.

We pushed forward with the BearCat, establishing a line of communication from behind the armored vehicle. This position was "danger close"—within sight of the residence—but it gave us the ability to speak with her directly while maintaining tactical cover.

At this stage, our objectives were threefold: Establish communication, confirm the safety and location of the children, and begin de-escalating the subject's emotional state. But the information flow was already clouded. Conflicting accounts came from family: One said both kids were inside, another insisted one had left earlier for the movies. Jennifer herself offered little clarity, alternating between denial, defiance, and vague statements that only deepened the uncertainty.

It was the kind of situation that tests doctrine. As with most special operation units, an outline of how to deploy assets such as who will be the Lead Negotiator, Tactical Liaison, Intel Officer? Radio call signs will be assigned to team members. How and where will the negotiation operations center be established? Everything that goes into establishing an operational footprint for the team to work the incident effectively. The Optimum Deployment Model (ODM) was difficult to apply cleanly—containment was in place, but communication lines were strained, and the intelligence picture was incomplete. We would have to adapt in real time.

Confusion and Resistance

Jennifer's voice carried a mix of anger and defensiveness when we first made contact. She was quick to vent her frustrations—not just at law enforcement but at her family. She railed against her estranged husband, accusing him of being a drug user and unfit father. She spoke bitterly of her father-in-law, saying he meddled in her life and didn't deserve to be near her children. Her words were sharp, layered with years of resentment, and she made it clear that she had no intention of simply complying.

The children became the center of our concern. Reports had them both inside, but Jennifer contradicted that. At one moment, she insisted her daughter wasn't even home, claiming she had gone to the movies with friends. Minutes later, she referred to her daughter being upset in another room. The contradictions were more than frustrating—they were dangerous. We needed proof of life and clarity on who was actually inside the residence. Without it, tactical planning risked being based on guesswork.

When pressed, Jennifer doubled down on her hostility. She accused us of lying, siding with her husband, and trying to "take her kids away." She circled her grievances again and again, often raising her voice as though volume would make her case stronger. Her tone fluctuated between defiant rage and wounded self-pity, a pendulum swing common in barricade negotiations.

The temptation in these moments is to hammer on the facts—insist on direct answers about the children and confront every contradiction. But facts alone rarely move people who are entrenched in emotion. So we shifted strategy. Instead of arguing over details, we began reframing the conversation toward her role as a mother.

We told her we understood she saw herself as protective. We acknowledged her claim of being a "good mom" and gave space for her to describe what that meant. Each time she circled back to grievances about her husband or in-laws, we gently redirected to her children: "You've worked hard to take care of them. What's the next best step you can take to show them you're still that steady mom?"

Slowly, the temperature began to cool. The contradictions didn't vanish, but the tone softened just enough to give us an opening. She wasn't ready to surrender, but she was beginning to see the possibility of doing so without losing her identity.

Danger Close

Negotiating from the BearCat meant we were close—too close by doctrinal standards. The Optimum Deployment Model emphasizes distance, containment, and layered communication whenever possible. Yet here we were, parked within clear view of the residence, our voices carrying across the lawn to a woman whose emotions swung unpredictably by the minute.

This deviation from doctrine created tension within the team. Some questioned whether pushing forward so near the house invited unnecessary risk. Others argued that establishing direct communication outweighed the dangers. Both perspectives had merit. From the inside of the BearCat, the stakes felt real—one rash move, one impulsive decision by Jennifer, and the situation could spiral.

Compounding the risk was the lack of clarity on the children. If both juveniles were truly inside, a forced breach could mean tragedy. If one was gone and the other remained, we risked over-committing resources unnecessarily. If neither were inside, then the barricade itself was built more on fear than fact. This fog of uncertainty magnified every decision, making caution both necessary and frustrating.

Coordination with tactical command was critical. We kept them updated on Jennifer's emotional tone, her contradictory statements, and any small cues we could glean about the kids' presence. They, in turn, adjusted their posture, balancing readiness with restraint. Everyone knew that a breach was a last resort. But everyone also knew that if proof of life went in the wrong direction, we had to be ready to act.

Through it all, our role was to maintain calm consistency. Jennifer could see the BearCat, and she knew we were close. If we projected aggression, she would interpret it as betrayal. If we projected indifference, she would escalate to force our attention. Instead, we chose steady, measured presence. Each word was deliberate, designed not to inflame but to coax.

Looking back, the decision to go "danger close" was not perfect. It was a calculated risk, a reminder that doctrine provides a framework but not a straitjacket. Sometimes the ground truth demands flexibility. That day, flexibility kept the dialogue alive, even as uncertainty pressed in from every side.

The Breakthrough

Hours into the standoff, Jennifer's energy began to shift. The anger that had fueled her earlier rants gave way to fatigue. Her voice cracked more often, and instead of shouting, she lingered in long pauses. Fatigue is not always a weakness to exploit, but it can open the door for redirection. We chose that moment to press gently on a different angle: dignity.

We told her she could show her children what strength really looked like by walking out on her own terms. We reminded her that good mothers don't let chaos define the moment—they take control of it. Instead of framing surrender as a loss, we reframed it as proof of her ability to protect her kids by keeping the situation calm.

Jennifer resisted at first. She said she didn't want her daughter to "see her like that," afraid that coming out in front of her would be humiliating. That hesitation gave us a pivot. We worked with tactical to arrange a face-saving solution: She could come out the front near the garage, out of sight of her daughter. She would not be paraded, but treated with restraint and respect.

This offer mattered. It wasn't about giving her control of the outcome—custody was inevitable. But it gave her the perception of choice, a small island of dignity in a storm of shame. That perception was enough to tip the scales.

On the phone, her breathing slowed. "If I walk out," she asked, "you promise my daughter won't see me?" We confirmed the plan, coordinated the timing with tactical, and assured her that her request would be honored.

Moments later, the front door creaked open. Jennifer stepped onto the porch, phone still pressed to her ear. She moved cautiously, scanning the yard as though waiting for betrayal. But instead of chaos, she found order. Officers moved swiftly, taking her into custody without incident.

Inside, her daughter was secured and brought out safely. The relief on her face said everything—fear giving way to calm, uncertainty replaced with safety. No one was injured, and the barricade ended with dignity intact.

For negotiators, the breakthrough was not a single phrase or tactic. It was the culmination of hours of listening, reframing, and patience. It was the proof that even in volatility, controlled surrender is possible when leaders balance firmness with respect.

Doctrine: Lessons from Choctaw

Every barricade teaches lessons, but not every lesson comes neatly packaged. The Choctaw case reminded us that doctrine is a guide, not a script, and that real-world crises demand both discipline and flexibility.

Flexibility within Doctrine

The Optimum Deployment Model (ODM) provides the gold standard for staging, containment, and communication. Yet this case did not fit neatly within that model. Negotiating "danger close" from the BearCat was a calculated deviation, born out of necessity. It carried risk—visible proximity, heightened emotions—but also provided access we would not have had otherwise. The doctrine lesson is simple: Know the standard, but recognize when the ground truth requires adaptation. Flexibility is not failure; it is wisdom applied in real time.

Proof of Life in the Fog

Confusion about the children's presence underscored the critical importance of proof of life. Without it, tactical decisions risk being built on guesswork. Jennifer's contradictory statements—one moment insisting her daughter was at the movies, the next hinting she was upset in another room—forced us to operate in uncertainty. Doctrine reinforces the necessity of relentless pursuit of clarity, even when direct answers are elusive.

Face-Saving as a Strategy

Surrender is never easy for a subject, especially when family is watching. Jennifer's refusal to come out in front of her daughter reflected more than stubbornness; it revealed a human need to preserve dignity. By arranging her surrender near the garage, out of sight, we provided a path that allowed her to comply without humiliation. The doctrine here is powerful: When leaders give people a way to save face, resistance often transforms into cooperation.

Reframing Surrender as Strength

The language we chose mattered. Instead of portraying surrender as giving up, we reframed it as proof of Jennifer's role as a mother—calm, protective, choosing peace over chaos. That reframing gave her a reason to see compliance not as weakness but as a demonstration of strength. Doctrine reminds us that words are tools of influence; they can cast the same action as shameful or dignified, depending on how they are framed.

The Choctaw barricade reaffirmed that doctrine is alive, not static. It must be carried in principle but applied with creativity. Flexibility, proof of life, face-saving, and reframing are not tricks—they are the disciplines that allow negotiation to succeed when rigid confrontation would fail.

Operating in Uncertainty

Few things test a negotiator more than foggy intelligence. In Choctaw, every decision was clouded by Jennifer's contradictory statements about her children. One minute, we believed two juveniles were inside. The next, perhaps only one. At one point, maybe none at all. That uncertainty demanded restraint. It reminded us that rushing to action without clarity risks compounding the crisis. Doctrine teaches us to move deliberately, even when the pressure to act feels overwhelming. Uncertainty is not permission to gamble; it is a signal to slow down.

Negotiator–Tactical Alignment

The Choctaw case also underscored the importance of seamless communication between negotiators and tactical command. Our updates about Jennifer's tone, contradictions, and shifting demands allowed the tactical team to posture appropriately—neither overcommitting to an unnecessary breach nor relaxing into false security. The alignment was not perfect; tensions rose when doctrine was bent. Yet the lesson was clear: Negotiation without tactical trust is fragile. Tactical without negotiation is dangerous. Alignment is not optional—it is the backbone of safe resolution.

The Weight of Family Dynamics

Unlike suspects barricaded against police, Jennifer was barricaded against her family. Her anger at her estranged husband and distrust of her father-in-law drove much of her behavior. This dynamic made her volatile in ways not easily addressed with traditional tactics. Family-driven barricades carry a unique burden: The conflict is deeply personal, and the negotiator is often drawn into years of unresolved resentment. The doctrine here is sobering—negotiators must navigate not only the crisis at hand but the decades of pain that fuel it.

Patience as a Shield

At several points, Jennifer's hostility spiked. She accused us of plotting against her, siding with her enemies, and trying to steal her children. It would have been easy to argue back, to defend ourselves against false claims. Instead, patience absorbed the blows. Each surge of anger eventually ebbed, leaving space to redirect. Patience is not passive; it is an active shield that protects the process until a better opportunity arrives.

The Choctaw barricade revealed that uncertainty, family conflict, and deviation from doctrine are not anomalies—they are realities. Negotiators who thrive are not those who cling rigidly to plans but those who adapt principles with patience, alignment, and discipline under pressure.

Doctrine Expansion: Family Dynamics as Barricades

One of the clearest lessons from Choctaw was how deeply family dynamics shape crisis. Jennifer was not barricaded against police alone; she was barricaded against years of resentment, mistrust, and fractured relationships with her husband and father-in-law. Her anger toward them bled into every word she spoke to us. In many ways, law enforcement became a proxy target—the face she could rage at when she could not face her family.

This matters for doctrine because negotiators must see beyond the surface of resistance. What looks like defiance against authority is often pain directed at those who are not even in the room. When Jennifer accused us of plotting with her husband or siding with her in-laws, she was not evaluating facts. She was replaying the betrayals and disappointments that defined her private life. To argue against those claims would have been futile. What she needed was redirection—a shift from grievance to identity.

For leaders outside of negotiation, the same truth applies. Employees who resist change are often not fighting policy; they are reacting to a sense of betrayal by former managers. Children who lash out at parents are often carrying anger from another relationship. Communities that resist leadership often do so because of wounds inflicted long before the current leader arrived.

Doctrine must account for this reality: People rarely resist because of the surface issue alone. They resist because of the unresolved history beneath it. Leaders who recognize this can reframe the moment—not by trying to fix the past but by anchoring people to values that still matter in the present.

Reader Application: Face-Saving Leadership

The Choctaw barricade may have involved armored vehicles, tactical teams, and police radios, but the principles that carried it to resolution are not confined to law enforcement. They are principles of leadership, human behavior, and influence that matter wherever trust and conflict collide.

Flexibility Without Weakness

Leaders in business, education, or community life often face situations where the "manual" doesn't match reality. Policies are important, just as the Optimum Deployment Model is in negotiation, but rigid adherence in the face of new facts can do more harm than good. The lesson is not to abandon doctrine but to bend wisely, adapting without breaking. Flexibility, when grounded in principle, is not weakness—it is strength applied with discernment.

Saving Face as a Universal Need

Jennifer's fear of being humiliated in front of her daughter mirrors a truth that crosses every field: People resist most fiercely when they feel their dignity is at stake. In the workplace, an employee who made a mistake may dig deeper into denial if correcting it means public embarrassment. Families experience the same dynamic when arguments turn into contests of pride. Leaders who provide face-saving exits create conditions for resolution. A quiet conversation, a private correction, or an alternate path can unlock cooperation where confrontation would only harden resistance.

Reframing Weakness as Strength

To Jennifer, surrender felt like defeat—until it was reframed as proof of her strength as a mother. Leaders must master the art of reframing. A failed project can be cast as wasted effort or as the foundation of lessons that lead to success. An apology can be painted as humiliation or as courage to repair what was broken. Reframing shifts the meaning of an action, and meaning is what drives behavior.

Patience Over Reaction

When anger or false accusations surface, leaders face the temptation to react. But patience—the deliberate choice to absorb heat without striking back—preserves space for resolution. Silence, measured pauses, and steady composure often communicate more than words. Leaders who master patience create climates where others can calm down enough to move forward.

The Choctaw barricade was resolved without injury not because we had the perfect script, but because we applied timeless principles. Leaders across every arena can do the same—bending without breaking, protecting dignity, reframing outcomes, and holding steady with patience when pressure mounts.

The Choctaw confession is a stark reminder that truth does not surface by accident—it must be cultivated. That principle extends far beyond criminal interviews. Whether leading a company, raising a family, or guiding a team, the same dynamics unfold in quieter ways.

Business Leadership

In corporate settings, leaders often face employees or teams barricaded behind excuses. Missed deadlines become "supply chain issues," poor communication becomes "the client's fault." Pushing harder with data sometimes makes the denial stronger. The Choctaw barricade teaches that progress comes when leaders pivot from facts to values: "You've always been someone who delivers. What do we need to get back to that?" The reframing preserves dignity while still demanding accountability.

Family Leadership

Parents know well the tension between confrontation and connection. A teenager caught lying may respond with defiance if the focus is purely on the lie. But when parents say, "You're better than this—I know the kind of person you want to be," they appeal to identity, not just behavior. In Choctaw, Jennifer yielded when surrender was framed not as failure but as strength in protecting her daughter. Families thrive when leaders see beyond resistance to the deeper needs of dignity and belonging.

Coaching and Mentorship

On the field or in the gym, athletes sometimes resist correction out of pride. A coach who humiliates a player in front of teammates risks making the barricade stronger. But one who says, "You're the leader here—the younger players are watching you," reframes accountability as an opportunity to show strength. That mirrors Choctaw: Surrender became possible only when reframed as leadership rather than weakness.

Community and Civic Leadership

When communities face crises—whether natural disasters, scandals, or political divisions—leaders must manage resistance without stripping dignity. Public shaming hardens divisions. Private conversations, controlled messaging, and respect for face-saving allow resolution without unnecessary escalation. Just as Jennifer needed to walk out on her own terms, communities often need to feel that solutions preserve their identity, not destroy it.

The Aftermath Matters

The barricade ended with safe custody, but the story did not stop there. Trauma lingered—for the child, the family, and for Jennifer herself. Leaders in every setting must plan not only for resolution but for recovery. Winning the moment without preparing for what follows leaves scars unhealed and problems unresolved.

The Choctaw case showed that leadership is not about forcing compliance but about creating conditions for voluntary cooperation. In every domain—business, family, coaching, or community—the principles hold: Preserve dignity, reframe outcomes, and remember that resolution is only the first step.

Closing Compass

The Choctaw barricade was not the most violent call we have faced, nor the longest. But it was one of the clearest reminders that leadership in crisis is rarely about force—it is about influence. No shots were fired. No tactical breach was ordered. The resolution came through listening, reframing, and preserving dignity long enough for compliance to feel possible.

The doctrine was not followed perfectly. Negotiating "danger close" from the BearCat was not the textbook application of the Optimum Deployment Model. The fog of uncertainty about the children's presence complicated decision-making. Yet the outcome was safe, because principles were honored even when the framework bent. Flexibility within discipline is not a compromise of doctrine; it is its living application.

For leaders outside law enforcement, the Choctaw barricade underscores that not every problem is solved by pushing harder. Some situations demand space for the other side to save face and step forward without humiliation. Leaders who understand this unlock cooperation that confrontation alone can never achieve.

The Warrior-Guardian ethos is not about domination. It is about controlled presence, disciplined patience, and the courage to see people not only as obstacles but as human beings who still value dignity, even in failure. Jennifer did not surrender because she lost a contest of wills. She surrendered because she was given a way to see herself as a mother, not just a suspect. That reframing was enough to tip the balance.

Every leader will face their own version of Choctaw—a moment where policy, pride, and pressure collide. The choice in those moments is whether to hammer harder or to reframe with patience and respect. Only one of those choices leads to resolution without scars.

Epilogue and Ethos Connection

The Choctaw barricade may not have ended with headlines or dramatic force, but it carried lessons just as powerful. It reminded us that leadership in crisis is less about proving who is right and more about creating the conditions where people can step into resolution without losing their humanity.

Jennifer did not surrender because she was crushed by overwhelming force. She surrendered because she was given a path that preserved her dignity. That principle reaches beyond negotiation into every form of leadership. People resist when they feel humiliated, but they cooperate when they see a way forward that allows them to stand tall, even in failure.

For negotiators, Choctaw reaffirmed the Warrior-Guardian ethos: strength under control, discipline in the face of volatility, and compassion woven into firmness. We did not see an adversary that day; we saw a mother consumed by fear and resentment, yet still tethered to the identity of protector. By appealing to that identity, we moved her from resistance to compliance.

The lesson is not confined to barricades. Leaders in business, education, families, or communities all face moments when pride builds walls higher than logic. The temptation is to force compliance—to prove authority through power. But the greater strength lies in patience, reframing, and the protection of dignity.

As Warriors, our role is not merely to win. It is to preserve life, protect dignity, and lead in ways that leave fewer scars when the conflict ends. The Choctaw barricade did not finish with a tactical breach or broken bodies. It ended with a controlled surrender, a child unharmed, and a mother given the chance to face consequences without being stripped of her humanity.

This is the compass for leaders everywhere: Flex where needed, preserve dignity at every turn, and remember that resolution without destruction is the highest form of victory.

CHAPTER 13

The Shepherd's Burden

Shepherd's Maxim: "The shepherd does not drag the lost; he walks beside them until they find their own way."

A Different Kind of Strength

If the warrior's task is to stand firm and the guardian's task is to shield, then the shepherd's task is to stay. Not to conquer. Not to command. To remain present when others withdraw.

In crisis, people are stripped of dignity, clarity, and often the will to live. The shepherd's ethos is to refuse abandonment—to guide with patience, restore dignity through presence, and remind the lost that surrender is not defeat but survival.

This burden is heavy because it demands endurance, not force. It calls for the kind of strength measured not in decisive action but in stubborn presence.

Doctrine Principle: Presence Over Performance

The shepherd knows this: People in despair don't need speeches. They need presence.

- *Parents:* Your children may not remember every word of advice. They will remember that you stayed when they failed.

- *Leaders:* Your team may not recall every strategy. They will remember that you did not abandon them when the heat rose.

- *Coaches:* Athletes may not quote your pep talks. They will remember that you believed in them when others doubted.

- *Spouses:* Your partner may not remember every argument. They will remember that you refused to walk away in silence.

The shepherd's doctrine is simple: Stay. Be there when others are tempted to flee.

Case Reflection: The Midnight Negotiation

In one long standoff, a subject whispered only a handful of words across twelve hours. Many wanted to end it by force. But the shepherd negotiators stayed through the silence, the fatigue, and the temptation to press.

When dawn broke, the subject whispered, "You didn't leave me." He surrendered without a shot fired.

The shepherd's presence saved him. It wasn't about eloquence. It was about endurance.

Reader Application: Shepherd in Daily Life

- *Parents:* When your child withdraws, resist the urge to lecture. Sit with them. Let your presence heal more than words.

- *Leaders:* When your team struggles, don't disappear into optics. Stand beside them, even in silence.

- *Coaches:* When your athlete falters, sometimes the best support is a hand on the shoulder, not a speech.

- *Spouses:* When your partner is hurting, don't demand explanations. Sit beside them. Stay.

Presence over performance. Patience over pressure. That is the shepherd's burden.

Closing Maxim: "When words fail, presence speaks louder."

Doctrine of the Shepherd

"Guidance is not dragging the lost forward. It is walking beside them until they choose to move."

The Discipline of Patience

The shepherd's work is not flashy. It rarely earns medals or headlines. Instead, it demands patience that stretches longer than comfort allows. It means breathing through long silences, absorbing frustration from commanders, and enduring the weight of doubt from others in the room.

The shepherd is often misunderstood. Some see their stillness as weakness, their refusal to push as indecision. But the shepherd knows: Presence is power, and dignity takes time to restore. His discipline is not to rush, not to lecture, not to abandon.

Case Reflection: The Daughter's Voice

A barricaded suspect shouted threats through the night. But then, in quieter moments, he mentioned his daughter. Again and again.

Instead of pouncing on it, the negotiators noted the repetition. They gave him space. Hours later, they asked gently: "What would your daughter want you to do?"

He fell silent for a long time. Then, softly, "She'd want me to live."

That moment was not won by force. It was shepherding— listening, waiting, then guiding with patience toward dignity.

Doctrine Principle: Dignity Restored

The shepherd's ethos is to restore dignity when people feel stripped of it.

- *Parents:* Guide children through failure by affirming worth, not amplifying shame.

- *Leaders:* Restore trust when teams stumble by reminding them of their value, not just their mistakes.

- *Coaches:* Help athletes reset after loss by reinforcing growth, not berating them.

- *Spouses:* When conflict cools, honor dignity before demanding resolution.

People surrender to dignity, not to domination.

Case Reflection: The Unseen Negotiator

In one negotiation, a subject refused to speak for hours. The tactical team grew impatient. Yet the negotiator stayed—repeating, in calm tones: "We're here. We'll stay as long as it takes."

Finally, after nearly twelve hours, the door creaked open. The subject stepped out silently, weapon lowered. He never spoke a single word of negotiation.

Later, he admitted: "I only walked out because you didn't leave me."

That is shepherding—presence without pressure.

- *Parents:* Instead of demanding answers from a withdrawn teenager, sit with them. Quiet presence speaks more than interrogation.

- *Leaders:* When the board demands optics, remind your team they are valued beyond numbers. Stay steady while they rebuild.

- *Coaches:* After a crushing defeat, don't rush to analysis. Let the silence breathe. Presence steadies before strategy teaches.

- *Spouses:* When words break down, sometimes the act of staying in the room is the truest form of love.

Doctrine Principle: Patience Builds Trust

The shepherd does not demand. They invite. They do not push. They steady. Their patience creates the space where trust can grow again.

This is why shepherds are remembered. Not for their speeches but for their presence. Not for their orders but for their willingness to walk beside the broken until dignity returns.

"Shepherds restore dignity not by dragging but by staying."

Shepherd's Discipline Under Fire

"Patience under fire is harder than courage in the charge."

The Pressure to Act

Few moments test the shepherd more than when time stretches thin and pressure mounts thick. Commanders want updates. Media howl outside. Tactical grows restless. Families plead for resolution.

In those moments, the shepherd's discipline is forged. To stay calm when everyone demands speed is not weakness—it is strength under fire. Shepherds know: Surrender is often a marathon, not a sprint. If we abandon patience, we abandon hope.

Case Reflection: The Command Post Clash

During one tense standoff, the subject spoke only in erratic bursts. Hours passed with little progress. The command post began to fracture. Tactical officers demanded entry. Leaders whispered about optics.

But the negotiator in the shepherd's role stood steady. He slowed his cadence, reassured both the subject and the team, and absorbed the scorn of impatient voices behind him.

After fourteen hours, the subject surrendered without injury. Later, one tactical operator admitted: "I thought you were wasting time. Turns out, time was the tactic."

Doctrine Principle: Absorbing the Heat

The shepherd's discipline is to absorb the heat of the room—not by shouting louder but by staying steady.

- *Parents:* When children collapse under emotion, parents can model steadiness instead of reacting in kind.

- *Leaders:* When markets shake or shareholders panic, leaders can stabilize the team by refusing to let fear dictate.

- *Coaches:* When a team unravels in the heat of competition, a steady presence from the sideline steadies them.

- *Spouses:* When conflict escalates, presence and calm restore clarity faster than words can.

Case Reflection: The Whispered Breakthrough

In another incident, a subject screamed threats for hours before collapsing into quiet sobs. Many thought progress was lost. But the negotiators, shepherding with patience, let the silence sit.

Finally, a whisper: "I don't know what to do."

That was the turning point. The subject had not surrendered to force. He had surrendered to presence.

The shepherd's discipline was rewarded—not with glory but with life preserved.

- *Parents:* In moments of family crisis, pause before acting. Let patience, not fear, guide your words.

- *Leaders:* When pressured by headlines or deadlines, protect your team from rash decisions.

- *Coaches:* When players choke under stress, don't pile on. Hold steady until confidence returns.

- *Spouses:* When emotions boil, choose patience. Let silence cool the air before speaking.

The shepherd's gift is not simply staying present. It is staying steady under fire—when pressure tempts everyone else to break.

Doctrine Principle: Presence Outlasts Panic

The shepherd knows: Panic burns hot but burns out fast. Presence is slower, but it endures. To outlast panic is the truest strength.

"Panic runs out of breath. Presence never does."

Restoring Dignity

"We do not hand people their dignity. We remind them it was never lost."

The Heart of Shepherding

At the center of the shepherd's ethos is the conviction that every human being carries dignity—even when hidden beneath rage, despair, or shame. The shepherd's work is to uncover it, remind it, and hold space until the person reclaims it themselves.

This is not weakness. It is the most difficult form of strength. To believe in dignity when others see only danger is to walk the hard path of the shepherd.

Case Reflection: The Broken Father

A father barricaded himself after a violent outburst against his family. His voice cracked between rage and grief. He declared himself "a monster" unworthy of forgiveness.

The shepherd negotiator refused to argue. Instead, he acknowledged the pain but reminded the man of his identity: father, provider, human.

Hours later, after a long silence, the man repeated the words back: "I'm still a father." That recognition opened the door to surrender.

The shepherd did not give him dignity. He reminded him it was always his to reclaim.

Doctrine Principle: Naming Worth

The shepherd restores dignity by naming worth, even in brokenness.

- *Parents:* Tell your child who they are beyond their failure—loved, valued, capable.

- *Leaders:* Remind employees that mistakes do not erase identity or potential.

- *Coaches:* Affirm that a loss on the scoreboard is not a loss of character.

- *Spouses:* See beyond flaws in conflict, calling out the worth in your partner that hardship may obscure.

When people are reminded of their worth, surrender becomes possible—not surrender to defeat but to healing.

Case Reflection: The Veteran's Shame

A veteran who had lost everything sat in silence with a gun in his lap. He whispered only fragments: "failure," "worthless," "done."

The negotiator responded not with arguments but with empathy. He spoke of the man's service, his sacrifice, the lives already touched by his courage.

At last, tears broke through. The veteran whispered: "You still see me."

That recognition was the pivot. The shepherd's gift was not persuasion but restoration.

- *Parents:* When children stumble, remind them of their strengths instead of magnifying weaknesses.

- *Leaders:* When teams collapse under pressure, reinforce identity before performance.

- *Coaches:* After a crushing loss, highlight growth, courage, or discipline that remains intact.

- *Spouses:* In the midst of conflict, speak to who your partner is, not just what they did.

The shepherd sees beyond the moment to the person—and helps them see it too.

Doctrine Principle: The Mirror of Presence

The shepherd's presence acts as a mirror. Where despair shows only failure, the shepherd reflects worth. Where shame clouds vision, the shepherd clears it. Where hopelessness whispers, the shepherd counters with dignity.

This is not manipulation. It is restoration.

"Dignity cannot be taken. It can only be forgotten. The shepherd helps us remember."

The Shepherd's Trials

"The burden of staying is heavier than the glory of leaving."

The Cost of Staying

The shepherd's path is noble, but it is not easy. It comes with fatigue that lingers long after the crisis ends. It comes with misunderstanding from peers, pressure from leaders, and the gnawing question of whether patience will ever yield results.

The shepherd's trial is endurance. To stay when every instinct screams to move. To wait when adrenaline demands action. To carry someone else's despair while still managing your own fatigue.

This is why the shepherd ethos requires courage as much as the warrior's charge or the guardian's shield. Patience is not passive. It is active endurance under crushing weight.

Case Reflection: The Endless Night

A subject barricaded himself in a small house after firing shots. For fourteen hours, negotiators heard nothing but silence, curses, and the rattling of nerves inside the command post.

The shepherd negotiator stayed steady. Every thirty minutes, he reminded the subject of his presence: "We're still here. You're not alone."

At dawn, exhausted and broken, the subject opened the door unarmed.

Later, he said: "I didn't think anyone would wait for me."

That is the shepherd's burden: to wait when no one else will.

Doctrine Principle: Endurance as Courage

The shepherd's discipline reframes endurance as courage. It is not glamorous. It rarely gets applause. But it is the quiet courage that changes outcomes.

- *Parents:* Stay in hard conversations with your children when silence feels easier.

- *Leaders:* Stand with a struggling team when critics circle.

- *Coaches:* Believe in an athlete through failure until they believe in themselves again.

- *Spouses:* Remain present in seasons of strain instead of fleeing into distraction.

Endurance is what makes shepherds rare—and what makes them essential.

Case Reflection: The Command Post Fatigue

In another incident, a subject alternated between rage and despair. The night dragged on. Commanders pressed for resolution. The negotiator absorbed the pressure, kept his tone steady, and bore the weight of ridicule from those who wanted force.

Finally, the subject surrendered. No gunfire. No funerals.

The cost was not visible to the public. It was borne in the negotiator's fatigue—the shepherd's trial of endurance.

- *Parents:* Endure through the long season of adolescence. Presence across years steadies more than words in a moment.

- *Leaders:* Carry your team through downturns. Endurance in lean times creates loyalty in prosperous ones.

- *Coaches:* Stay patient with players who struggle. Endurance builds growth that quick fixes destroy.

- *Spouses:* Remain faithful through storms. Endurance deepens bonds that abandonments can never repair.

The shepherd's trial is not about being brilliant. It is about being steadfast.

Doctrine Principle: The Power of Refusal

Sometimes the greatest act of strength is the refusal to leave. The shepherd says: "You may give up on yourself. But we will not give up on you."

That refusal becomes a lifeline stronger than any argument.

"The shepherd's greatest courage is not action but endurance."

Shepherd's Practice: Field Drills for Readers

"Presence is a discipline, not an accident."

Why We Train

The shepherd's ethos is not reserved for negotiators in command posts. It is a discipline for every parent, leader, coach, and spouse who faces moments of despair, silence, or conflict. Like any discipline, it requires practice—because in crisis, we do not rise to the occasion; we fall to our level of training.

The shepherd's practice teaches us to embody presence in small, ordinary ways, so that in extraordinary moments, patience and dignity come naturally.

Drill: Sitting with Silence

Choose one difficult conversation this week. When silence arrives, resist the urge to fill it. Count to ten in your head. Breathe. Notice how silence, when held with calm presence, invites others to speak deeper truths.

- *Parents:* Sit with your child when they withdraw. Silence steadies them.

- *Leaders:* When your team hesitates, let silence draw out what fear conceals.

- *Coaches:* In practice, give players the pause to self-correct.

- *Spouses:* In conflict, let silence soften emotion before words return.

Drill: Mirror of Dignity

Each day, find someone carrying shame or fatigue. Speak directly to their worth. Remind them of what is intact, not just what is broken.

- *Parents:* Call out your child's effort, not just their results.

- *Leaders:* Affirm value even in failure.

- *Coaches:* Celebrate discipline as much as victory.

- *Spouses:* Acknowledge resilience before pointing out flaws.

Dignity restored is power renewed.

Drill: Patience Rehearsed

Practice patience before crisis demands it. Choose one situation where your impulse is to rush. Delay your response by sixty seconds. Breathe. Observe how often clarity emerges when impatience is restrained.

Patience practiced becomes patience lived.

Drill: Carry with, Not For

Take one burden you normally shoulder alone—a decision, task, or fear. Share it with a trusted ally. Notice how its gravity lessens when carried together.

The shepherd's gift is not removing weight but refusing to let others carry it alone.

Drill: The Ethos Check

At day's end, reflect: Did I act as shepherd today? Did I remain present when leaving was easier? Did I restore dignity instead of stripping it? Did I walk beside, or did I drag?

This simple reflection transforms ethos from theory into daily practice.

Case Reflection: The Family That Stayed

A suicidal subject once told negotiators: "Everyone always leaves. Why should you be different?"

The negotiator responded: "Because staying is who we are."

That line, repeated patiently through the night, broke despair. The subject surrendered. Later, he said: "It wasn't your words. It was that you never left."

This is the shepherd's power: presence as proof of worth.

When presence becomes habit, its ripple endures long after the crisis.

Children remember parents who stayed through storms.

Teams remember leaders who walked beside them through failure.

Athletes remember coaches who refused to abandon them in defeat.

Spouses remember partners who endured when walking away seemed easier.

The shepherd's legacy is not applause. It is breath still drawn, dignity still intact, and lives still held together by the simple act of presence.

"The shepherd's burden is not to fix every life but to refuse to abandon any."

Closing Call of the Shepherd

"The shepherd's strength is measured not in victories won but in lives not lost."

The Quiet Victory

The shepherd's victories rarely make headlines. They are quiet, unseen, sometimes even misunderstood. There are no parades for the one who stayed, no medals for the one who waited, no spotlight for the one who bore the weight in silence.

But the shepherd knows: The quiet victory is the truest victory. Every surrendered weapon, every life preserved, every family spared from grief—these are the fruits of presence. The shepherd's legacy is measured not in applause but in breaths still drawn.

Doctrine Principle: Refusing to Abandon

At the heart of the shepherd's ethos is refusal. Refusal to abandon the broken. Refusal to let despair dictate. Refusal to surrender patience when the world demands speed.

This refusal is not stubbornness. It is faith—faith that dignity, when given time and space, will rise again.

- *Parents:* Refuse to give up on your child when they falter.

- *Leaders:* Refuse to abandon your team when critics circle.

- *Coaches:* Refuse to discard an athlete who struggles.

- *Spouses:* Refuse to leave when love requires endurance.

The shepherd's gift is simple but rare: presence that outlasts despair.

Case Reflection: The Silent Acknowledgment

In one negotiation, a subject surrendered without ever speaking a word. He simply opened the door, laid down his weapon, and walked out.

Later, he explained: "I heard your voice. You never left. That was enough."

No eloquent arguments. No brilliant strategies. Just presence— patient, unbroken, steadfast. That is the shepherd's way.

The shepherd's code belongs not just to negotiators but to anyone willing to walk beside another human being in struggle.

- *Parents:* Sit with your children in silence, not just in conversation.

- *Leaders:* Stay visible in crisis, not just in triumph.

- *Coaches:* Hold steady when your team collapses.

- *Spouses:* Choose presence over withdrawal, even when words fail.

Every one of us carries the shepherd's charge: to remain present when walking away feels easier.

The Shepherd's Burden and Gift

The shepherd's burden is heavy: fatigue, criticism, and the ache of waiting without certainty. But the shepherd's gift is greater: lives preserved, dignity restored, hope reborn.

Presence is the greatest influence. Patience is the greatest shield. Endurance is the greatest courage.

The shepherd does not drag, force, or abandon. The shepherd walks beside, reminding the broken of their worth until they are ready to walk on their own.

Closing Charge

We stand in a lineage of protectors who bore the burden of presence. Warriors carried strength. Guardians carried shields. But shepherds carried presence—the quiet force that turned despair into survival.

Together, we carry the shepherd's ethos beyond the command post. Into homes, teams, boardrooms, marriages, communities. Into every place where dignity falters and despair tempts people to give up.

Because the shepherd's truth is eternal: No one should ever face the storm alone.

The Shepherd's Legacy

"Presence outlives performance."

The Legacy of Staying

The shepherd's greatest gift is not measured in moments but in memory. Long after the crisis has passed, what people remember is not the brilliance of our arguments or the cleverness of our words. They remember that we stayed.

Time erases speeches. But it never erases presence. The quiet choice to remain when others would have walked away becomes the memory that steadies someone in the years to come.

This is the shepherd's legacy: to be remembered not for glory but for endurance.

Case Reflection: The Officer's Son

Years after a tense negotiation, an officer's teenage son approached the negotiator who had once convinced his father to surrender. He didn't remember the words spoken that night—he had been too young, too scared.

What he remembered was this: "You stayed until my dad put the gun down. Because you stayed, I still have a dad."

The negotiator had long forgotten the tactical details. But the son's life was forever marked by presence.

That is the legacy of the shepherd.

Doctrine Principle: Generations Remember Presence

- *Parents:* Children rarely remember the exact lectures. They remember who sat with them through the storm.

- *Leaders:* Employees may forget strategies, but they remember who stood with them in failure.

- *Coaches:* Players may forget every drill, but they remember who stayed after practice when they were ready to quit.

- *Spouses:* Partners may forget arguments, but they remember who stayed when it would have been easier to leave.

Shepherding is not only about crisis. It is about planting memories that outlive the moment.

Case Reflection: The Athlete's Return

A young athlete spiraled into despair after repeated injuries. His coach, embodying the shepherd's ethos, refused to give up. Instead of pushing harder, he simply stayed—showing up to every rehab session, encouraging through silence more than words.

Years later, when the athlete returned to competition, he told the coach: "I didn't come back because of my talent. I came back because you never left me."

This is the power of shepherding presence. Its impact is not temporary. It shapes the trajectory of lives.

Ask yourself: What do I want my legacy to be?

- *Parents:* Will your children remember the rules you made or the presence you carried?

- *Leaders:* Will your team remember the quotas you set or the loyalty you showed when things broke?

- *Coaches:* Will your players remember the plays you called or the patience you modeled when they failed?

- *Spouses:* Will your partner remember the words of arguments or the endurance of love through strain?

Legacy is not built in grand gestures. It is built in staying power.

The Cost of Legacy

The shepherd's legacy is not free. It costs time, energy, comfort, and sometimes reputation. It requires saying no to optics and yes to endurance. It demands bearing criticism for staying too long, waiting too patiently, believing too stubbornly.

But the return is immeasurable. A life spared. A family whole. A future still intact. These are the legacies that outlive applause.

Doctrine Principle: Legacy Is Presence Remembered

Performance fades. Presence remains. The shepherd knows that true success is not found in the record books but in the lives quietly steadied by endurance.

Closing Transition

And so, as we consider the shepherd's way, we recognize this truth: Presence is the legacy we carry forward. It is the gift we give to the next generation. It is the story that will be told long after the details of the crisis are forgotten.

The shepherd's code does not end with the moment. It echoes into the future, carried in the lives of those who will one day say: "Because you stayed, I survived."

Final Maxim: "It is us—together—who are charged with carrying the Shepherd's Code forward."

CHAPTER 14

Nicoma Park AAR: Anchor Point

The call came late on a Sunday night, just as most families were winding down for the week ahead. Dispatch relayed that a man had barricaded himself inside a small home on the edge of a quiet Oklahoma community. He was armed with a rifle, had already fired shots, and was holding his partner against her will. By the time my phone rang, the first responding officers were already in position outside, reporting gunfire and an escalating crisis.

I was serving as lead negotiator that evening. The initial information was stark: a barricaded suspect with a hostage, shots fired, and a history of volatility. What set this situation apart, however, was not just the threat to the hostage, but the very real possibility that if we were forced to breach, several of our own operators might not make it out. The house was small. Each operator would be responsible for providing cover for a specific area that overlapped the officer to their left and right sides. These overlapping "fields of fire" were very restricted, and the suspect had already demonstrated both intent and capability to use lethal force.

We rallied at the staging area under tense conditions. Officers briefed me on what they knew: The suspect was armed with a semi-automatic rifle and had threatened to kill his partner. The hostage had been able to whisper messages during brief moments of contact, confirming the danger she was in. "He's going to kill me," she said at one point—words that cut through the noise of radio chatter and settled like a stone in the pit of my stomach.

The first hour of negotiations was a flurry of attempts to establish meaningful dialogue. We made call after call to the hostage's phone—sometimes the suspect answered, other times, she did. Each conversation was tense, with the suspect refusing to leave the house and refusing to surrender his weapon. He alternated between silence, anger, and vague declarations that he wasn't ready to come out.

As negotiators, we always balance hope against reality. In this case, the reality was sobering. Our assessments told us that if this turned into a forced entry, the likelihood of casualties—both the hostage and our operators—was high. Every decision, every phrase on the phone, every directive to the tactical team had to be weighed against that risk. It wasn't just about words anymore; it was about keeping people alive long enough for an exit strategy to emerge.

As the minutes stretched into hours, we worked every angle to keep the suspect engaged. The phone calls came in bursts—sometimes answered, sometimes ignored, often placed on speaker so both the hostage and suspect could hear. Each time I spoke, I chose my words carefully, threading a narrow path between de-escalation and direct instruction. The goal was simple in principle but difficult in practice: Keep the suspect talking, keep the hostage alive, and keep our team outside the threshold of that house.

At one point, the hostage whispered that the suspect had the rifle leveled at her chest. She said it calmly, almost flat, as though resignation had settled in. A moment later she added, "Tell my mom I love her." That single phrase froze the command post. Every man and woman listening understood the weight of those words. It was more than a plea; it was preparation for death.

The tactical operators tightened their perimeter, knowing that if her voice suddenly went silent, the next sound might be gunfire. They were prepared to move, but we all knew what that movement would mean. The floor plan was tight, the fields of fire were short, and the suspect had already demonstrated he was willing to pull the trigger. If we breached, we would be forcing our people into a kill box.

In those moments, the concept of protection took on two faces. On one hand, the hostage demanded our absolute commitment; she was innocent, trapped, and terrified. On the other, our operators—men ready to put themselves in harm's way—required leadership that valued their lives as much as hers. My responsibility was not simply to secure the release of one but to prevent the loss of many.

I kept circling back to what the suspect valued most: his children, relationships, and his ability to "do the right thing." These became my hooks, repeated often, in hopes of sparking something within him that could outweigh his anger. Every call, every text, every phrase was another strand in a rope we were throwing across the divide—hoping he would take hold before the thin thread of safety snapped.

The longer the night stretched, the more the suspect withdrew into silence. Where the first calls carried bursts of defiance or argument, now he responded only in fragments, letting the hostage speak on his behalf. She relayed his moods in clipped sentences: "He's getting angrier." "He won't let me go." Each update was unnervingly calm, her voice steady even as the danger grew sharper.

We tried to parse every tone, every pause, every faint sound in the background. Was he pacing? Reloading? Crying? The audio gave us little, forcing us to lean heavily on the hostage's words—words that might have been filtered by fear or control. We never truly knew if she was free to answer or was repeating what he told her to say. That uncertainty was as dangerous as the rifle itself.

Family members gathered near the command post, desperate for updates. Some confirmed what we already feared: He was capable of killing her. Others pleaded for us to use relatives as third-party intermediaries, believing their voices might get through where ours could not. We weighed those options carefully. Every seasoned negotiator knows the risk: Introduce the wrong person, and the suspect might react violently, shifting blame to them or seizing it as justification to act. In this case, the risk outweighed the reward. We held the line.

The tactical team worked quietly in the shadows, adjusting lighting around the residence, shifting positions to tighten containment, mapping possible breach routes. At one point, I was asked to prepare the suspect and hostage for a sudden change in exterior lighting, to reassure them it wasn't gunfire. Even small tactical adjustments required a layer of communication, lest a flicker of light trigger panic inside the house.

The hostage continued to communicate through texts as well as phone calls. At 2:42 a.m., one came through that rattled every member of the team: "He's going to kill me." It was short, final, and void of emotion. She followed it minutes later with another message: "Tell my mother I love her."

Those words hit like a gut punch. Negotiators, commanders, and operators all felt the clock ticking louder. We knew the margin between life and death had narrowed to minutes. Still, the strategy held: Maintain pressure through presence, offer a path of dignity through surrender, and buy just enough time for an opening to appear.

By the early morning hours, the suspect's world had narrowed to the four walls of that small house and the voice on the other end of the phone. The calls became shorter, his responses less frequent, but the hostage remained our lifeline. Her steady voice, calm despite the fear, gave us windows of communication we desperately needed.

Every time she answered, we reassured her that she wasn't alone and that we were working to keep her safe.

I reminded her, and by extension the suspect listening on speakerphone, that their children needed both parents alive. I wove his own words back into the conversation—things he had once said about "doing the right thing" and setting an example. Hooks like these are fragile; sometimes they hold, sometimes they snap. But in that house, with tension mounting, they were the only leverage we had short of force.

The tactical commander requested regular updates, and I passed along each shift in tone, each fragment of dialogue, so the operators could be ready. Everyone knew the stakes. If the breach order came, men would move forward into a confined space against a suspect who had already fired his weapon. We carried no illusions about the cost of that entry. Protection demanded that we keep the shield up as long as possible, buying every minute we could through negotiation.

Around 4:30 a.m., a break finally came. The hostage sent a short text: "I'm fine. We are talking." It was the first sliver of hope we had seen in hours. I replied simply: "Good. Maybe you can both come outside. Let me know before you walk. He must leave the rifle inside."

Moments later, radio traffic lit up: The hostage was at the front door. Operators rushed forward, guiding her to safety. Relief swept the command post, but only briefly. The suspect was still inside, still armed, still unpredictable.

We turned our focus back to him, calling repeatedly, giving clear, simple instructions: "You can walk out. Leave the weapon behind. Come to the door empty-handed." For ten long minutes, he stayed silent. Then, just before dawn, the front door opened again. He stepped out slowly, hands visible, leaving the rifle inside. The operators secured him without firing a shot.

The standoff had ended. Hostage alive. Suspect in custody. No operators lost.

The surrender phase brought with it a strange quiet. After hours of tension, adrenaline, and the constant buzz of radios and phones, silence filled the staging area as the suspect was secured. The hostage was quickly escorted for medical evaluation, then brought back to the command post for a brief debrief. She was exhausted but alive—shaken, bruised by fear, yet intact. Her first words to us were simple: "Thank you."

The operators, sweat-soaked and wired from holding their positions all night, allowed themselves a moment of relief. They knew just how close this had come to tragedy. Inside the command post, commanders replayed the timeline: the near-misses, the crucial moments where negotiation bought seconds, and the thin margin between control and chaos.

For me, the lessons were immediate and sobering. The hostage's calm voice had masked the reality that she was under the barrel of a rifle for most of the night. Every text and whispered word could have been her last. At the same time, our tactical assessment was clear: A forced entry would have placed multiple operators in direct danger of being cut down. This was not an abstract calculation—it was a reality we carried in every decision.

The role of the negotiator in that moment was not only to safeguard the hostage but to shield our team. Words became armor, buying distance between danger and the men who were ready to breach. That balance—the life of the innocent and the safety of those sworn to protect—was the weight we carried through the long hours.

When it was over, no one celebrated. There were no cheers or back slaps. Just a quiet recognition that lives had been spared, the worst outcome had been averted, and the cost of failure had been high enough to demand humility. Every operator, every commander, every negotiator knew how close we had come to tragedy.

The Meadow Drive barricade became one more story written into the ledger of hard calls and harder nights. For me, it reinforced a truth that threads through every crisis: Protection is not one-dimensional. It is the simultaneous duty to shield the innocent, guide the guilty toward surrender, and guard the men and women standing at the breach.

The Meadow Drive incident illustrates a central reality of the Protector Ethos: Protection is not singular. It is layered, multidirectional, and often paradoxical. In this case, protection meant safeguarding the hostage, protecting the tactical operators, guiding the suspect toward surrender, and preserving community trust in law enforcement. Every action we took was judged against these competing imperatives.

From a negotiation standpoint, the doctrine that carried us was time, presence, and hooks. Time is always a negotiator's ally. Every minute the suspect delayed pulling the trigger was a minute closer to exhaustion, reconsideration, or surrender. Presence mattered just as much—not only physical containment but the steady voice on the line, reminding both hostage and suspect that they were not forgotten, and that the outside world was waiting. And hooks—those personal connections to children, family, or identity—gave us levers to pull when logic and demands failed.

But doctrine also had to expand beyond the suspect. In this case, our assessments showed a high likelihood of operator casualties if forced entry became necessary. That demanded a broader view of protection. A negotiator cannot become so tunnel-focused on saving a hostage that they forget the lives of their own team. Balance, not blinders, defines a true protector.

Another doctrinal insight was the use—or deliberate non-use—of third-party intermediaries. Family voices can sometimes reach where ours cannot, but they can also inflame, confuse, or be exploited. The principle we applied was simple: Do no harm by proxy. Unless a third-party voice could add clear value without introducing unacceptable risk, the shield of negotiation remained with us alone.

Finally, the Meadow Drive call highlighted the importance of command communication. Negotiators cannot work in isolation. Every shift in tone, every phrase of threat or resignation, had to be relayed to tactical and command leaders so that decisions were informed, synchronized, and measured. In this case, the decision not to breach was not rooted in fear but in calculated protection—protection of both hostage and team.

Doctrine here teaches that the protector is not reckless, but neither are they paralyzed. They seek resolution that spares life where possible and count the cost when force becomes unavoidable. The shield is always raised, but it is guided by wisdom, patience, and the courage to stand in the gap between chaos and collapse.

What separates the protector from the warrior is not courage alone but the willingness to absorb complexity for the sake of others. A warrior can act swiftly, decisively, even violently if required. A protector must carry all of that capacity while also weighing the invisible lives balanced on every choice. The Meadow Drive call underscored this truth: If I pressed too hard, a hostage might die. If I failed to press enough, operators might be ordered through a fatal breach. Protection demanded I hold both realities at once and refuse to let either slip from view.

This balance highlights a second element of doctrine: restraint under pressure. In negotiation, silence can feel unbearable, especially when the clock is ticking. Yet restraint often preserves life where haste destroys it. When the hostage texted, "He's going to kill me," the natural impulse was to force action. The doctrine of restraint reminded us that unless the threat became immediate and observable, words could still work. The suspect's silence was not a void; it was space—space we had to occupy with steady patience instead of panic.

Leadership under risk also defines the protector. Tactical operators are trained to go forward, to accept danger as part of their oath. But leaders must guard that willingness, ensuring it is not squandered. A protector-leader does not spend lives recklessly. They recognize that those standing ready with shields and rifles are not disposable, but sons, daughters, husbands, wives. Protecting them is as much a duty as protecting the innocent behind a barricade.

Doctrine also teaches that protection extends beyond the incident. Every decision echoes into the future—in the lessons learned by the team, the trust of the community, and the reputation of the agency. The Meadow Drive resolution without loss of life reinforced public confidence and reminded every operator that their sacrifice had meaning even when restraint, not force, carried the night.

The final doctrinal insight is that the protector accepts burden without resentment. In moments like these, negotiators often feel the crushing weight of responsibility: One wrong word, one misjudged pause, one phrase too sharp or too soft could ignite catastrophe. Yet that burden is not optional. It is the very essence of the protector ethos—to carry the risk so others might live.

You may never find yourself standing outside a barricaded home at three in the morning, balancing the life of a hostage against the lives of your own team. Yet the essence of the protector's role reaches far beyond law enforcement. It is lived every day by parents, teachers, leaders, coaches, neighbors, and anyone entrusted with the care of others.

Protection begins with awareness. In the Meadow Drive incident, awareness meant listening for faint shifts in tone, sensing unseen threats, and anticipating consequences. In daily life, awareness is the same discipline. Parents notice the unspoken struggles of their children. Leaders pay attention to the subtle signs of burnout in their teams. Friends sense when silence masks pain. A protector does not wait for danger to announce itself; they learn to see it forming in the shadows.

Protection also demands restraint. Just as negotiators resist the urge to force action before its time, protectors in everyday life learn patience. It is easy to overreact, clamp down with authority, and demand instant change. But true protection often means buying time, creating space for calm, and allowing others the dignity to make a safe choice. A father who listens before judging, a supervisor who coaches instead of condemns, a neighbor who de-escalates a conflict instead of escalating it—all reflect the same principle of restraint under pressure.

Equally, protectors must weigh multiple lives in tension. In negotiation, it was the hostage and the operators. In life, it might be the balance between family and work, or between one employee's need and the well-being of an entire team. Protectors refuse to choose the easy path of saving one while sacrificing the many. They search for solutions that preserve as much life, dignity, and future as possible.

Finally, protectors accept the burden of responsibility. Carrying the shield is not optional. Whether you are a parent staying up late with a sick child, a teacher standing in defense of a struggling student, or a citizen stepping between anger and violence in your community, the burden falls on your shoulders. It may feel heavy, thankless, and unseen, but it is the weight that proves your calling.

The Meadow Drive barricade reminds us all: Protection is not about power but about presence. It is not about domination but about devotion. Every protector—uniformed or not—writes a story of safety with the choices they make when others cannot stand for themselves.

The Meadow Drive barricade left behind no medals, headlines, or applause. What it left was something quieter but far more enduring: lives that were not lost. A hostage returned to her family. Operators went home to their loved ones. A suspect, still dangerous but still breathing, faced justice in a courtroom instead of in a grave.

This is the measure of the protector: not in what they conquer but in what they preserve. The world often glorifies decisive victories and bold advances, yet protection is defined more by what never happens—the tragedy that is avoided, the wound that is prevented, the life that continues unseen. To stand in the breach and hold the line long enough for others to survive is a victory of its own.

The protector ethos calls each of us to embrace this quiet strength. It is not glamorous. It rarely earns applause. At times, it may even be criticized as hesitation or weakness. But the protector knows better. They understand that patience, restraint, and selfless courage are not signs of fear but of conviction. To protect is to absorb risk so that others are spared. To protect is to shoulder the weight of decision so others may remain free of it.

For those reading this outside the uniform, the lesson is the same. You are called to be the shield in your own sphere—for your children, community, team, faith, or values. You may never face the muzzle of a rifle, but you will face the hard choice of when to act and when to wait, when to speak and when to remain silent, when to absorb the cost yourself so that someone else does not bear it.

The maxim that emerges from Meadow Drive is simple: "The protector's greatest victories are the tragedies they prevent."

Carry that truth with you. Remember that your strength is measured not by what you take but by what you preserve. The shield you raise may never be seen by others, but its impact will echo in the lives that continue because you stood firm.

Doctrine Expansion

Beyond the immediate dynamics of the Meadow Drive barricade, the incident also underscores how doctrine shapes institutional resilience. Communication between negotiators and tactical commanders was not just an exchange of updates but a living demonstration of synchronized protection. In any crisis, command clarity prevents fractured decision-making. When leaders in the command post understand the negotiator's intent, tactical teams can posture with confidence, ready to move but also restrained by wisdom.

Another facet often overlooked is the emotional stewardship of a team standing ready on the perimeter. Operators are trained to move toward danger, but the doctrine of the protector demands leaders prevent unnecessary sacrifice. This responsibility requires continual reinforcement through training, debriefs, and culture-building long before the crisis occurs. Doctrine lives not just in policy binders but in the habits that thought leaders instill in their people.

Reader Application: The Weight of Protection

Everyday protectors can take lessons from this call by examining how they lead during unseen crises. For instance, in workplaces, leaders may be tempted to act impulsively when an employee fails or when tension builds within a team. The doctrine of restraint teaches that sometimes listening and buying time yields better outcomes than immediate confrontation. Similarly, parents often balance competing duties—protecting one child's needs without neglecting the well-being of the whole family. True protection is not about choosing one at the expense of the many but holding space for all to flourish.

This chapter also challenges readers to think about communication in moments of pressure. Just as negotiators had to select each phrase carefully, protectors in daily life must be intentional with words when stakes are high. A single harsh remark can escalate conflict, while a well-timed pause or empathetic phrase can preserve dignity and open a path forward. This is not just professional negotiation—it is human stewardship.

Closing Compass Expansion

The Nicoma Park incident remains a vivid reminder that protection is measured not in headlines but in lives preserved. The quiet victories of restraint rarely appear on the evening news, but they resonate in the families who were spared grief and in the teams who returned home intact. For protectors of all kinds, this is the deeper compass: Choose the harder path of patience, trust in presence when others demand speed, and measure success not in conquest but in continuance.

In the end, the Meadow Drive barricade was not simply a tactical win; it was a moral one. It reinforced that courage is not always forward motion—sometimes it is the discipline to hold ground until a door opens that spares life on both sides. This is the kind of victory that defines the protector ethos and ensures the code is carried into every future call, crisis, and community.

CHAPTER 15

Systems Over Scenarios

Protector's Maxim: "Strength without purpose is chaos. Protection without courage is surrender. True protection is legacy, not applause."

The Protector's Role

If the warrior embodies courage, the guardian embodies discipline, and the shepherd embodies presence, then the protector embodies purpose. The protector is the unifying ethos, the thread that binds the others together.

The protector's purpose is not conquest or recognition. It is preservation—of life, dignity, and legacy. When the world calls for spectacle, the protector calls for substance. When politics demand speed, the protector demands patience. When pride demands action, the protector demands outcomes that endure.

This ethos is not about defense alone. The protector does more than shield. The protector ensures that survival is not just physical but moral and communal. A life preserved at the cost of dignity is only half-protected. The protector insists on both.

Case Reflection: The Pressure of Optics

During a prolonged standoff, command staff faced relentless pressure from media and politicians demanding resolution. "Do something" became the cry, not because the situation had worsened, but because patience looked weak on camera.

The protector negotiator stood firm. He reminded the room: "We measure success by breaths, not headlines."

Hours later, the subject surrendered alive. The news cycle was already chasing other stories, but the family of the man who walked out carried a different headline: He was still breathing.

That is the protector's work: choosing outcomes over optics and lives over applause.

Doctrine Principle: The Protector's Compass

The protector brings clarity when confusion tempts leaders to drift.

Purpose over Pride: Success is not about proving rightness but preserving life.

Outcomes over Optics: Protectors act for results, not appearances.

Legacy over Applause: Victory is measured in lives preserved, not headlines written.

This compass steadies the team when storms of politics, fear, or ego rise.

Reader Application: Protector in Daily Life

The protector's ethos transcends crisis response. It is a discipline for every domain where leadership requires endurance.

- *Parents:* Protection is not about controlling your children but about preserving their dignity while guiding them through storms.

- *Leaders:* True leadership is measured not in quarterly reports or press releases but in the people who thrive under your care.

- *Coaches:* Winning at the cost of an athlete's health or confidence is not victory; it is betrayal. The protector insists on outcomes that build, not break.

- *Spouses:* Protection is not guarding your partner from hardship but walking with them through it, ensuring they emerge whole.

In one case, a negotiator persuaded a subject to surrender peacefully after hours of dialogue. No shots were fired. No one was hurt. Yet when the team packed up, some scoffed: "All that time for nothing."

But for the mother reunited with her son, the protector's work was everything.

The protector knows this truth: The measure of success is not in dramatic endings but in the quiet continuation of lives.

Closing Thought

The protector ethos is the culmination of all others. Warriors act with courage. Guardians hold with discipline. Shepherds endure with presence. But protectors measure it all by purpose: life preserved, dignity intact, legacy carried forward.

The Protector's Burden

"The shield does not choose its battles. It bears them."

The Weight of Responsibility

To be a protector is to accept a burden heavier than steel. Unlike the warrior who thrives in action, or the shepherd who thrives in presence, the protector carries responsibility for the final measure of success.

Every decision weighs: If we hold too long, lives may be lost; if we act too soon, lives may be destroyed. Protectors live in that tension.

The protector's burden is not only external. It is internal—the sleepless nights, the second-guessing, the haunting of "What if?" Protectors carry the unseen cost of lives preserved and lives lost, even when outcomes are beyond their control.

Case Reflection: The Double Edge

In one crisis, negotiators secured the surrender of a barricaded suspect after eighteen exhausting hours. The subject lived. The community was spared.

But the family of a hostage who had been killed before police arrived asked bitterly: "Why didn't you get there sooner?"

For the protector, both realities coexist: victory for some, grief for others. Success is never absolute. The burden is carrying both without letting either break you.

Doctrine Principle: The Protector's Three Weights

The Weight of Choice: Knowing every decision closes one door while opening another, and none are free of risk.

The Weight of Criticism: Bearing the blame of those who do not understand why restraint or patience was chosen.

The Weight of Memory: Carrying scars of the ones you could not save, even as you preserve the ones you did.

The protector must learn to bear these weights without crumbling, because the shield is no good if it shatters.

- *Parents:* You carry the burden of guiding children through choices they cannot yet see clearly. Sometimes they will resent the boundaries, even as those boundaries protect them.

- *Leaders:* You will be criticized for restraint as much as for action. Protectors endure the weight of unpopular but necessary decisions.

- *Coaches:* You must balance pushing athletes toward growth with protecting them from harm. Push too little and they fail. Push too much and they break. Both outcomes rest on your shoulders.

- *Spouses:* You carry the unseen burdens of family well-being, finances, and stability. Even when unthanked, the weight remains yours.

The protector's burden is not unfair. It is simply part of the calling.

Case Reflection: The Night of No Applause

A negotiator once described a standoff where the subject finally surrendered, alive and unharmed. No shots fired, no officers injured.

When the debrief came, command simply moved on to the next item on the agenda. No applause. No gratitude.

The negotiator later said: "I realized then the burden of the protector. When you succeed, no one notices. When you fail, everyone remembers."

That is the lonely weight of the protector.

Doctrine Principle: Strength Without Applause

Protectors must cultivate strength that does not rely on applause. If they wait for recognition, they will falter. If they seek validation, they will bend under pressure.

True protectors know that silence is often the only acknowledgment they receive—and they carry on anyway.

Closing Thought

The protector's burden is not proof of weakness; it is proof of calling. To bear weight no one else sees, stand in storms that others flee, and protect without expectation of applause—this is the cost, and this is the strength, of the protector.

The Protector's Compass

"When the storm rages, the compass must point true."

The Need for a Compass

A protector cannot rely on instinct alone. Instinct is reactive, swayed by adrenaline, ego, or fear. The protector must instead carry a compass—a set of unchanging principles that guide decisions when the storm howls loudest.

The compass does not erase the weight of choice, but it ensures the direction of travel remains true. Without it, protectors risk drifting into pride, haste, or despair. With it, they anchor themselves and those they lead.

Doctrine Principle: The Protector's Compass

Purpose Over Pride: Protectors act not to prove themselves right but to preserve life and legacy. Pride seeks victory; purpose seeks outcomes.

Outcomes Over Optics: When political or public pressure demands spectacle, protectors return to the outcome: Is life preserved? Is dignity intact?

Legacy Over Applause: Applause fades, headlines vanish, but legacy endures. Protectors aim not for momentary recognition but for generational impact.

Truth Over Comfort: Protectors speak what must be spoken, even when unpopular, because deception corrodes protection.

Discipline Over Impulse

Impulse may win the moment; discipline wins the day. Protectors slow the tempo until clarity can guide action.

This compass gives direction when emotion, politics, and fear threaten to pull leaders off course.

Case Reflection: The Mayor's Demand

In one critical incident, a city mayor demanded immediate action to "end it quickly." The command post was tense; tactical teams were ready. But the protector negotiator replied: "We should continue working to save lives more than optics. We should hold and continue to peacefully resolve this incident."

The delay was agonizing, but hours later, the subject surrendered without loss of life. The mayor later complimented the team. "It was right to hold life in the highest of regard! You were right to suggest waiting."

The compass had held true: outcomes over optics.

Protectors in everyday life also need this compass.

- *Parents:* Your compass reminds you that the goal is raising resilient children, not winning every argument. Purpose over pride.

- *Leaders:* The compass keeps you from chasing quarterly optics at the cost of long-term health. Outcomes over optics.

- *Coaches:* The compass reminds you to build athletes for life, not just for one game. Legacy over applause.

- *Spouses:* The compass steadies you to speak truth even when it is uncomfortable, because honesty is the foundation of protection.

Case Reflection: The Quiet Leader

A business leader faced enormous pressure to lay off hundreds to satisfy shareholders. Instead, she slowed the process, found alternatives, and preserved jobs. Critics attacked her patience, but years later, her company thrived on loyalty and morale.

She later said: "The compass was simple: I wouldn't trade lives for headlines."

That is protector leadership—not optics, not applause, but legacy.

Doctrine Principle: Teaching the Compass

Protectors must pass their compass on to the next generation. Doctrine without compass becomes brittle. Compass without doctrine becomes vague. The two together create leaders who can endure storms without drifting.

Teaching the compass means:

Speaking the principles daily.

Modeling them in small decisions, not just big ones.

Holding yourself accountable to them when no one is watching.

Closing Thought

The protector's compass does not make storms easier. It makes storms survivable. In the chaos of crisis, pride, ego, or fear will try to pull leaders off course. The compass points them back to purpose, outcomes, legacy, truth, and discipline.

When storms come—and they always do—the compass must point true.

Case Reflections of the Protector

"A protector's victory is often invisible, but its absence is always obvious."

Case Reflection: The School Standoff

A middle-aged man barricaded himself inside an empty elementary school, threatening violence if anyone approached. The community was panicked. Parents demanded immediate resolution. The media hovered like vultures.

Inside the command post, tension mounted. Tactical units pressed for entry. Leaders worried about optics. The protector negotiator urged restraint. "He is isolated, armed, but not resolved. If we hold, fear will break before he does."

The hours dragged into night. The suspect's anger ebbed and flowed. Finally, near dawn, he surrendered. No shots fired.

The public never knew how close it had been to a tragedy. The protector's burden was invisible—but his victory was absolute.

Doctrine Principle: Protectors Absorb Pressure

Protectors act as buffers between external pressure and life-preserving patience. They absorb the demands of politics, the restlessness of tactical, the impatience of media, so others don't have to bear it. Their shoulders carry what the room cannot.

Case Reflection: The Corporate Collapse

A CEO faced a catastrophic financial shortfall. Advisors demanded layoffs to save appearances. Investors wanted spectacle to calm the markets.

The CEO, acting as protector, refused. "We do not solve crisis by sacrificing people." Instead, she restructured, cut executive bonuses, and held the line.

Months later, the company recovered. The employees she had shielded remained fiercely loyal. The layoffs never came.

The public applauded the recovery, but never knew the hours of agony she bore. Her protection was invisible. But her absence would have been obvious.

The protector's work is not only found in hostage standoffs or boardrooms. It lives in the small, daily acts of choosing outcomes over optics.

- *Parents:* When you take criticism for giving your child space instead of punishment, you are protecting their dignity.

- *Leaders:* When you shield your team from political noise so they can focus, you are protecting their capacity.

- *Coaches:* When you hold a player back to heal instead of chasing a win, you are protecting their future.

- *Spouses:* When you endure tension rather than abandon commitment, you are protecting your home.

These decisions may not win applause, but they shape lives.

Case Reflection: The Call No One Praised

During a crisis, a negotiator persuaded a desperate man to surrender after hours of dialogue. The man was unarmed when he walked out. No one was injured.

At the debrief, command dismissed the event: "That wasn't much of a threat."

The negotiator carried the sting of those words. He knew the truth: The man had been one trigger pull away from suicide. The victory was quiet. The applause never came.

Protectors must learn this lesson: If you require recognition, you will falter. If you rest your worth on applause, you will break. The true measure is not the praise of the room but the breath still in a chest.

Doctrine Principle: Quiet Success, Loud Failure

For protectors, success is invisible but failure is deafening. That is the paradox of protection. You cannot enter the role expecting recognition. You enter it because you accept the burden that life matters more than acknowledgment.

Case Reflection: The Family Shield

A father carried the protector's ethos into his home. His daughter battled addiction. The community whispered. Friends drifted away. Yet he refused to abandon her. He bore the criticism of those who said he should cut ties.

Years later, she recovered. At her wedding, she told him: "You saved my life, not because you fixed me but because you never left."

That is protection: not fixing, not forcing, but staying with enough strength that the other person can one day rise.

Closing Thought

These reflections remind us: The protector's work is rarely glamorous, often misunderstood, sometimes mocked. But its absence is catastrophic. Protectors shield families, teams, organizations, and nations not through noise or spectacle but through quiet endurance.

The Protector's Practice

"Protection is not a reaction. It is a discipline."

Why Practice Matters

Protection cannot wait until the crisis erupts. By then, instincts will betray, fear will overwhelm, and impulse will dominate. Protection must be trained daily in the small arenas of life so it becomes reflex in the larger ones.

The protector ethos is lived, not proclaimed. Doctrine becomes real only when practiced.

Field Drills for Protectors

The Breath Shield: In your next conflict, focus not on winning but on slowing your breath. Set the tempo of the room with calm cadence. This is the shield of physiology: When your body steadies, others will unconsciously follow.

Optics vs. Outcomes Drill: At the end of the day, ask: Did I choose outcomes or optics? Write down one moment where you faced the temptation to act for appearances and one where you resisted. Over time, you will see a pattern that strengthens your compass.

Burden-Carrying Exercise: Choose one responsibility you typically shoulder alone. Share it with someone you trust. Notice how the weight lightens. Protectors divide burdens not only in crisis but in daily life.

The Silent Watch: Practice presence without words. Sit with someone in difficulty without offering solutions. Endure the discomfort of silence. This trains you to resist the impulse to fix, and instead to protect through presence.

Legacy Ledger: Keep a simple journal of lives you've influenced not by power or applause but by presence and restraint. Reread it on days when you doubt the value of your quiet work. This is your legacy in ink.

Case Reflection: The Protector in Practice

A coach once resisted the urge to play his star athlete too soon after an injury. Fans shouted, parents questioned, rivals mocked. But he held the line.

Months later, the athlete returned stronger, unbroken, and more resilient than before. Years later, that athlete thanked him: "You cared more about my future than about your record."

That is protector practice in action: optics sacrificed, outcomes preserved.

Doctrine Principle: Practice Is Prevention

Protectors do not wait for the storm to learn how to stand.

Daily disciplines become automatic shields under pressure.

What feels ordinary in training becomes extraordinary in crisis.

Just as negotiators practice silence, warriors practice endurance, and guardians practice discipline, protectors practice presence and restraint until they are second nature.

You don't need a hostage scene to practice the protector ethos. You can begin today.

- *Parents:* When your child tests your patience, ask: Am I protecting their dignity or just defending my pride?

- *Leaders:* When your team falters, resist the impulse to blame. Instead, shield them and guide them.

- *Coaches:* Protect your players not just from opponents but from short-sighted decisions that trade their long-term growth for short-term gain.

- *Spouses:* Protect not by controlling but by carrying—bearing weight when your partner is too weary to stand.

Every act of protection plants legacy.

Closing Thought

Protection is not about grand gestures. It is about the ordinary disciplines practiced until they become extraordinary under fire.

The protector who practices daily is ready when the storm comes. Not because they are flawless, but because discipline has replaced impulse, and presence has replaced panic.

The Protector's Legacy

"The truest measure of protection is not in the moment but in the memory."

The Long Arc of Protection

Every ethos carries weight, but the protector's weight is unique: it stretches beyond the moment into the generations. Warriors inspire courage. Guardians create discipline. Shepherds bring presence.

Protectors weave all three into a legacy that endures long after the crisis has faded.

Protection is never just about the present danger. It is about shaping futures. The lives spared today ripple into tomorrow—children raised, communities rebuilt, leaders inspired to carry the shield forward.

The protector's legacy is not headlines or awards. It is the quiet testimony of those whose lives remain intact.

Case Reflection: The Officer's Daughter

Years after a tense standoff, a negotiator was approached by the daughter of the man who had surrendered that night. She said simply: "Because you stayed, I still have a father. And now my children have a grandfather."

The negotiator realized then that his legacy was not the debrief notes or commendations. His legacy was standing in that gap long enough for a family to remain whole. Protection had multiplied across generations.

Doctrine Principle: Legacy Beyond Applause

Protectors measure success differently than the world.

Applause is temporary. Legacy is permanent.

Optics vanish. Outcomes endure.

Recognition fades. Relationships remain.

The protector knows that the world may never thank them—and yet families reunited, futures preserved, and dignity protected are gratitude enough.

Case Reflection: The Business Leader's Stand

In the corporate arena, one leader faced immense pressure to cut jobs for short-term profit. Instead, she sacrificed executive bonuses and shielded her employees.

Years later, many of those same employees were still with the company, fiercely loyal. One told her: "You saved my family. You didn't just protect my job. You protected my future."

This was not a corporate decision. It was a legacy decision.

The protector's legacy is not reserved for negotiators, officers, or CEOs. It belongs to anyone willing to carry weight for others.

- *Parents:* Your children may not remember every rule, but they will never forget whether you stood by them when they were lost.

- *Leaders:* Your teams will forget quarterly numbers, but they will never forget whether you protected them when politics or pressure came crashing down.

- *Coaches:* Your players will forget play calls, but they will never forget whether you safeguarded their health and dignity when others demanded sacrifice.

- *Spouses:* Your partner may forget arguments, but they will remember whether you carried the family when storms hit.

The protector's legacy is lived in the stories others will one day tell about you.

Case Reflection: The Teacher's Choice

A teacher once stayed late every night to tutor a struggling student. The student later said: "I don't remember the lessons. I remember that you didn't give up on me."

That student went on to become a teacher herself. The legacy of protection is multiplication—one act of endurance echoing into countless others.

Doctrine Principle: Legacy Is Multiplication

Protectors plant seeds of dignity that others will carry forward.

Protection multiplies not because of applause but because of presence.

One shield raised today becomes many shields raised tomorrow.

Closing Thought

The protector's legacy is not found in the crisis logs, in commendations, or in fleeting recognition. It is found in the quiet continuity of life. Families whole. Futures intact. Dignity preserved.

Protectors accept the burden not for themselves but for those who will never know their names—and yet will live because they stood.

The legacy of protection is not in what the world sees but in the lives that remain unseen yet unbroken.

The Protector's Closing Charge

"The measure of our lives is not in what we gain but in what we preserve for others."

The Protector's Call

Every ethos in this code has carried us to this point. The warrior teaches courage without ego. The guardian embodies discipline under fire. The shepherd brings presence that refuses to abandon.

But it is the protector who binds them all into a single charge: life preserved, dignity intact, legacy carried forward.

The protector's ethos is not optional. It is the anchor that keeps courage from becoming recklessness, discipline from becoming rigidity, presence from becoming passivity. It is the unifying call that ensures every act of strength serves a purpose higher than self.

Case Reflection: The Line We Hold

In one standoff, a subject threatened to kill himself if police did not withdraw. Commanders debated storming in to "take control." The protector negotiator countered: "Our role is not control. Our role is protection. We hold."

The team endured hours of unbearable tension. In the end, the subject laid down his weapon and surrendered.

The negotiator later said: "We didn't win. We didn't lose. We protected."

That is the protector's charge. Not victory. Not defeat. Protection.

Doctrine Principle: The Protector's Shield

The protector's ethos can be summarized in three truths:

Protection Is Active: It is not standing by. It is standing firm. It is the discipline of presence with purpose.

Protection Is Costly: It demands sleepless nights, harsh criticism, and burdens borne in silence.

Protection Is Eternal: Its fruits may not appear today or tomorrow, but they ripple into generations unseen.

The protector's ethos is not confined to negotiators or officers. It belongs to anyone willing to bear weight for another.

- *Parents:* Protect not just your child's safety but their dignity, their confidence, and their hope.

- *Leaders:* Protect not just the bottom line but the people who make it possible.

- *Coaches:* Protect not just performance but health and character.

- *Spouses:* Protect not just the household but the bond of trust that holds it together.

The charge is clear: In every arena, choose outcomes that preserve life, dignity, and legacy over optics, pride, or ego.

Case Reflection: The Protector in Legacy

One negotiator spoke of a case where, years later, he attended the wedding of a young man he had once talked out of suicide. The man introduced him to his bride and whispered: "I wouldn't be here without you."

The negotiator did not boast. He only nodded, knowing this truth: Protection's victories are often invisible, but their echoes are eternal.

The Final Charge

Protectors do not wait for applause. Protectors do not seek medals. Protectors do not measure their worth in headlines.

We measure our worth in breaths still drawn, families intact, futures preserved, and legacies carried forward because we chose the shield over the sword, patience over impulse, life over pride.

This is the charge every protector must carry: to stand when others demand action, wait when others demand speed, and preserve when others demand spectacle.

The protector's voice is not singular. It is collective. The shield is never held by one. It is borne together, shoulder to shoulder, generation to generation.

We are warriors who do not confuse volume with strength. We are guardians who hold the line when fear demands spectacle. We are shepherds who refuse to abandon the lost in the darkest hour. We are protectors who measure success not by applause, but by breath still drawn in a chest that might have been stilled.

This is the protector's charge. This is the Code we carry.

Case Reflection: The Apartment Murder/Attempted Suicide

It was a Sunday just before noon when we got the call: An armed man had shot and killed someone in the parking lot of a large apartment complex, then barricaded himself inside. Reports confirmed he had also shot himself in the stomach. Now he was bleeding, armed, and desperate.

At staging, intel trickled in—refrigerator against the front door, weapon somewhere inside, suspect unable to move far. When contact was made, his voice carried agony. He pleaded for us to end it, groaning that prison awaited him and his children already hated him.

We shifted our tempo. Long conversational bridges wouldn't hold. Instead, we broke the dialogue into small, clear steps: short questions, simple requests, immediate affirmation. "Good job. Thanks for working with us." The call became about clarity under duress.

He claimed the gun was on the bedroom floor. We tested his word through FaceTime. The image was dim, but it revealed what we needed: He lay on the floor, wounded and weak. At our request, he raised one hand, then both, showing them empty.

With an open mic keyed up, tactical commanders heard it in real time. "Hands visible. Compliant. Not armed." Minutes later, the entry team moved. He was taken into custody and rushed to medical care.

No further shots were fired.

***

Lessons in the Code

- Adaptation is survival. Adjust communication to the suspect's physical and mental state.
- Integration saves lives. Negotiation, intel, and tactical operated as one shield.
- Presence is power. Calm affirmation ("I see your hands") steadied the path to resolution.

Maxim: "Discipline adapts. Ego insists."

CHAPTER 16

Protector's Ethos

Protector's Maxim: "Command is not control. Command is responsibility."

The Command Post Beyond Crisis

Crisis negotiation taught us that protection is more than tactics—it is the steady presence that transforms chaos into survival. But the lessons of the command post cannot remain trapped in standoffs and negotiations. They must carry into every arena where leaders stand under pressure: boardrooms, classrooms, locker rooms, courtrooms, and homes.

Because here is the truth: Command exists everywhere.

A parent at the dinner table has a command post.

A CEO in the boardroom faces a command post.

A coach in the locker room stands in a command post.

A commander in the field is simply another version of the same reality.

Everywhere decisions are made under stress, there is a command post. And in every command post, doctrine decides outcomes.

The Illusion of Control

Many leaders enter crisis believing command equals control. They raise their voice, issue orders, enforce compliance, and demand results. For a time, it looks powerful. But control is brittle. It fractures under pressure.

Negotiators learned this lesson early. We cannot control a subject in crisis. We cannot force them to calm down. We cannot demand dignity into existence. Instead, we discovered that the role of command is not to dominate chaos but to direct energy.

The command post exists not to impose will but to create conditions where safety, dignity, and influence can flourish.

Doctrine Principle: Three Shifts of Command

From Control to Stewardship: Leaders are not owners of outcomes. They are stewards of people, resources, and time. Control is temporary; stewardship is enduring.

From Pressure to Presence: A leader under pressure can either transmit panic or steady the room. Presence is not passive. It shapes the tempo, steadies the storm, and directs attention to what matters.

From Authority to Responsibility: Authority is given; responsibility is chosen. Protectors understand that true command is not privilege but burden. The shield is carried for others, not self.

Case Reflection: The Command That Saved Lives

During one critical standoff, a commander faced intense pressure from political leaders and the media to storm the building. Hours had dragged into the night. Impatience grew like wildfire.

But instead of bowing to pressure, the commander anchored in doctrine: Contain. Stabilize. Influence. He refused to order an assault until negotiators had exhausted every path to life. His decision was unpopular, mocked in the press, and criticized by peers.

Yet in the end, the suspect surrendered without loss of life. The commander bore the criticism so his people could live.

This is the essence of protector command: refusing to exchange lives for optics.

Reader Application: Leading Beyond the Crisis

The lessons of command extend far beyond hostage scenes.

Parents face moments where control seems easier than connection. But command is not control; it is responsibility for shaping resilient children.

Leaders in business must resist the urge to chase short-term optics at the expense of long-term outcomes. Protection means stewarding both people and mission.

Coaches must resist the urge to push players for wins at the cost of their health and character. Protection means safeguarding futures, not just seasons.

Spouses lead in moments of family conflict. Control can silence for a night. Responsibility builds trust for a lifetime.

Every leader faces the same decision the command post faces: control or responsibility. The protector always chooses responsibility.

The command post beyond crisis is a reminder: Leadership is not about the power to demand but the courage to protect. Command is not control. Command is responsibility.

Pressure, Optics, and the Protector's Compass

"Optics fade. Outcomes remain."

The Weight of Pressure

No leader escapes pressure. In the command post, it roars from radios, commanders, and politicians. In the boardroom, it comes from shareholders, deadlines, and competitors. In homes, it rises from bills, fatigue, and expectations.

Pressure is relentless. It demands speed when patience is required. It demands action when restraint is wiser. It demands optics when outcomes matter more.

Negotiators learned early that pressure destroys clarity if we let it. Leaders collapse when they allow pressure to dictate tempo. The protector's compass is what prevents collapse.

The Temptation of Optics

Optics are the trap of leadership. They are the appearances, headlines, and illusions of strength. Commanders under scrutiny often give in, acting not because it is wise but because it looks decisive.

But optics are shallow. No family cares how tough a leader looked if their child never comes home. No employee celebrates quarterly stock photos if they lost their livelihood. No team remembers the show of anger; they remember whether they were protected.

The protector's compass demands that we reject optics as the measure of success.

Doctrine Principle: The Compass Under Fire

Purpose Over Pride: Leaders must act not to prove themselves right but to preserve the people entrusted to them.

Outcomes Over Optics: The question is never, "How do we look?" The question is, "Who is preserved?"

Legacy Over Applause: Today's headlines vanish. Tomorrow's lives endure. Protectors anchor in legacy, not noise.

Discipline Over Impulse: Impulse feels powerful. Discipline saves lives. Leaders slow down the tempo until clarity, not panic, dictates action.

Case Reflection: The Governor's Order

During one negotiation, a governor demanded swift action, convinced that patience made the state look weak. The command post braced for assault orders.

But the protector in charge replied: "With respect, Governor, optics are not outcomes. We will hold."

The hours dragged. Tension spiked. The media mocked the standstill. Yet in the end, the subject surrendered, alive. Families went home whole.

The governor's anger passed. The lives preserved endured.

Pressure does not only roar in hostage crises. It presses in classrooms, offices, and homes every day.

Parents feel pressure when outsiders judge their patience or discipline. But optics never raise children, consistency and presence do.

Leaders feel pressure when boards demand shortcuts for quarterly gain. But optics never save companies, wise stewardship does.

Coaches feel pressure from crowds screaming for quick results. But optics never build athletes, protection and patience do.

Spouses feel pressure to resolve conflict quickly to look harmonious. But optics never build marriages, responsibility and trust do.

In each case, the protector's compass steadies the leader. Outcomes matter. Optics fade.

Case Reflection: The Business Decision

A CEO faced a public scandal. Advisors urged him to "make a strong statement" that would quiet critics but betray an employee's dignity.

Instead, he chose silence until facts emerged. It looked weak. It looked indecisive.

Weeks later, truth vindicated the employee and the company's reputation. The CEO's refusal to bow to optics preserved not only integrity but trust.

The protector's compass had held.

The lesson is clear: Pressure will come, and optics will tempt. But protectors remember this maxim: Optics fade, outcomes remain.

It is not how the world sees us in the storm that matters. It is who still stands when the storm has passed.

Command Post Discipline Applied to Leadership

"The room does not steady itself. The leader steadies the room."

Command Post Discipline

The command post is often louder than the subject on the other end of the line. Phones ring. Radios crackle. Tactical teams press for entry. Politicians demand updates. Media chatter filters in. Adrenaline flows like electricity through every wire.

Without discipline, the command post collapses under its own weight. Negotiators learned that survival required not just talking to the subject but managing the chaos inside the room. The same principle applies to every arena of leadership.

A business can implode not from its competitors but from panic in the boardroom. A family can fracture not from outside threats but from discord at the table. A team can lose not from opponents but from the collapse of trust on the sidelines.

Command post discipline is not a negotiator's luxury. It is every leader's duty.

Doctrine Principle: Three Anchors of Discipline

Signal vs. Noise: Negotiators separate critical information (signal) from chatter, fear, or ego (noise). Leaders must do the same. Not every complaint, headline, or demand requires action. Signal demands response. Noise demands restraint.

Contain–Stabilize–Influence: Contain chaos by stopping new harm. Stabilize biology and emotion with tone, pacing, and presence. Only then influence behavior toward outcomes. Leaders who skip the first two steps fail at the third.

Truth to Authority: Negotiators learn to speak truth to commanders, even when unpopular. Leaders must speak truth to boards, teams, or families, refusing to let ego or fear dictate silence. Protection demands candor.

Case Reflection: The Command That Held

In one tense standoff, the command post boiled over. Advisors pushed action. Tactical teams stood ready. Voices rose, pressure spiked.

The negotiator calmly reminded the room: "This is noise. Signal is steady. He is talking. He has not hurt anyone in hours. Hold."

The room steadied. Hours later, the subject surrendered alive.

What changed the outcome was not only the dialogue with the suspect but the discipline inside the command post.

The same tools that protect negotiators under fire can protect leaders in every domain.

Parents must separate signal (a child's true fear) from noise (tantrums, resistance, or outside judgment). Respond to the signal; carry the noise without letting it dictate.

Leaders must contain chaos in their teams by preventing new harm first. Stabilize by listening, pacing decisions, and slowing panic. Influence follows only after calm is restored.

Coaches must hold players steady under pressure, filtering noise from crowds, critics, and media. Signal is in the team's body language and effort. Noise is in the stands.

Spouses must learn the difference between the urgent noise of arguments and the signal of deeper needs. Protecting the relationship means listening past volume to what is truly being said.

Every leader must ask: Am I responding to signal or chasing noise?

Case Reflection: The Boardroom Standoff

A company faced a financial shortfall. Executives shouted solutions: layoffs, cuts, restructuring. The noise was deafening.

But the CEO applied command post discipline. He asked: "What is signal? What is noise?"

Signal revealed the real issue: a broken supply chain. Stabilization came by calming fears of collapse. Influence came through a clear plan. Jobs were preserved. Trust was restored.

Command post discipline had moved from crisis to corporation.

Doctrine Principle: The Leader as Steadying Presence

Protectors understand the greatest influence in any room is not the loudest voice but the steadiest. Panic spreads quickly. Calm spreads faster when carried with discipline.

The command post teaches a truth every leader must embrace: Rooms do not steady themselves. The leader steadies the room.

The Burden of Responsibility

"The weight of command is invisible until it is carried."

The Invisible Load

Outsiders often imagine leadership as privilege—the corner office, the title, the authority. They see the medals, not the nights without sleep. They see the decisions, not the weight behind them.

Negotiators learned quickly that responsibility is heavier than authority. Authority gives you the right to decide. Responsibility forces you to live with the consequences. Protectors understand that command is not status; it is burden.

The burden is invisible to those who have never carried it. But once it rests on your shoulders, its weight becomes undeniable.

The Three Weights of Responsibility

The Weight of Choice

Every decision closes one path and opens another. No option is free of risk. The protector accepts that some will call them too slow, others too hasty. The weight lies in knowing both could be true.

The Weight of Criticism

Leaders who protect rarely receive applause. Success often means silence. Failure is loud, public, and enduring. The protector bears criticism, willing to be misunderstood to do what is right.

The Weight of Memory

Protectors carry the scars of those they could not save. Nights replay conversations, second-guessing every pause, every word. The burden is not erased by logic; it is carried with integrity.

Case Reflection: The Decision That Haunted

A negotiator persuaded a subject to surrender peacefully after hours of dialogue. Yet earlier in the standoff, one hostage had been killed before police arrived.

The commander was praised for saving many lives, but privately he carried the grief of the one lost. For years, he asked himself: "Could I have done more? Could I have been faster?"

The burden of responsibility is living with both victory and failure in the same breath. Protectors do not escape that weight. They carry it.

This burden does not belong only to command posts. Every leader carries it.

Parents carry the weight of choices that shape children's futures, knowing those choices may not be appreciated until decades later.

Leaders carry the burden of jobs preserved or lost, reputations built or shattered, cultures shaped or neglected.

Coaches carry the weight of athletes' health and character, knowing a poor decision can leave lasting scars.

Spouses carry the burden of decisions that shape the direction of family life, often with little recognition until years have passed.

Responsibility is invisible until you carry it. Then it shapes everything you do.

Doctrine Principle: Strength in Silence

The protector must learn to live with silence. Applause may never come. Gratitude may never be spoken. What matters is not recognition but fidelity to the burden.

Strength is not in the absence of weight but in the choice to carry it without breaking.

Case Reflection: The Night Without Applause

In one incident, negotiators resolved a crisis peacefully. No shots fired. No injuries. No funerals.

At the debrief, leadership simply moved on to the next agenda item. No recognition. No thanks.

The negotiator later said: "I realized then that the protector's burden is that success is invisible. We save lives, and no one sees. But if one life is lost, everyone remembers."

This is the cost of responsibility.

Accept that leadership means carrying unseen burdens.

Anchor yourself in ethos, not applause.

Surround yourself with allies who help divide the weight.

Remember that silence does not mean failure. It often means preservation worked.

The protector's burden is clear: Command is not about privilege. It is about responsibility. Authority may grant power, but responsibility demands weight. Protectors carry it not because it is easy, but because it is necessary.

The Cost of Courage

"Courage is not free. It costs—and protectors pay it."

The Nature of Courage

When people picture courage, they often imagine heroics: rushing into danger, standing tall under fire, winning against impossible odds. But the protector knows courage is often quieter, lonelier, and far more costly.

Courage is not only what you do in the spotlight. It is what you refuse to do in the shadows. It is the decision to say no when pressure screams for yes. It is the choice to stand steady when others demand you move. It is the conviction to protect when everyone else demands action for the sake of optics.

Courage, for the protector, is not about proving strength. It is about preserving life—even when it means losing popularity, status, or approval.

The Hidden Costs

The Cost of Criticism

Courageous protectors are often misunderstood. Their refusal to bow to optics or rush decisions invites ridicule. Leaders who demand speed label them weak. Politicians call them indecisive. Crowds grow restless. The cost of courage is carrying criticism without letting it erode conviction.

The Cost of Isolation

Courage sometimes means standing alone in the room. Protectors learn that allies may waver when pressure builds. In those moments, courage feels like exile. Yet the protector must still hold the line.

The Cost of Fatigue

Courage is rarely a single decision. It is endurance—holding the shield long after arms ache, long after sleep is gone, long after doubt whispers, "Just give in."

The Cost of Legacy

Courage often bears fruit long after the moment passes. Decisions that save lives may not be recognized until years later—or ever. The cost is leaving a legacy that few will see, but many will live.

Case Reflection: The Stand in the Command Post

During one prolonged standoff, a commander ordered negotiators to prepare for an assault. The lead negotiator respectfully disagreed: "We have time. We are making progress."

The commander, under political pressure, pressed harder. The negotiator stood firm: "With respect, sir, the assault will kill him. We will hold."

The commander relented, reluctantly. Hours later, the subject surrendered unharmed.

The negotiator was not applauded. Instead, he was criticized for "wasting time." But the family went home alive.

That is the cost of courage.

Courage is costly not only in command posts but in every domain where protectors stand.

Parents show courage when they say no to shortcuts that would quiet a child but erode their character.

Leaders show courage when they resist chasing numbers at the cost of people.

Coaches show courage when they protect an athlete's health, pulling them from a game while others demand victory.

Spouses show courage when they protect trust instead of "winning" arguments.

Courage is not glamorous. It is costly. But it is also necessary.

Doctrine Principle: The Currency of Courage

Courage must be counted not by what it gains, but by what it protects.

Protectors spend credibility to preserve dignity.

Protectors spend approval to preserve lives.

Protectors spend comfort to preserve futures.

The currency of courage is costly, but it is the only investment that yields eternal returns.

Case Reflection: The Quiet Protector

A negotiator once made the unpopular call to wait out a barricade. Hours stretched into days. Critics accused him of cowardice.

When the subject finally surrendered alive, the negotiator said simply: "I wasn't brave. I was patient. And patience is the hardest courage of all."

That truth remains: Courage is not loud. Courage is steady.

The cost of courage is real. Protectors know they will pay in criticism, isolation, fatigue, and obscurity. But they pay it willingly— because the lives preserved are worth the price.

The Protector's Compass in Legacy

"The measure of command is not applause today but lives preserved tomorrow."

The Compass That Endures

Negotiators discovered that the protector's compass was not just a tool for surviving the crisis in front of us. It was a guide for legacy— for shaping futures that others would walk into long after the radios went silent.

Leadership that protects does more than prevent loss in the moment. It sets conditions for resilience, trust, and dignity that endure across generations. The protector understands this: Today's discipline writes tomorrow's story.

Doctrine Principle: Four Bearings of the Compass

Safety as a Legacy: Each decision that prevents harm becomes a foundation others can build on. Protectors know they may never be thanked, but safety is its own testimony.

Dignity as a Legacy: Restoring dignity to people in their lowest moments creates ripple effects that last far beyond the incident. Families remember not only survival but how survival was achieved.

Trust as a Legacy: Every act of steady presence plants seeds of trust— in families, teams, and communities. That trust becomes capital for future crises.

Courage as a Legacy: The courage to protect when others demand haste becomes a story retold by those who witnessed it. Legacy is not theory. It is the memory of courage under fire.

Case Reflection: The Legacy of One Choice

In one standoff, negotiators held for sixteen hours while politicians, media, and commanders pressed for entry.

The choice to hold was mocked as weak, indecisive, even cowardly. Yet the subject surrendered alive. A child inside the home grew up with both parents alive rather than one killed in a raid.

Years later, that child wrote a letter thanking the department for giving her family back. The negotiator never saw headlines, but his choice shaped a life.

That is the compass of legacy.

Every leader leaves a legacy. The question is whether it is one of pressure and fear, or presence and protection.

Parents leave legacies not in perfect households but in children who remember safety, dignity, and trust.

Leaders leave legacies not in quarterly reports but in the careers preserved, the integrity upheld, and the futures secured.

Coaches leave legacies not in wins and losses but in the character of athletes who learned to compete with dignity.

Spouses leave legacies not in arguments won but in marriages protected through presence, patience, and honor.

The protector's compass ensures that legacy points not to optics but to outcomes that endure.

Case Reflection: The Coach's Legacy

A coach faced the decision to bench a star athlete for health reasons before a championship game. Pressure from fans and administrators demanded the athlete play.

The coach chose protection over optics. The team lost. Critics called him weak.

Years later, that athlete publicly thanked the coach, crediting him with preserving both his health and career. The loss faded. The legacy endured.

Doctrine Principle: Anchored in Tomorrow

Protectors understand the paradox of legacy: The choices that are least celebrated in the moment are often those most remembered in the future.

Command guided by the protector's compass does not chase applause. It anchors in outcomes that last.

The protector's compass points not to applause but to legacy. Protectors measure success not in the noise of the moment but in the lives preserved tomorrow.

Closing Charge and Final Maxim: "Command is not about how loudly you speak but about who still breathes when you are done."

The Closing Charge

The journey through the doctrine of command brings us to a truth that transcends standoffs, boardrooms, locker rooms, and homes: Leadership is never about you. It is about those entrusted to you.

Negotiators came to understand this the hard way. Every failed standoff, every scar carried, every moment of doubt etched the same lesson deeper: Command is not control. Command is responsibility. Command is stewardship of lives, dignity, and futures.

The protector's ethos anchors this truth:

Warriors steady themselves before steadying others.

Guardians shield chaos from the innocent.

Shepherds walk beside the vulnerable with patience.

Protectors unify it all—measuring success not in applause but in breaths preserved.

Now we carry these lessons forward, not as negotiators alone, but as leaders in every arena where people look to us in their darkest moments.

The Cost and the Call

The cost of command is heavy: criticism, fatigue, isolation, obscurity. Leaders who live the protector ethos will pay that cost. They will be misunderstood. They will be accused of weakness when they are practicing discipline. They will be mocked for silence when silence is strategy. They will be criticized for waiting when waiting saves lives.

But the call is greater than the cost. Protectors step into storms not for recognition but for preservation. They are willing to pay the price because the alternative—surrendering to optics, ego, and impulse—is far more costly in lives and legacies.

Every person stands in a command post, even if radios and rifles are not present.

Parents face crises of tantrums, choices, and futures that will outlast them. Their command post is the home.

Leaders face crises of markets, morale, and ethics. Their command post is the boardroom.

Coaches face crises of competition, character, and health. Their command post is the locker room.

Spouses face crises of conflict, forgiveness, and trust. Their command post is the family.

In each arena, the question is the same: Will you bow to pressure and optics, or will you hold the protector's compass steady?

Case Reflection: The Legacy Commander

One veteran commander summarized his career at retirement with words that shocked his audience. He did not list medals or promotions. He said simply: "Every person who walked out alive— that is my legacy. Nothing else matters."

That statement is the protector's compass in its purest form. The true measure of command is not in titles or applause but in lives preserved.

Doctrine Principle: The Shield Passed On

Negotiators eventually pass the phone to the next generation. Leaders eventually pass the baton to successors. Parents eventually pass wisdom to children. Coaches eventually pass culture to new teams.

The protector understands that leadership is temporary, but legacy is not. The shield must be passed on, intact, unbroken, carrying doctrine and ethos with it.

This is the essence of protector command. Not one person. Not one team. Not one generation. But all of us carrying the code, refusing to let it be diluted by ego, forgotten under pressure, or abandoned for optics.

The command post taught us that rooms do not steady themselves; leaders steady the room. Futures do not secure themselves; protectors secure them. The code does not carry itself; we must carry it—together.

And when history looks back, the measure will not be how loudly we commanded but how faithfully we protected.

CHAPTER 17

Protector Lessons Carried Forward

Protector's Maxim: "The protector does not stand above the storm. He stands within it, absorbing its force so others may endure."

The Protector Defined

Every ethos—warrior, guardian, shepherd—finds its ultimate convergence in the protector. The warrior provides courage, the guardian steadiness, the shepherd presence. But the protector unifies them all. They are the weight-bearer, the one who carries not just their own discipline but the sum of all others.

To be a protector is to carry pressure most will never see. The glare of media, the panic of families, the impatience of commanders, the fatigue of teammates, the despair of the subject—all at once, all bearing down. Most would crack under that load. The protector absorbs it.

The protector is not thanked for it. They are not applauded for it. They are not usually remembered for it. Their victories are invisible—not in the headlines of lives lost but in the silence of lives preserved. Their discipline is simple, but brutal: They do not pass the weight down the chain. They carry it, ground it, and steady the storm so others can stand.

A long barricade stretched deep into the night. The subject raged, sobbed, and threatened. Tactical teams stood by, adrenaline sharp. Reporters pressed microphones against the glass. Phones rang with city officials demanding resolution. Families outside wept. The weight was unbearable.

In the middle of that pressure, the protector negotiator spoke with deliberate calm:

"We will not move tonight. His cadence is breaking. Time is bending. Hold your positions."

The command post bristled. Operators groaned. Politicians cursed. Everyone wanted movement. But the protector anchored the storm. Hours later, the subject surrendered alive. Families reunited. The city never knew how close it had come to catastrophe.

The negotiator wasn't praised in the papers. His name wasn't in the mayor's press conference. But that didn't matter. His legacy was carried in breaths still drawn—in a daughter hugging her father, in officers who went home instead of to funerals.

The protector is not defined by words, tactics, or personality. They are defined by absorption. Pressure must go somewhere. Weak leaders pass it down. Fearful leaders lash it out. The protector grounds it.

Reader Application: Grounding the Storm

- *Parents:* Your children need you to carry storms so they don't drown in them.

- *Leaders:* Your team needs you to absorb executive heat so they can focus.

- *Coaches:* Your athletes need you to ground noise so they can perform.

- *Spouses:* Your partner needs you to hold steady when storms threaten to divide.

To absorb is not weakness. It is strength refined by discipline.

When criticized unfairly, absorb it without retaliating.

When pressured to move rashly, ground the storm instead of passing it down.

When the room grows restless, let your steadiness set the tempo.

Closing Maxim: "The protector absorbs storms so others may breathe."

"The protector stands last, so others may stand at all."

The Protector as Convergence

The protector is not a new ethos; they are the culmination of all that came before.

The Warrior's Courage: strength without ego, courage under control, the refusal to let fear or pride dictate decisions.

The Guardian's Steadiness: the shield between chaos and the innocent, absorbing weight so others can function.

The Shepherd's Presence: the companion who will not abandon, who restores dignity, who guides without coercion.

The protector unites them. They are the warrior without rage, the guardian without paralysis, the shepherd without sentimentality. They are the ones who carry the Code intact when storms would shatter it.

In one high-profile standoff, the subject held a family inside while reporters swarmed outside. Phones in the command post buzzed without pause. At one point, the governor himself called, demanding resolution.

"Go in," he said. "End it now."

Tactical operators were ready. Their adrenaline was sharp. The command post nearly tipped.

But the protector negotiator said quietly:

"If we move now, people die. Hold steady. Let time work. His cadence is shifting."

The words were not popular. They were not applauded. Yet hours later, the subject surrendered alive. The governor took credit at the press conference. The negotiator's name was never mentioned.

But the family went home together. That was the legacy.

Pressure is electricity. If you don't ground it, it arcs—downward, outward, and destructively.

Weak leaders pass it to subordinates.

Fearful leaders pass it to peers.

Selfish leaders pass it to the public.

Protectors absorb it. They are the ground.

- *Parents:* Absorb work stress so children feel safety, not chaos.

- *Leaders:* Absorb investor panic so teams can stay focused.

- *Coaches:* Absorb crowd noise so athletes play free.

- *Spouses:* Absorb hardship so relationships endure storms.

After a long surrender where no one was harmed, a tactical operator leaned over and said, "That could've been my funeral today."

The negotiator nodded and replied: "And the best part is—it wasn't."

There were no headlines. No medals. No fanfare. Just a quiet victory. A family that didn't mourn. An officer who didn't bleed. That is the protector's measure: lives that go on quietly.

When tension escalates, absorb it instead of transmitting it.

When pressured for rash answers, respond with grounded steadiness.

When recognition is denied, remember that legacy is measured in lives, not applause.

Protectors know the truth: If the room stays steady, they have succeeded, even if no one notices.

"The protector is remembered not for what they achieve but for what they prevent."

The Cost of Abandonment

"When the protector leaves, chaos wins."

It was hour twelve of a grueling barricade. The subject had slowed, cycling between muttering and silence. Fatigue was heavy in the command post. One negotiator—worn down by pressure and convinced nothing more could be done—stepped out for air.

In that gap, pressure surged. Tactical pressed: "Now or never." A leader, eager to show decisiveness, nodded. Within minutes, the breach was ordered.

The subject panicked. Gunfire erupted. A hostage was injured. The suspect died.

The debrief was brutal. Everyone knew the truth: If the negotiator had stayed, the pressure might have been absorbed. The protector cannot abandon the line. Even in silence, presence itself steadies the storm.

Protectors understand this: Their presence anchors the team. Even if they are not speaking, even if progress feels stagnant, their very steadiness prevents collapse.

When the protector leaves, impatience fills the vacuum. Chaos surges in.

- *Parents:* A child doesn't always need words. They need presence. Walking out leaves fear. Staying grounds security.

- *Leaders:* Teams don't always need speeches. They need steady eyes and calm posture.

- *Coaches:* Athletes don't always need correction. They need belief embodied in presence.

- *Spouses:* Sometimes silence together is protection enough. Absence leaves wounds deeper than words ever could.

Protectors stay because staying is its own discipline.

Another negotiator described a different night. Hours of silence dragged on. The subject offered nothing. The command post buzzed, impatient. Yet the negotiator remained at the line. Calm. Present. Unmoved.

At dawn, the subject opened the door and walked out unarmed. Later, a young officer asked: "What made him surrender? You didn't even talk for hours."

The veteran replied: "We didn't leave. That was enough."

- *Parents:* Stay in the room when your teenager rages. Presence outweighs lectures.

- *Leaders:* Sit with the discomfort of silence before making hasty decisions.

- *Coaches:* Stay with your athletes in the low moments; don't vanish after defeats.

- *Spouses:* Stay engaged even when words fail; presence is the shield.

The protector is defined less by words than by the refusal to leave.

When protectors step out, chaos takes permission to enter. But when protectors remain, their steadiness communicates: "Not yet. We hold."

Protectors know that their role is not to rush resolution but to preserve options—to keep doors open until dignity and survival can walk through them.

"Leaving the line invites the storm. Staying steadies the shield."

The Weight of Silence

"Silence carried with steadiness is strength."

The standoff had stretched into its second night. The subject raged in bursts, then fell into stretches of heavy silence. Hours passed with no movement. The command post grew restless. Leaders whispered about optics. Tactical prepared to move.

One negotiator leaned forward, calm and unwavering. "Let the silence work," he said. "He isn't gone. He's recalibrating."

The room hated it. Silence felt unbearable, like surrender. Yet the negotiator held firm, refusing to let impatience dictate the moment.

Hours later, the subject's voice finally returned, low and tentative: "Are you still there?"

"Yes," came the answer. "We're not going anywhere. We're here to help you."

Minutes later, the door opened. The subject laid down his weapon and stepped out alive.

The surrender did not come through clever words. It came through silence carried with discipline—silence the protector was willing to shoulder while everyone else tried to escape it.

To the protector, silence is not absence. It is a tool, a tactic, a shield. Where others see a void, protectors see a vessel.

Silence allows biology to reset. The human nervous system cannot sprint forever. Silence slows adrenaline and restores thought.

Silence restores dignity. By not rushing to fill the void, we show respect for the other person's process.

Silence communicates presence. Even without words, the steady "withness" of a protector is clear: I am here. I am not leaving.

One subject in crisis went silent for nearly three hours. Commanders pressed for entry. The negotiator simply stayed, breathing slowly, speaking only once every half hour to remind: "We're still here."

When the subject finally surrendered, he told the negotiator: "I didn't give up, because you didn't give up. I knew you were still there."

That is the protector's truth: Silence steadies storms more than speeches ever could.

- *Parents:* Resist filling every quiet moment with words. Sometimes silence is the medicine your child needs to feel safe.

- *Leaders:* In tense meetings, pause before responding. Let silence cool the room.

- *Coaches:* In the huddle, don't always bark commands. Sometimes stillness gives athletes space to reset.

- *Spouses:* Share silence without fear. Sometimes presence speaks louder than explanation.

Silence does not mean doing nothing. It means carrying weight others cannot—the weight of waiting, restraint, and presence.

Protectors train themselves to embrace silence, not fear it. They know:

Words can close doors; silence can keep them open.

Noise can fracture trust; silence can heal it.

Rash speech can wound; silence can protect.

Protectors discipline themselves to resist the temptation to perform. They choose presence over performance, patience over pressure.

"Silence is not absence. Silence is presence. Silence is protection."

The Protector's Legacy

"The protector's legacy is not carved in stone but in lives that continue."

A father barricaded himself after striking his wife. His teenage daughter was inside. Tactical wanted to breach. The command post buzzed with panic. Reporters hovered outside, cameras rolling.

The protector negotiator absorbed it all. "She is alive," he said. "That means time is still on our side. Hold."

Hours dragged by. Pressure mounted. But the team held. At dawn, the father surrendered. The daughter stumbled out, shaken but alive.

The media ran headlines about leadership. Politicians claimed credit. Almost no one mentioned the negotiator. But the daughter did. She hugged her mother and whispered, "He stayed. He didn't leave me."

That was legacy. Quiet. Invisible. Yet carved into lives that endured.

Protectors accept that they may never be celebrated. Their victories live in the things that do not happen.

No funerals.

No folded flags.

No obituaries.

Their names are rarely in print. Their faces rarely on camera. Their success is measured in the absence of loss.

- *Parents:* Legacy is in the safety your children never knew was threatened.
- *Leaders:* Legacy is in the careers you quietly shielded from collapse.
- *Coaches:* Legacy is in the athletes whose character outlived the game.
- *Spouses:* Legacy is in the storms you carried so your partner could breathe.

That exchange was never reported. But it lived in the lives that continued. That is the protector's burden: to be forgotten by history, but remembered by families who still have their people.

The protector does not chase applause. They know applause is shallow. Their victories are measured in:

The absence of violence.

The breath still drawn.

The child who grows up with both parents.

The officer who goes home safe.

In a city high-rise, a subject surrendered after two days of dialogue and silence. No one was harmed. No shots were fired. The press called it "uneventful."

But every officer in the command post knew: Lives had been preserved.

That is the paradox of the protector: Their greatest triumphs are the ones that leave no visible mark.

- *Parents:* Protect your children's sense of safety. It will echo for decades.

- *Leaders:* Protect your team's trust. It will outlast quarterly reports.

- *Coaches:* Protect your athletes' integrity. It will shape who they are beyond the scoreboard.

- *Spouses:* Protect your home's stability. It will outlast every argument.

Legacy is not an event. It is the accumulation of quiet choices that keep others standing.

"The protector's greatest victories are the ones no one notices—because nothing went wrong."

"The protector carries weight others never see—and would never survive if they did."

A barricade dragged into its fourteenth hour. The subject's voice faded into mutters. Tension thickened. Tactical whispered: "He's done. Let's end it."

A commander, red-faced with impatience, pounded the table. "If this goes bad, it's on us."

The negotiator answered, voice low and steady: "No, it's on me. I'll carry it."

He absorbed the pressure of leadership, the frustration of tactical, the impatience of politicians. He carried it himself so the team could stay steady. Hours later, the subject surrendered alive.

Pressure is never neutral. It seeks release. If not absorbed by a protector, it explodes somewhere else.

Passed down, it crushes subordinates.

Deflected outward, it destroys trust.

Pushed upward, it fractures leadership.

The protector holds it, containing the surge until it dissipates. This is not glamour. It is grit.

- *Parents:* Carry stress without unloading it on children.
- *Leaders:* Carry investor panic without dumping it on your team.
- *Coaches:* Carry external noise without transferring it to athletes.
- *Spouses:* Carry financial or emotional strain without turning it into bitterness.

The protector is not fragile. They are a vessel built to absorb. Where others break, they ground the surge.

This is not martyrdom. It is discipline. The protector does not resent the weight. They embrace it, knowing others could not withstand it.

- *Parents:* When work overwhelms, resist unloading anger at home. Carry the stress; protect the family.

- *Leaders:* When deadlines tighten, resist shouting at the team. Carry the strain; protect trust.

- *Coaches:* When pressure mounts, resist scapegoating players. Carry the heat; protect confidence.

- *Spouses:* When storms hit, resist detachment. Carry the burden together; protect unity.

Carrying is not glamorous. It is the quiet discipline that preserves lives, teams, and futures.

One veteran negotiator told a rookie: "You won't be thanked for the weight you carry. But you'll know when the storm breaks and no one else felt it. That's the measure."

The rookie asked: "And if no one notices?"

The veteran smiled: "That means you did it right."

"The protector's burden is invisible—but it saves lives all the same."

The Protector in Daily Life

"Protection is not an event. It is a way of living."

Not every story of protection makes headlines. One negotiator recalled a conversation with his teenage son:

"You don't yell when you're stressed at work," the boy said. "You just get quieter. Why?"

The negotiator smiled. "Because if I pass it to you, it becomes your burden. And it's mine to carry."

That is protection in daily life—absorbing strain so others are not crushed beneath it.

The protector's ethos does not belong only in hostage standoffs. It belongs in every room, every home, every workplace.

- *Parents:* Protection is patience, not perfection. It is creating a home where children feel safe even when storms rage outside.

- *Leaders:* Protection is absorbing pressure so teams can focus on performance instead of politics. It is shielding them from unnecessary storms.

- *Coaches:* Protection is teaching athletes that character outlasts competition. It is valuing their dignity more than the scoreboard.

- *Spouses:* Protection is bearing weight together, refusing to let storms fracture unity.

One business leader described inheriting a team under crushing corporate pressure. Executives demanded immediate results. The leader absorbed the demands privately, then turned to the team and said: "I've got this. You just do the work you know how to do."

Months later, the team thrived. They never felt the corporate chaos because their leader carried it. That is protection in leadership.

- *Parents:* Absorb work stress so your children feel stability. Say, "I'm here, and you're safe."

- *Leaders:* Absorb executive pressure so your team feels clarity. Say, "I've got the heat. You've got the mission."

- *Coaches:* Absorb crowd noise so athletes feel focus. Say, "Ignore them. Play your game. I'll carry the rest."

- *Spouses:* Absorb storms so your partner feels partnership. Say, "We'll carry this together."

Protectors rarely get applause. Most of their victories are invisible. But that invisibility is the point. If others never felt the storm, then protection worked.

The child who grows up without fear.

The team that succeeds without chaos.

The athlete who plays with freedom.

The spouse who feels secure.

That is legacy.

In one championship game, the crowd roared with anger. Referees blew call after call. Players lost focus. The coach called time-out.

He didn't rant. He didn't argue. He steadied his voice and said: "The noise. I'll take it. You just play."

The players returned calm, refocused, unshaken. They won the game.

Later, one athlete said, "Coach carried the crowd for us. We just played."

That was protection in its purest form.

Reader Challenge: Protect Where You Stand

This week, ask yourself: Where can I absorb storms instead of passing them down? Where can I shield others instead of sharing my chaos?

Protection is not a role assigned. It is a choice made—daily, deliberately, with discipline.

"The protector's legacy is not applause. It is the lives that never felt the storm."

The Protector's Ethos

Doctrine alone cannot hold the line. It is checklists, steps, and techniques. But under pressure, checklists tremble. Procedures bend. If all we have is doctrine, the storm will prevail.

Ethos is what holds. Ethos is character in practice, conviction under fire. Doctrine tells us what to do. Ethos decides whether we stand or fold when the storms come... and they will come!

The protector knows: Their strength is not just in tactics but in ethos.

Protectors live by the discipline that:

Optics are temporary. They fade with the news cycle.

Lives are permanent. They endure.

Ethos is eternal. It carries forward long after both optics and lives are forgotten.

This is not just true in the command post. It is true everywhere.

- *Parents:* Ethos matters more than convenience.

- *Leaders:* Ethos matters more than quarterly numbers.

- *Coaches:* Ethos matters more than scoreboards.

- *Spouses:* Ethos matters more than winning arguments.

A rookie once asked a veteran: "How do you know what to do when everyone screams at you to move?"

The veteran protector smiled. "That's when you stop listening to them, and listen to the Code inside you. That's ethos."

When tempted to cut corners for speed, remember: Ethos outlasts expedience.

When pressured to perform for optics, remember: Ethos protects lives, not reputations.

When uncertain which path to choose, ask: Which choice honors the Code?

Ethos transforms negotiation from tactics into character. It transforms life from reaction into discipline.

In another crisis, a governor personally demanded: "Resolve it tonight. I don't care how."

The protector negotiator held firm: "Sir, with respect, if we move tonight, people die. We hold."

The governor hung up, furious. The negotiator carried the weight. Hours later, the subject walked out alive.

That is ethos. It doesn't bow to rank, optics, or fear. It anchors decisions in protection.

"Tactics may falter. Procedures may bend. But ethos does not break."

Why Practice Matters

Protectors know this truth: Crisis does not create discipline, it reveals it. By the time the storm breaks, your instincts are all you have left. That is why practice is not optional. It is survival.

Negotiators rehearse silence, cadence, and patience daily. Warriors drill under weight until calm is reflex. Guardians practice separating signal from noise. Shepherds rehearse presence until it becomes second nature.

And protectors—they practice all of it, so when the world shakes, their hands do not.

"We do not rise to the level of crisis. We fall to the level of our training."

A rookie once confessed: "I thought the hard part would be learning what to say. But the real discipline is practicing what not to say."

The veteran smiled. "That's why we drill silence, not speeches. That's why we carry burden daily. Words will come. Presence must be practiced."

- *Parents:* Practice patience in daily stress so it is muscle memory in crisis.

- *Leaders:* Practice restraint in meetings so you can hold steady in storms.

- *Coaches:* Practice stillness on the sidelines so your team learns calm by osmosis.

- *Spouses:* Practice carrying together, not apart, so the bond is unbreakable when tested.

"Practice in calm what you will need in chaos. That is how protectors are made."

Closing Call: Carry the Code Forward

"The Code is not ours to own. It is ours to carry—and pass on."

In one long, tense incident, the subject finally opened the door after nearly two days of negotiation. He placed his weapon on the ground and walked out alive. There were no gunshots, no injuries, no funerals.

The media didn't care. They had already packed up. The story wasn't dramatic enough. But the negotiators, the tactical officers, the families waiting outside—they knew.

The protector's presence had carried the storm. The legacy was not a headline but a life still lived.

That is the essence of carrying the Code. Not glory. Not applause. But life preserved, dignity restored, futures protected.

The protector's work does not end at the command post. The Code is not bound by radios and rifles. It belongs in boardrooms, classrooms, homes, and marriages.

Parents Carry the Code when they choose patience instead of anger.

Leaders Carry the Code when they protect their team from chaos instead of feeding it.

Coaches Carry the Code when they value character over the scoreboard.

Spouses Carry the Code when they refuse to abandon one another in silence or in storms.

Every one of us faces negotiations—not always with hostages but with fear, ego, and despair. The protector's Code is the same everywhere: stay, steady, shield, preserve.

A rookie, after his first real surrender, asked his mentor: "So what now? What happens next?"

The veteran replied: "Now you carry it. And you pass it on. That's the oath."

This book is not just a record of battles fought in crisis. It is a blueprint for how to live.

When fear presses down on your family, will you be the warrior who steadies?

When chaos demands rashness at work, will you be the guardian who shields?

When despair silences someone you love, will you be the shepherd who stays?

When pride demands spectacle, will you be the protector who chooses legacy over optics?

The Code is not just for negotiators. It is for anyone who chooses courage under control, presence over performance, life over applause.

The Universal Challenge

The protector's Code is not words on paper. It is a charge, a discipline, a way of life.

Carry it at work. Shield your team from noise.

Carry it at home. Protect your children from storms.

Carry it in marriage. Refuse to abandon.

Carry it in leadership. Preserve dignity when ego tempts you otherwise.

Carry it in yourself. Be the steady presence when chaos rages.

This is not theory. This is not metaphor. This is the discipline of protection, lived daily.

Final Call

We stand where generations of protectors taught us to stand—at the edge of harm, courage under control, ready to shield.

We are warriors who do not confuse volume with strength.

We are guardians who hold the line when fear demands spectacle.

We are shepherds who refuse to abandon the lost in the darkest hour.

We are protectors who measure success not by applause but by breath still drawn in a chest that might have been stilled.

It was just before one in the morning when we staged outside an apartment complex. The call was clear: armed suspect, confirmed hostage inside. The subject was volatile, but the hostage's family was close by—too close—watching events unfold from their car.

When we approached, the sister clutched her phone. A FaceTime call was active with the hostage inside. The feed showed only a ceiling fan, but every so often, figures passed across the screen. It was a narrow window into a crisis we couldn't yet touch.

We built trust quickly with the family, treating them not as bystanders but as partners. They were cooperative, steady, and ready to help. That became our advantage.

Through a modest text string, we made discreet contact with the hostage. The question was simple: "Are you being held against your will?" Her reply, in body language and in courage, was enough. We pushed one more step: "If it is safe, walk outside."

Minutes later, she spoke to the suspect about needing to check his car for his phone. He agreed. The door opened. She stepped out. Tactical secured her immediately. She was safe.

The suspect remained inside, but the hostage was out—alive, uninjured, preserved.

***

Lessons in the Code

- Creativity is a weapon. Sometimes the tool is not a tactic but a text message.
- Families can be allies. When treated with respect and guidance, third parties can extend the negotiator's reach.
- Freedom can be negotiated step by step. One safe exit may be the resolution needed to save a life, even if the standoff continues.

Maxim: "Presence creates options. Creativity turns them into exits."

CHAPTER 18

Adaptive Leadership

Protector's Maxim: "The protector measures success not in medals or headlines but in breaths still drawn."

The Final Pillar

If the warrior ethos is courage, the guardian ethos is weight-bearing, and the shepherd ethos is presence, then the protector ethos is purpose. The protector is the unifying force. Warriors may act, guardians may endure, shepherds may guide—but protectors hold all three together under one principle: life preserved over ego, outcomes over optics, legacy over applause.

Protectors are those who decide that the measure of victory is not recognition but survival. They do not fight for medals. They do not argue for credit. They do not count headlines. They count heartbeats still beating because restraint prevailed, breath still drawn because patience held, dignity restored because presence endured.

Case Reflection: The Mayor's Demand

During a standoff in a small city, a mayor stormed into the command post, demanding quick resolution. Media vans lined the street.

Cameras broadcasted live. The subject inside was armed, suicidal, and threatening violence. Pressure was overwhelming.

The mayor snapped: "Do something! The city is watching. I won't have us look weak!"

The protector negotiator stood firm. "We will act," he said, "but we should act with mission purpose and not act for cameras. We should act for the preservation of lives."

Hours later, the subject surrendered. No shots fired. No one harmed. The mayor left unsatisfied, but the team knew the truth: The protector ethos had prevailed. Lives were preserved, even if applause was not.

Doctrine of the Protector

Life Over Optics: Success is measured in survival, not spectacle.

Outcomes Over Ego: Protectors set aside personal pride for the sake of mission.

Legacy Over Applause: Protectors build doctrine that outlasts them, rather than chasing recognition.

Discipline Over Pressure: Protectors absorb political heat without breaking ethos.

Case Reflection: The Commander's Crossroads

A commander once told a negotiator: "I need this resolved before the press briefing." The negotiator replied: "Lives don't run on your clock."

The subject eventually surrendered alive, long after the briefing ended. It was a victory no cameras captured, but families remembered forever.

Reader Application: Protector Ethos in Daily Life

- *Parents:* Protection is not raising children for applause but raising them with values that endure after you're gone.

- *Leaders:* Protection is making decisions that preserve integrity, even if shareholders or optics push for shortcuts.

- *Coaches:* Protection is teaching athletes that true success is legacy—who they become, not the scoreboard.

- *Spouses:* Protection is standing firm in storms, not for recognition but for the quiet preservation of family.

The protector ethos asks the hardest discipline of all: Resist the applause of the moment in service of the legacy of tomorrow.

Why This Matters

Warriors may save lives through courage. Guardians may save lives through bearing weight. Shepherds may save lives through presence. But without protectors, all three risk collapse under ego, politics, or optics.

The protector ethos ensures that courage, weight-bearing, and presence serve a higher aim: survival with dignity.

Closing Maxim: "True victory is quiet—a subject alive, a family intact, a team unbroken."

Case Reflection: The Subject No One Thanked

"The protector seeks no applause, only survival."

The Forgotten Victory

It was an incident that barely made the news. A man had barricaded himself inside a small apartment after a bitter divorce, threatening to end his life. There were no hostages, no gunfire, no dramatic standoff. Just hours of silence punctuated by bursts of despair.

The negotiators stayed, patiently carrying the silence with him. Finally, in the early hours of the morning, he stepped outside, exhausted, alive.

The next day's paper carried only a small line: "Police resolve disturbance without incident." No interviews. No headlines. No praise.

But the team knew what had been preserved: a man's life, a family spared another funeral, a community spared another scar.

Doctrine of Unseen Victories

Protectors understand that many of their greatest victories will never be celebrated. They will be forgotten by media, overlooked by commanders, unnoticed by the public. But the measure of success is not in recognition—it is in survival.

Preservation Over Recognition: Protectors accept invisibility if lives are spared.

Endurance Without Applause: Protectors hold the line even when no one notices.

Quiet Victories Last: The quiet victories that go unrecognized still ripple outward for generations.

Case Reflection: The Officer's Frustration

A young officer once asked after such an incident: "Why do we even do this if no one notices?"

The veteran replied: "Because the point is not for people to notice us. The point is for people to live."

That conversation shifted the officer's perspective forever. He learned that protection is not about applause. It is about survival, legacy, and dignity.

- *Parents:* The most important acts of protection are often invisible: late-night talks, steady presence, sacrifices no one else sees.

- *Leaders:* The best leaders protect teams from burnout and mistakes quietly, without seeking credit.

- *Coaches:* The most meaningful coaching moments are often invisible to fans—character built in practice, integrity nurtured in losses.

- *Spouses:* Protection is often unrecognized—being the steady one when your partner falters, carrying unseen weights so the family endures.

The protector ethos teaches us to measure success not by how loudly it is applauded but by how long it endures.

Case Reflection: The Subject's Daughter

Years after one such "quiet victory," the negotiator received a letter. It was from the daughter of the man whose life had been preserved. "You probably don't even remember me," she wrote, "but because you stayed that night, my dad walked me down the aisle at my wedding."

The negotiator wept. The victory had gone unreported, but its legacy was immeasurable.

Doctrine of Legacy Over Applause

Applause Fades. Legacy Endures. Media cycles last a day. Lives saved last generations.

Recognition is Optional. Protection is Mandatory. The protector ethos does not depend on credit to function.

Purpose Over Performance. Protectors act for the sake of life, not for the stage of optics.

Closing Reflection

Protectors know that the world rarely thanks them. But the lives still lived, the families still whole, and the futures still preserved are their reward.

The protector ethos accepts invisibility in exchange for survival. It is the most difficult discipline—to give everything, receive nothing, and know that nothing matters more.

"Applause fades. Legacy remains."

Doctrine: Absorbing Pressure Without Breaking

"The protector absorbs pressure so others may endure."

The Weight of Pressure

Negotiators and commanders alike face pressures beyond the immediate crisis. Cameras circle outside. Commanders demand quick results. Politicians demand optics that look strong. Families beg for safety. Tactical teams strain under readiness. The storm of voices threatens to fracture the command post.

In that storm, the protector ethos becomes the anchor. Protectors absorb pressure without breaking, ensuring that the focus remains on preservation, not performance.

Doctrine of Absorbing Pressure

Shielding the Team: Protectors bear the brunt of external demands, shielding tactical and negotiators so they can work with discipline.

Filtering the Noise: Protectors separate signal (real changes in risk) from noise (political heat, media optics, emotional pressure).

Maintaining Compass: Protectors hold doctrine steady even when the room sways under fear or ego.

Carrying Heat Without Passing It Down: Protectors prevent outside pressure from fracturing the team inside.

Case Reflection: The Governor's Call

During one long incident, a governor phoned the command post directly, furious that the standoff had stretched into its second day. "Why are you not doing anything?" he barked.

The protector commander absorbed the blow. He did not pass it down to negotiators or tactical. He simply said: "We are doing everything. And we will act when it preserves life, not before."

The negotiators never even knew the call came until after resolution. The protector had absorbed the pressure, shielding the team.

Case Reflection: The Tactical Team Held Back

At another barricade, tactical officers grew restless after hours of waiting. "Let us go in," one insisted. The protector negotiator walked perimeter, reminding them: "Your discipline is as protective as your rifles. Holding is protection."

The reminder calmed the team. When the subject eventually surrendered, the tactical unit understood: Their restraint had been as valuable as action.

- *Parents:* Absorb stress from work or conflict without unloading it on children. Shield them from unnecessary weight.

- *Leaders:* Absorb pressure from executives or shareholders without breaking your team's morale. Translate stress into clarity.

- *Coaches:* Absorb the roar of the crowd, shielding athletes from panic. Let them focus on the game, not the noise.

- *Spouses:* Absorb outside stress—financial, professional, personal—without letting it poison the home.

The protector ethos means carrying the heat so those around you can stay steady.

Doctrine in Leadership

Protectors in leadership know: Not every pressure must be passed downward. Pressure is energy—it can be dissipated or magnified. Leaders who pass it downward fracture teams. Leaders who absorb it preserve cohesion.

Signal vs. Noise: Ask: Does this demand represent real danger, or is it optics?

Translate Before Passing: If pressure must be passed down, translate it into clear, mission-focused language.

Model Calm: The team will mirror the protector's posture. Calm steadies; panic multiplies.

Without protectors, pressure fractures teams, rushes decisions, and produces casualties. With protectors, pressure is absorbed, filtered, and transformed into focus.

The protector ethos ensures that life is preserved not only by negotiation skills but by the discipline of leadership under fire.

"Pressure breaks the unprepared. Protectors turn pressure into patience."

Case Reflection: The Commander Who Refused to Bend

"The protector stands firm when others demand spectacle."

The Call for Action

It was late into the second night of a barricade. Media vans still lined the street. Families of nearby residents demanded resolution. Commanders were tired. Politicians were angry. Tactical officers shifted restlessly, ready to move.

In the command post, the pressure was unbearable. "We can't look weak," one official said. "We need action. We need resolution. People are watching."

The protector commander stood up. His voice was steady, deliberate: "People are not watching as closely as you think. They will forget by tomorrow. But if we act rashly tonight, families will live with it forever."

The room quieted. His refusal to bend shifted the momentum. Negotiators pressed forward with patience. By dawn, the subject walked out alive.

Doctrine of Refusing to Bend

Protectors know that sometimes the greatest act of leadership is saying no—to pressure, optics, and the illusion of urgency.

Spectacle Is Temptation: Protectors resist the urge to perform for the crowd.

Firmness Preserves Life: Saying no to rash action preserves options, dignity, and survival.

Legacy Over Headlines: Protectors understand that decisions made for optics rarely survive history.

Case Reflection: The Officer Who Spoke Truth

At another standoff, a senior officer quietly told a commander: "If you order an entry tonight, we'll be writing obituaries tomorrow."

It was bold. It was risky. But it was true. The commander held back. Hours later, the subject surrendered alive.

That officer's courage was not loud or flashy. It was protector ethos embodied: refusing to bend when pressure screamed for action.

- *Parents:* Refuse to bend when culture pressures you to raise children for applause instead of character.

- *Leaders:* Refuse to bend when executives demand shortcuts that sacrifice integrity.

- *Coaches:* Refuse to bend when fans scream for spectacle instead of discipline.

- *Spouses:* Refuse to bend when storms tempt you to abandon the commitment of presence.

The protector ethos teaches us that refusing to bend is not stubbornness—it is discipline under pressure.

Doctrine in Action

Protectors in every field face crossroads: bend to pressure or hold for purpose.

Ask: Who Benefits? Does this action serve lives and legacy or just optics and ego?

Ask: What Lasts? Will this decision still look wise in five years, or will it be regretted?

Ask: What is at Risk? Count survival before counting applause.

Case Reflection: The Forgotten Heroism

After one long incident ended without casualties, a reporter mocked the "inaction." The commander smiled. "If you think patience is inaction, you've never carried lives on your shoulders."

The article faded in a day. The lives preserved remained for decades.

Without protectors, teams bend to fear, optics, and ego. With protectors, teams hold the line long enough for life to be preserved.

The protector ethos is not about stubbornness—it is about steadfastness. It is about standing unyielding in the storm so others may survive it.

"Spectacle fades. Survival endures."

Doctrine and Reader Application: Legacy Over Applause

"Legacy outlives applause."

Doctrine of Legacy

Protectors are driven not by the praise of today but by the endurance of tomorrow. They know applause is fleeting, headlines are temporary, and recognition fades. What endures is legacy—principles passed on, lives preserved, doctrine written in scars and stories that outlast the individual.

Applause Fades: Media cycles vanish in hours.

Legacy Remains: Lives preserved ripple for generations.

Doctrine Outlives Personality: What we leave behind is stronger than who we were in the moment.

Case Reflection: The Retirement Speech

At the retirement of a veteran negotiator, no media were present. No politicians attended. It was a quiet gathering of officers, families, and peers.

When he spoke, he didn't list statistics, medals, or cases. He said simply: "There are dozens of people alive today who don't know my name. That's my legacy."

The room fell silent. It was a reminder: Applause fades, but lives preserved endure.

Doctrine in Leadership

Protectors in leadership think beyond immediate recognition. They build systems, doctrines, and cultures that last.

- *Parents:* Legacy is raising children with values, not applause.

- *Leaders:* Legacy is building organizations that endure after you step down.

- *Coaches:* Legacy is shaping character that outlasts the scoreboard.

- *Spouses:* Legacy is preserving a family that thrives long after storms pass.

Applause can be manufactured. Legacy must be lived.

Case Reflection: The Family That Endured

A negotiator once intervened in a suicide attempt. The subject survived. Years later, he quietly built a new family, raised children, and lived a quiet, unremarkable life.

The negotiator heard nothing more until decades later, when one of the man's sons became an officer. "You don't know me," he said, "but you once kept my father alive. Because of that, I'm here today."

Applause never came for that incident. But legacy endured.

- *Parents:* Ask, What will my children carry when I am gone?
- *Leaders:* Ask, What culture will remain when I step away?
- *Coaches:* Ask, What character will my players carry into life beyond sport?
- *Spouses:* Ask, What memories will remain when words are forgotten?

The protector ethos challenges us to live for legacy, not applause.

Case Reflection: The Medal That Never Came

An officer was once recommended for a medal after a peaceful resolution. The award was denied. He shrugged: "If my worth depends on a ribbon, I've missed the point. My worth is in the people who walked away alive."

The denial of the medal did not diminish the legacy. Recognition was denied. Purpose was preserved.

Doctrine of Protector Legacy

Measuring Success: Count survivors, not headlines.

Defining Purpose: Value long-term dignity over short-term applause.

Anchoring Ethos: Remember that legacy is built one life, one moment, one choice at a time.

The protector ethos teaches us the hardest lesson: to give everything, and receive nothing, except the quiet knowledge that lives were preserved.

That is the essence of legacy: invisible to many, immeasurable to those who live it.

"Applause is momentary. Legacy is eternal."

Why We Train This Way

The protector ethos cannot be theory. It must be lived, rehearsed, and repeated until it becomes reflex. Under pressure, we do not rise to the level of our intentions—we fall to the level of our training.

Protectors know that legacy is built not in dramatic moments but in daily discipline. Ordinary choices, repeated with consistency, prepare us for extraordinary storms.

"The protector builds habits today that preserve lives tomorrow."

Field Drills for Living the Protector Ethos

The Integrity Drill: When tempted to cut corners for convenience, stop. Choose integrity over speed. Protectors train integrity in small things so it holds under great pressure.

The Shielding Drill: When pressure comes from above, filter it before it reaches others. Practice translating stress into clarity. Protectors shield teams and families from unnecessary weight.

The Courage Drill: Say no when pressured to act against your principles. Protectors rehearse courage daily so they can stand firm when the stakes are highest.

Case Reflection: The Silent Protector

A negotiator once carried the weight of a commander's impatience. The team never knew. He absorbed the criticism, shielded his colleagues, and let them work without distraction.

After resolution, his partner said: "I don't know how you stayed so calm with all that pressure." He smiled. "You didn't feel it because I carried it."

That is the protector's practice: shielding others so they can perform.

- *Parents:* Shield children from unnecessary stress. Carry financial or professional burdens quietly when you can. Teach integrity in small, daily choices.

- *Leaders:* Absorb pressure from above, filter it, and deliver clarity to your teams. Protectors steady organizations by carrying storms at the top.

- *Coaches:* Teach players that discipline now builds legacies later. Help them measure success in character, not applause.

- *Spouses:* Protectors in marriage absorb storms without letting them fracture the home. They carry weight with steadiness and love.

Case Reflection: The Officer's Example

One veteran negotiator was known for his calm under fire. Asked how he managed it, he answered: "Because I practiced in traffic. I practiced in arguments at home. I practiced in meetings. By the time I reached the command post, I wasn't practicing anymore—I was living it."

The protector ethos is not born in crisis. It is built in the everyday.

The protector's practice is about building reflexes that hold when the storm breaks. Legacy is not a single act of heroism. It is thousands of small acts of discipline that preserve life, protect dignity, and outlast applause.

Without practice, protectors crack under pressure. With practice, protectors absorb storms and hold steady.

"Protection is not one act of heroism. It is daily discipline that becomes legacy."

The Protector's Closing Call

"The protector measures success not by applause but by breath still drawn."

The Quietest Victory

When a negotiator walks away from a scene where no shots were fired, no one was injured, and no headlines were made—that is the protector's greatest triumph. It is a victory so quiet that the public rarely notices, yet so profound that families live with its impact for generations.

Protectors understand that the world will often miss their victories. They do not fight for recognition; they fight for survival. Their creed is not written in medals but in lives that go on quietly, uninterrupted.

The Protector's Creed

We are protectors.

We measure success not by headlines but by survivors.

We absorb storms so others may stand.

We refuse to bow to optics when life is at stake.

We choose legacy over applause, purpose over pride.

We carry courage, weight, and presence, uniting them under one principle: survival with dignity.

We do not act for recognition. We act for life.

Case Reflection: The Family That Never Knew

A negotiator once ended a long standoff peacefully. The subject surrendered. The family was reunited. The media called it a "routine resolution."

Years later, the negotiator reflected: "That family never knew how close they came to tragedy. And that's the point. If they never knew, we did our job."

Protectors do not need the story told. They need the story to continue—with lives intact.

Doctrine of the Closing Call

Quiet Victories Matter Most: A peaceful surrender is always greater than a dramatic assault.

Legacy Is Invisible: Most lives preserved never know they were spared.

Ethos Must Prevail: Without protector ethos, fear and optics fracture judgment.

- *Parents:* Your greatest victories may never be noticed—the nights you steadied, the moments you stayed, the quiet presence you carried.

- *Leaders:* Your team may never see the storms you absorbed, but they will feel the steadiness that allowed them to thrive.

- *Coaches:* Your players may never thank you for the discipline you demanded, but years later, they will live by it.

- *Spouses:* Your partner may never know the burdens you carried silently, but they will live in the stability you preserved.

The protector ethos is the unifying force. Without it, courage fractures into pride, weight-bearing collapses under fatigue, and presence bends under pressure. With it, all three—warrior, guardian, and shepherd—unite into a shield that endures.

The protector ethos ensures that success is not temporary applause but lasting survival. It is the anchor, the compass, and the creed that carries the code forward.

Closing Call

We stand where generations of protectors have stood—at the edge of chaos with courage under control.

We choose life over optics, legacy over applause.

We measure success not in headlines but in lives still breathing.

We carry the weight not for recognition but for survival.

Final Maxim: "Applause fades. Legacy remains. The protector carries the Code."

CHAPTER 19

Closing Compass:
Carry the Code

Protector's Maxim: "The code is not mine. It is ours. Together, we carry it forward."

The Final Ascent

Every journey has a summit. For us, this book has been a climb through the four great ethos—the Warrior, Guardian, Shepherd, and the Protector. Each chapter has built discipline, revealed scars, and distilled doctrine forged in the crucible of crisis.

Now we arrive at the summit: the charge to carry the code forward.

This is not a code to be admired on the page but one to be lived in practice. It is not the property of negotiators, soldiers, or law enforcement alone. It is a code for parents, leaders, coaches, spouses, and anyone who chooses presence over absence, discipline over chaos, protection over pride.

The question is no longer whether the code works in a command post. We have seen that it does. The question now is whether we are willing to live it daily—in boardrooms, on ballfields, across kitchen tables, and in moments when no one but us will ever know.

Doctrine Principle: From Craft to Calling

Negotiation began as craft: words sharpened under fire, doctrine forged by trial and error, maxims born of scars. But the longer we lived the code, the clearer it became: This was never just about a profession. This was about calling.

A calling is what you cannot set down, even when the world moves on. A calling is what you carry not because it is easy, but because it is right.

The code is our calling. It demands that we do more than memorize doctrine. It demands that we embody it, every day, everywhere, with everyone.

Case Reflection: The Quietest Charge

One of our most senior negotiators, on the eve of retirement, was asked what he remembered most. He did not speak of medals, commendations, or headlines. He spoke of one call where nothing seemed to happen.

A man in despair sat in silence for hours. The negotiator stayed. At dawn, the man walked out alive. Years later, the negotiator said, "That was my proudest moment. Because I knew I had carried the code when no one else cared."

That is what it means to carry the code. Not for recognition. Not for glory. Simply because presence is the duty of protectors.

Reader Application: The Universal Charge

The code is not locked in crisis; it belongs everywhere. To carry it forward means to embody it in places where doctrine feels distant but ethos is vital.

Parents carry the code when they refuse to let failure define their children.

Leaders carry the code when they resist the temptation of optics and instead choose presence with their teams.

Coaches carry the code when they place dignity above victory and character above statistics.

Spouses carry the code when they stand unyielding in love, refusing to let silence or pride fracture the bond.

The code is carried every time we divide burdens, restore dignity, and choose presence when retreat would be easier.

The summit is not a place where we rest. It is a place where we decide.

The decision is simple: Will we carry the code forward—or let it remain only ink on a page?

The protector's maxim lights the way: The code is not mine. It is ours. Together, we carry it forward.

The Four Ethos Revisited: One Code, One Charge

"Strength without purpose falters. Shield without courage breaks. Presence without endurance fades. Protection without legacy fails. Together, they endure."

Why We Return to the Four

The code is not a collection of disconnected sayings. It is a living system. The Warrior, Guardian, Shepherd, and Protector are not separate roles to be picked up or set down. They are facets of one unifying charge: to preserve life, restore dignity, and lead with courage under control.

As we close, we must revisit these four ethos—not as fragments but as a single shield.

The Warrior: Strength Under Control

The Warrior's essence is courage without ego. Strength that could dominate but chooses restraint. In negotiation, the Warrior refused to let anger or fear dictate decisions. In life, the Warrior refuses to let pride dictate leadership.

The Warrior's gift is discipline. Their legacy is strength under control.

The Guardian: Shield for the Innocent

The Guardian's essence is protection. A shield between chaos and the vulnerable, between rash action and disastrous consequence. In negotiation, the Guardian absorbed the anxiety of the command post, calming others so that wisdom could guide decisions.

The Guardian's gift is steadiness. Their legacy is the quiet weight carried so others can breathe.

The Shepherd: Presence That Refuses to Leave

The Shepherd's essence is presence. A refusal to abandon, even when silence stretches, criticism mounts, or patience feels impossible. In negotiation, the Shepherd waited through silence until hope returned. In life, the Shepherd stays when everyone else walks away.

The Shepherd's gift is dignity. Their legacy is lives preserved through presence.

The Protector: Purpose That Unifies

The Protector's essence is legacy. The unifying purpose of the code. Life over optics. Outcomes over pride. Legacy over applause. In negotiation, the Protector ensured that all other ethos fused into one mission: life preserved. In life, the Protector ensures that strength, shielding, and presence serve a greater purpose.

The Protector's gift is unity. Their legacy is the code carried forward.

Doctrine Principle: Four Into One

The Warrior without the Guardian becomes reckless.

The Guardian without the Shepherd becomes rigid.

The Shepherd without the Warrior becomes fragile.

The Protector without the others becomes hollow.

But together, the four are unbreakable.

This is why the code is carried forward not as fragments but as one ethos. Warrior, Guardian, Shepherd, Protector—fused into one shield, one compass, one code.

The four ethos are not a menu. They are a system. They are us.

We do not choose between being Warriors, Guardians, Shepherds, or Protectors. We embody all so that strength is guided by purpose, shields are backed by courage, presence is carried with endurance, and protection leaves legacy.

Together, they endure. Together, we endure. Together, we carry the code.

Case Reflection: The Last Call

"In the end, what remains is not the noise of the crisis but the lives preserved by those who stayed."

The Call That Tested Everything

It was late in a long career. A man had barricaded himself in his own home after losing his job, his marriage, and his sense of worth. He fired two shots through the ceiling to prove he was serious. Commanders grew anxious. Tactical tightened their posture. The room thickened with pressure.

This was not the first time we had been there. But it might have been the last.

We gathered as one team. No longer negotiators on one side and SWAT on the other. No longer doctrine separate from ethos. We gathered as one shield.

The man's voice shook with despair. He cursed. He demanded. He broke into long silences. At one point he screamed, "You don't care about me! You just want this over!"

That was the moment the code was tested. Not in the textbooks. Not in the training rooms. In the test of one man's despair.

The Warrior's Presence

The Warrior spoke first, but not with firepower. With discipline. The negotiator's voice stayed calm, even when rage was hurled back. Courage was not found in commands but in restraint.

"Sir, you are safe where you are. No one is rushing you. We will stay with you."

Strength under control. Courage without ego. The Warrior was alive in that voice.

The Guardian's Shield

As hours passed, commanders pressed for resolution. Optics loomed. Tactical prepared for a breach. The Guardian stepped in— not with weapons but with steadiness.

"We hold the line. His life is worth more than a headline."

The Guardian absorbed the heat so others could breathe. The shield was raised, invisible but unbreakable.

The Shepherd's Refusal

Silence settled in. Minutes stretched. Pressure built. The man stopped speaking, and some feared it was over.

But the Shepherd knew silence is not absence. Silence is presence.

"We are still here," the voice said into the quiet. "We are with you. You are not alone."

Patience over pressure. Presence over performance. The Shepherd refused to leave.

The Protector's Unity

At dawn, the man opened the door. His hands trembled, but they were empty. He stepped outside, and the team—tactical, negotiators, commanders—exhaled as one.

The Protector's ethos had unified everything. The Warrior's courage, the Guardian's shield, the Shepherd's presence—all woven together into one mission: Preserve life.

No one died that day. No one was forgotten. That was the last call—not because it was final in sequence, but because it carried the full weight of the code.

We all face last calls. Not with barricades and rifles but with moments where everything we believe is tested.

Parents face them when their child screams, "You don't care!" The last call is whether to walk away in anger or stay with presence.

Leaders face them when teams crumble under pressure. The last call is whether to sacrifice people for optics or absorb heat to preserve dignity.

Coaches face them when failure seems final. The last call is whether to define players by defeat or walk with them into growth.

Spouses face them in silence at the kitchen table. The last call is whether to retreat into pride or reach across with presence.

The last call is not about crisis alone. It is about whether we embody the code when it matters most.

The last call proved this truth: Doctrine may shape tactics, but ethos saves lives.

In the end, what remains is not the noise of the crisis but the lives preserved by those who stayed.

That is the last call. And it is the charge to all of us.

"The code cannot stay in the command post. It must be carried in the places we live, lead, and love."

From Doctrine to Daily Practice

Doctrine matters. Ethos matters more. And ethos only matters if it is lived. The danger of any book, any lecture, any training is that its wisdom ends on the page. The code cannot afford that fate. It must be carried into the fabric of daily life—into living rooms, boardrooms, locker rooms, classrooms, and communities.

To carry the code into daily life means to embody it in the ordinary, where no one is watching, where applause is absent, and where impact is often invisible until years later.

For Parents: The Code at Home

Parents live the code every time they refuse to abandon their children in moments of anger or despair.

Warrior: When you stay calm instead of shouting back, you model courage under control.

Guardian: When you absorb fear and frustration so your children can breathe, you become their shield.

Shepherd: When you stay beside them in silence, you remind them they are never alone.

Protector: When you teach values that will outlast your presence, you leave legacy.

The home is the first command post, and parents are its negotiators. Every word, every silence, every act of presence is a form of carrying the code.

For Leaders: The Code in the Workplace

Leadership is crisis work in disguise. Pressures mount, optics scream, stakeholders demand. The code is needed here as much as anywhere.

Warrior: Act with discipline, not ego. Courage without arrogance steadies teams under fire.

Guardian: Shield your people from optics-driven decisions that erode dignity. Take the heat so they can work with focus.

Shepherd: Stay present in the hard moments. Do not abandon your team when performance falters.

Protector: Build systems and legacies that endure long after your leadership term ends.

Great leaders are protectors, not performers. They preserve dignity and leave a legacy that speaks louder than any quarterly report.

For Coaches: The Code in Competition

Sports are classrooms of pressure. Coaches carry the code when they resist the temptation to define success by scoreboards alone.

Warrior: Teach athletes that discipline is greater than talent.

Guardian: Protect players from toxic cultures and unfair blame.

Shepherd: Walk with them through defeat as faithfully as through victory.

Protector: Build teams where character is measured as highly as championships.

Coaches who carry the code do more than win games. They win hearts and shape futures.

For Spouses and Families: The Code in Relationships

The most intimate command posts are in our homes. Here, the code is not about preserving strangers but about sustaining the people closest to us.

Warrior: Show strength not in dominance but in restraint.

Guardian: Protect one another from isolation, stress, and fear.

Shepherd: Stay in the room when silence stretches long. Refuse to abandon.

Protector: Build a marriage, a family, a bond that leaves a legacy for children and grandchildren.

The code in marriage is simple: Stay. Stay through storms, silence, and strain. Stay until tomorrow arrives.

For Communities: The Code in Society

Communities thrive or collapse on whether protectors rise.

Warriors: Citizens who master themselves before trying to master others.

Guardians: Neighbors who shield the vulnerable and absorb fear so others can breathe.

Shepherds: Volunteers, mentors, and friends who refuse to walk away from the lonely.

Protectors: Leaders and citizens alike who measure success not by popularity but by lives improved and dignity preserved.

The code carried into communities becomes culture. And culture, lived long enough, becomes legacy.

Doctrine Principle: Daily Habits That Carry the Code

Pause Before You Speak: Create silence that steadies.

Absorb Before You React: Take heat so others can function.

Stay When It's Hard: Endurance outlasts despair.

Share the Burden: Divide weights to make them survivable.

Choose Legacy Over Optics: Ask, "Will this matter tomorrow or only today?"

The code is carried not in speeches but in habits. Not in theory but in practice.

Every day offers us the chance to live as Warriors, Guardians, Shepherds, and Protectors. Every day offers us the chance to carry the code.

The final question is not whether the code works. It is whether we will live it.

Doctrine Principle: The Protector's Legacy

"Legacy is not what we keep. Legacy is what we leave in others."

The Long View

Doctrine gives us tactics. Ethos gives us presence. But legacy gives us permanence. The protector's legacy is not measured in headlines, medals, or applause. It is measured in lives carried forward, principles passed down, and cultures that endure because the code was not dropped.

Every protector must eventually ask: What will outlast me?

That question is the measure of legacy.

What Legacy Looks Like

Legacy is not abstract. It is specific. It is the child who remembers you stayed when anger would have been easier. It is the employee who recalls that you shielded them from politics so they could grow. It is the teammate who remembers that you absorbed the blow so they could find their footing.

Legacy is not about grand gestures. It is about consistent presence. The protector's legacy lives not in speeches but in scars, patience, and small acts of endurance that others never forget.

Case Reflection: The Next Generation

One young negotiator once told a story of shadowing a veteran. He expected to learn techniques, clever phrases, or polished lines. Instead, he watched the veteran sit in silence for almost two hours, saying little, breathing steadily, refusing to leave.

The subject surrendered alive. Afterward, the young negotiator asked, "Was that it? Just silence?"

The veteran answered, "That's the code. It's not tricks. It's presence. Someday, you'll pass it on."

Years later, that young negotiator became a trainer. He repeated those same words to rookies: "It's not tricks. It's presence. Someday, you'll pass it on."

That is legacy. Not personality. Not charisma. Not performance. Doctrine carried through ethos, passed intact, multiplied across generations.

The protector's legacy belongs to all of us.

- *Parents:* Your legacy is not what you give your children but what you instill in them— resilience, dignity, presence.

- *Leaders:* Your legacy is not your title but the culture you leave behind. Did you shield or did you abandon? Did you build trust or trade it for optics?

- *Coaches:* Your legacy is not trophies but the players who walk away believing in themselves.

- *Spouses:* Your legacy is not a perfect marriage but a faithful one. Staying through storms leaves a mark that ripples into generations.

Legacy is not measured in years. It is measured in endurance.

Doctrine Principle: Legacy Multiplied

Legacy multiplies in three stages:

Doctrine Preserved: Principles written down, taught, and remembered.

Ethos Embodied: Principles lived so that they are not just known, but seen.

Presence Multiplied: Others carrying forward what they saw in you, long after you are gone.

If any stage fails, legacy weakens. But if all three align, the code outlives us.

The Protector's Warning

Legacy is fragile. It can be lost in a single act of ego. It can be corrupted if influence replaces integrity. It can be forgotten if presence is abandoned.

That is why protectors must live daily with vigilance. Every act either strengthens or weakens the code we leave behind.

The warning is simple: Protectors cannot drop the shield. If we do, the next generation inherits fragments instead of a code.

The protector's legacy is not about us. It is about those who come after us.

When we carry the code, we are not just saving lives in the moment. We are writing doctrine into the future. We are handing courage, dignity, and presence to those who have not yet faced their storms.

Legacy is not what we keep. Legacy is what we leave in others. And the protector's legacy is to ensure that the code is never lost.

Closing Charge: Carry the Code Forward

"The code does not belong to the few. It belongs to all who choose to live it."

The Call to Action

We have walked through doctrine, ethos, case reflections, maxims, and drills. We have stood in the command post, carried silence through the night, shielded one another against pressure, and passed the code from generation to generation.

Now comes the moment where this book ceases to be mine and becomes ours.

The code is not owned by negotiators, officers, or warriors alone. It belongs to anyone who refuses to let ego rule, who absorbs the weight for others, who stays in presence when retreat is easy, and who measures victory not by applause but by lives preserved.

This is your charge: Carry the code.

The Battlefield Beyond the Command Post

The battlefield without bullets is not confined to barricades or hostage crises. It is in homes, workplaces, communities, marriages, locker rooms, and boardrooms. Every arena where fear rises, pressure mounts, or dignity is threatened is a battlefield waiting for protectors.

Parents who carry the code raise children who know presence.

Leaders who carry the code build organizations where integrity outlives profit.

Coaches who carry the code shape players who value character as much as victory.

Spouses who carry the code leave legacies that ripple into generations.

The code belongs everywhere. Because crisis belongs everywhere. And so must protectors.

Doctrine Principle: Courage Under Control

Courage under control is the unifying principle of the code. It is the essence of the Warrior, the steadiness of the Guardian, the patience of the Shepherd, and the unity of the Protector.

The charge is not to perform courage but to live it. Not to claim ethos but to embody it. Not to admire maxims but to act on them.

The code has no power unless it is lived.

Case Reflection: The Quiet Victory

In one of the last debriefs of his career, a negotiator was asked how many lives he thought he had saved. He paused, then shook his head.

"It's not the ones you count," he said. "It's the ones you'll never know. The ones who surrendered, went home, and lived quiet lives with their families. That's the real victory."

The room fell silent. Because everyone knew he was right. The code is not measured in medals but in quiet victories.

The reader's charge is simple, but it is not easy.

Pause before reacting. Create space where dignity can survive.

Absorb pressure. Shield others from the heat so wisdom can prevail.

Stay present. Refuse to abandon in silence, in conflict, in despair.

Pass the code. Teach, model, and live ethos so it outlasts you.

This is not a checklist. It is a calling.

The Shared Burden

Every protector learns the same truth: No one carries the code alone. Burdens are divided. Shields are shared. Legacies are written in plural, not singular.

That is why the closing charge is not "I will carry the code." It is We will carry the code.

Together, we stand as Warriors who master ourselves.

Together, we stand as Guardians who shield the vulnerable.

Together, we stand as Shepherds who refuse to abandon.

Together, we stand as Protectors who measure success by breaths preserved.

Together, we carry the code.

This is the moment where the book hands the shield to you.

The code is not a story to be admired. It is a life to be lived.

The code is not a maxim to be quoted. It is a discipline to be embodied.

The code is not a doctrine to be stored. It is a legacy to be carried.

The protector's maxim lights the way: The code does not belong to the few. It belongs to all who choose to live it.

Carry the code forward. Because the world will always need protectors.

Final Maxim: The Torch We Carry

"The code survives only if we choose to carry it."

The Last Word Before Legacy

Every book ends. Every command ends. Every mission ends. But the code cannot end. It survives only if it is carried—forward, outward, and into the lives of those who come next.

The code is not ink on a page. It is not a speech or a slogan. It is a way of standing when storms hit, a way of holding when pressure builds, a way of staying when others walk away.

This maxim is the final reminder: The code survives only if we choose to carry it.

What the Code Requires

The code does not require perfection. It requires presence. It requires the courage to show up, absorb weight, and stand steady when fear and chaos demand collapse.

Warriors: Master yourselves before trying to master others.

Guardians: Shield the vulnerable even when it costs you.

Shepherds: Stay present in silence and despair.

Protectors: Choose legacy over optics, life over pride, others over self.

These are not tasks. They are choices. Choices made daily, quietly, consistently. Choices that seem small until you see their weight in another person's survival.

Case Reflection: The Torch Passed

At a retirement ceremony, a veteran negotiator was asked what he hoped would remain after his departure. He held up a single page of notes, worn and stained.

"This is nothing special," he said. "Just the reminders I carried on every call. But it kept me steady. And if it steadied me, maybe it can steady you."

He handed the page to a younger negotiator. No speeches, no headlines. Just presence passed forward.

That is the essence of the code. Not grand monuments but torches passed hand to hand, life to life, generation to generation.

This final maxim is not a farewell. It is a commissioning.

- *Parents:* Your torch is the patience you model for your children.

- *Leaders:* Your torch is the integrity you protect under pressure.

- *Coaches:* Your torch is the discipline you instill in players when no one is watching.

- *Spouses:* Your torch is the faithfulness you choose, day after day.

Your torch may seem small. But every protector learns the same truth: Even the smallest torch pushes back the dark.

The Shared Legacy

The code is not mine. It is not yours. It is ours. The code is not carried by one protector but by a community of protectors—parents, leaders, coaches, citizens, spouses—who together ensure it survives.

This is why the final maxim is written in plural: We carry the code.

The Final Line

The closing call is clear:

We are Warriors who master ourselves.

We are Guardians who shield the vulnerable.

We are Shepherds who refuse to abandon.

We are Protectors who choose legacy over pride.

And together, we carry the code.

Clearly, it is you—me—we who are charged with carrying the code forward.

The Code does not require perfection . . . only a relentless pursuit of excellence!!

We will Carry the Code . . . Forward . . . Together!!

Commitment Page

(Carry the Code: My Contract with Myself)

As Warrior, I will fight with courage under control.
As Guardian, I will shield the weak and stand against chaos.
As Shepherd, I will guide, protect, and preserve life with wisdom and patience.
As Protector, I will preserve what matters most and carry forward this doctrine.

I choose to live my life aligned with these four-Pillar ethos.
I do not seek perfection—that is beyond reach.
Instead, I commit to the relentless pursuit of excellence.

I accept that being "average" is not a failing, so long as I choose a peer group of integrity, courage, and honor.

This book is the Code brought to life—my compass and my conviction.

I choose a life of service.
I choose a life of honor.
I hold myself accountable to this Code.

Signature: _____ Date: _____

Acknowledgments

No book is written alone, and this one certainly was not.

To Nathan, you are an exceptional warrior and gentleman. I always welcomed every class, every scenario, every change just to share ideas and philosophy. Your commitment to readiness and your willingness to prepare for the worst gave me confidence that what we teach truly matters.

To Rick, who penned the Foreword and who walked with me down many challenging paths. Your courage and trust are woven into every page of this book. Thank you for sharing what you hold most dear. Your voice strengthens mine.

To my credit union colleagues and board leaders, thank you for showing me that courage and character are not just needed in the streets but in boardrooms, classrooms, and every corner where trust must be built. You reminded me that leadership is not limited to one sphere; it transcends professions and positions. I appreciate the faith and encouragement you each offered.

To my colleagues in law enforcement, especially my brothers and sisters in the tactical and negotiation teams, thank you for trusting me in the hardest moments. First Chair negotiator was not just a title; it was a responsibility, and you made it possible for me to carry the faith you placed in me.

To my martial arts family, decades on the mat have given me more than rank or recognition. The discipline of a fifth-degree journey and the honor of Hall of Fame inductions pale in comparison to the friendships, respect, and resilience earned alongside you. Those lessons in humility and perseverance flow through these pages.

To my friends, peers, and readers who encouraged me to capture these lessons, this book exists, in part, because of your supportive nudging. You saw value in the stories and ethos before I believed they could be bound into a book.

And finally, to my family. Maria, my beautiful, amazing warrior princess bride, thank you for patience, grace, sacrifice, and unwavering support. This project took time, energy, and heart, and you gave me all three without complaint. My mom, her faith and example laid the foundation that still steadies me today. She was strong when it was the only choice and truly has lived a life of honesty and enduring value.

This book is dedicated to you, but it was also made possible because of you.

About the Author

Michael Davenport is a seasoned law enforcement professional, senior crisis negotiator, and crisis negotiation unit team leader with a large Midwestern sheriff's office. Over decades of service, he has trained and led officers through high-stakes incidents where presence, patience, and principle determined life-or-death outcomes. His role as First Chair negotiator placed him at the center of moments where words, timing, and conviction mattered more than weapons, and where lives depended on the ability to lead with calm clarity.

Beyond law enforcement, Michael has also served as president and CEO of a five-star-rated federally chartered credit union, guiding staff, members, and boards through seasons of growth and challenge with the same ethos of courage, accountability, and trust that defined his tactical career. His leadership philosophy in the financial sector emphasized service before self, protecting people's futures, and helping organizations thrive with integrity. He believes leadership in business, like leadership in crisis, is measured by the lives it strengthens and the legacies it leaves behind.

A fifth-degree black belt and martial arts Hall of Fame inductee, Michael has spent more than forty years teaching resilience, discipline, and honor. For him, that recognition was never about trophies or titles but about building legacies—shaping fighters into leaders, and students into men and women of character.

Michael and his bride, Maria, are also the founders of Children Deserve Christmas, a charitable program that for more than twenty-five years has brought love, hope, and happiness to abused, neglected, and otherwise needy children. Their mission is to ensure that every child is well-fed, warmly clothed, and cared for during the Christmas season and throughout the year.

Michael is also an adjunct university instructor and a nationally certified ALERRT active attack response trainer. He has dedicated his life to preparing others for the unthinkable and guiding them through the unimaginable.

At home, he is a husband to Maria, whose presence and support have been his anchor, and a proud son who still draws strength from the faith and example of his mother.

Carry the Code is his first book, but it is also a legacy—a challenge to leaders in every sphere to live with courage, guard what matters, shepherd with presence, and protect with conviction.

www.ingramcontent.com/pod-product-compliance
Lightning Source LLC
Chambersburg PA
CBHW030906120626
46554CB00001B/31